Reading the Homeless

Reading the Homeless

The Media's Image of Homeless Culture

Edited by
Eungjun Min

Westport, Connecticut
London

Library of Congress Cataloging-in-Publication Data

Reading the homeless : the media's image of homeless culture / edited
  by Eungjun Min.
     p.   cm.
  Includes bibliographical references and index.
  ISBN 0–275–95950–3 (alk. paper)
  1. Homelessness in mass media. I. Min, Eungjun, 1957–
P96.H62R43   1999
305.5′69—dc21   98–35370

British Library Cataloguing in Publication Data is available.

Library of Congress Catalog Card Number: 98–35370
ISBN: 0–275–95950–3

First published in 1999

Praeger Publishers, 88 Post Road West, Westport, CT 06881
An imprint of Greenwood Publishing Group, Inc.
www.praeger.com

Printed in the United States of America

The paper used in this book complies with the
Permanent Paper Standard issued by the National
Information Standards Organization (Z39.48–1984).

10 9 8 7 6 5 4 3 2 1

Copyright Acknowledgments

The author and publisher gratefully acknowledge permission for use of the following material:

Chapter 1 reprinted from J. Fiske (1991) "For Cultural Interpretation: A Study of the Culture of Homelessness." *Critical Studies in Mass Communication* 4, 455–474. Copyright by the Speech Communication Association. 1991. Reproduced by permission of the publisher.

Chapter 2 reprinted from R. Campbell and J. L. Reeves (1989) "Covering the Homeless: The Joyce Brown Story." *Critical Studies in Mass Communication* 1, 21–42. Copyright by the Speech Communication Association. 1989. Reproduced by permission of the publisher.

To my parents

Contents

Introduction

Eungjun Min

In the past decade, no single subject has been put under such a microscopic examination like the issue of homelessness. Homelessness has become one of our country's major social problems. From an emotional "letter to the editor" to a systematic scientific research, the issue has touched virtually every sector of America. "The press fell in love with the symptom of homelessness," a journalist observed (Terzian, 1999). The image of the homeless, however, has not been entirely accurate. They have been portrayed as drunk, stoned, crazy, sick, and drug abusers by the media and by many social science researchers. Although the portrayal is partly accurate, these images are indeed obstacles in better understanding the homeless. When a researcher examines the homeless with monologic views, it introduces, as Foucault (1979) explains, "the constraints of conformity that... homogenizes and excludes" (1979, p. 184). We become crusaders for compulsory objectification. It is not surprising that the homeless are generally portrayed as socially dysfunctional given researchers' and journalists' preoccupation with problems the homeless presumably have, but that preoccupation can lead to a general distortion of the issue of homelessness. As Rossi (1994), one of leading scholars in the study of homelessness, indicates, homelessness is not just about the absence of a physical shelter. Homelessness has multiple meanings on socioeconomic conditions that include the homeless themselves (1994, pp. 342–343). It is essential to allow the homeless describe their conditions in their own discourses to provide a more accurate and balanced depiction of the homeless.

The portrayal of the homeless by the media is equally disturbing. Media narrative is a mode of communication which usually contains a story (or stories) made up of a series of events and which always involves some kind of audio and/or visual narrations and portrayals. Any study on narrative basically examines two aspects of it, its content (story) and expression (discourse). Television, for example, is a medium in which the quality of a story is enriched and elaborated by means of various audio-visual devices for expression, the adequate explanation and understanding of it can be reached when it is examined at both levels of expression and of story. In the same way, news can be defined as a set of symbols which, on the one hand, consist of historically transmitted conceptions and which, on the other hand, conceptualize reality by giving meaning to it, make it understandable and thus provide the guidelines and sources for maintaining our reality. In other words, news provides a symbolic communication system by which "reality is produced, maintained, repaired and transformed" (Carey, 1975, p. 10).

This book does not attempt to cover a wide range of noxious conditions of the homeless, nor provide an alternative approach to study the homeless. Instead this book begins with the assumption that media narrative and image blur and distort the distinction between fact and fiction, between information and entertainment, between nature and culture, and finally provides a systematic frame of reference through which the world view is created, maintained, and transformed. The study of news as a form of narrative, however, is not to claim a total rejection of a traditional "transmission view of communication" (Carey, 1975) but to look into the other side of it, that is, to realize that there is something more than the functions of informing and explaining. It attempts to understand the fictional narrative quality of the news, by means of which the viewers as well as the news makers organize our experiences, bring order to events, and thus make sense of the world. News reporting does not merely relates story events, it makes stories themselves. Making stories does not occur in a vacuum; rather, it depends on a set of rules and symbols embedded in a particular sociocultural milieu. As Manoff and Schudson (1986) argue, "Journalism, like any other storytelling activity, is a form of fiction operating out of its own conventions and understandings and within its own set of sociological, ideological, and literary constraints" (p. 6). Seen from this perspective, Newcomb's (1974) suggestion is worth noting:

It should be clear by now that the relationship between fact and fiction, between reality and fantasy in the popular arts, is much more complex than the simple distinction would indicate. In order to understand the unreal quality of TV's "real" programs, one should not turn to the ideology of a particular set of writers or reporters, but to *the fictional structures* that news, sports, and documentary reflect. (p. 184).

John Fiske begins in chapter 1 by demonstrating how the conjunctural interpretive analysis may be utilized in the study of the culture of homelessness. Following the tradition of Gramsci and Hall, he calls for an analysis that is multilevel (ranging from macrostructures to micropractices), multimodal (encompassing texts, practices, empirical data, among others), and explicitly theoretical and political. Since the issue of the homelessness is structural, it requires an analysis that seeks to understand the variety of social forces that come together and conflict at any one particular historical moment. Fiske also attempts to relate his interpretation of material conditions of homelessness with that of the homeless's cultural practice of "watching television" (specifically, the film *Die Hard*). He contends that "the cultural analysis studies instances of culture in order to understand both the system that structures 'the whole way of life' and the ways of living that people devise within it." Speaking of cultural practices of the homeless, Jeremy Reynalds, the executive director of Joy Junction, Albuquerque's (New Mexico) largest and most successful homeless shelter, in chapter 5 shares and examines his own experiences working with the media as a homeless provider. He also investigates whether local and regional newspapers have a tendency to treat the homeless as former mental hospital patients who were deinstitutionalized in the 1970s. Reynalds contends that the misrepresentation of homeless in media can be improved if personnel and scholars make a concerted effort to inform and educate the media about the homeless.

In chapter 2, Richard Campbell and Jimmie L. Reeves examine how network news makes sense of the homeless. They interpret three conventional news narratives and a "60 Minutes" story about Joyce Brown, a homeless woman who, against her will, was institutionalized by the City of New York. They also analyze how television news marks boundaries between the marginal and the mainstream, between a major socioeconomic problem demanding collective engagement, and a personal problem requiring private remedy. In his separate analysis of hindsights on the Joyce Brown story, Reeves deploys a similar strategy in chapter 3 in treating the story as a significant moment in the flow of television news reports between 1981 and 1988 that, collectively, gave expression to the Reagan-era homeless narrative. In this macro-level critical analysis, Reeves treats 246 different news stories on the homeless as a kind of grand mosaic that took shape around the economic instabilities, cultural conflicts, and political rivalries of the day.

Gerald Power in chapter 4 attempts to integrates the two theoretical traditions of media effects and cultural studies to explain differential levels of viewer identification with a range of network news reports depicting homeless people. His findings suggest that the role that culture plays in societal definitions of poverty goes beyond the characteristics of the environment within which poor people live, rather culture raises its ugly head in television's and consequently viewer's inability to go beyond individual explanations for homelessness. Yet television can generate meanings and understandings which are very much tied to a larger culture where poverty is understood in terms of lack of individual effort and achievement. In a computational linguistic analysis, Rebecca Ann Lind and James A. Danowski in chapter 7 use a form of computerized network analysis which provides a unique qualitative analysis by using quantitative procedures. To guide their investigation of the representation of the homeless in American electronic news and information media, they use Power's concepts of stigmatization (discrediting the homeless based on appearance, character, and so on) and attribution (identifying the cause of homelessness as relating to either individual or societal factors). Danowski's own "Wordlink" program allows them to discover and map the relationships among words within television and radio messages: the underlying themes and structures present in mediated representations of the homeless. It also allows them to discern the frequency with which certain words, terms, concepts, attitudes, and values are associated with the homeless.

In a structuralist analysis of media discourse, Insung Whang and Eungjun Min in chapter 6 attempt to interpret and understand the news narrative as a form of a cultural system, which, along with other cultural forms, participates in creating and maintaining our reality. The public's growing antagonism against the homeless people portrayed in television news is examined by using narrative theories. It is found that the status of the homeless tended to be transformed from that of victim of the social problems into that of cause of the social disruption itself. Furthermore, this transformation seems to have been achieved particularly when the narrative closures slipped away from the "burden of proof" and then joined the "populistic" sentiment, which only functioned as confirming our common sense stock of knowledge. Whang and Min in chapter 8 also examine the populist aspect of television narration, that is, for example, how socially and politically important issues are transformed into trivial stories about personal events. On the whole, it can be argued that the issue of the homeless has not been taken seriously. Put another way, the structural and serious nature of the issue has been altered to appeal to our emotions. During this process, the issue itself, as is often the case, seems to have disappeared, since the narrative has dealt with the issue in such a way that only provides us with some isolated examples to show the problem's immediate effects on the personal level.

The motion pictures probably have the longest history of dealing with the underclass of the homeless from Edwin Porter's *The Twentieth Century Tramps* (1902) to *Sunday* (1997), a grand jury prize winner at the Sundance Film Festival. In her study in chapter 10, Linda K. Fuller analyzes seventy motion pictures dealing with the homeless and homelessness by using the theory of intracinematology. Intracinematology, according to Fuller, is envisioned as penetrating into the deepest aspects of uncovering the many aspects and layers of film that can provide clues to our better understanding both its manifest and latent content. The idea is to explore film by means of conventionology. Fuller argues that film directors and producers continually impose their ideological assumptions. In turn, we as audience members are let off from caring about the homeless in this capacity, later representations of them as lowlife and /or street smart, worldly-wise mystics provide an equally easy allowance for keeping our distance from both the people and their problems. From the motion pictures to still pictures, Andrew Mendelson in chapter 11 explores the effect of still photographs of newspapers on the homeless by examining college students' responses in terms of Iyengar's attribution theory and other related researches. Attribution theory focuses on how people use incoming information to form judgments about the causes of events or situations. Unlike previous researches, he found that one or two pictures with newspaper articles may not be strong enough to create a framing effect and move a subject to action. Perhaps, Mendelson contends, still pictures do not have the power they once had. People have become so reliant on moving images they are no longer "literate" to the meanings in still pictures. It is, however, true that today's photojournalists are still using episodically framed pictures to tell the stories of social problems in this country.

In a phenomenological analysis, Eric Mark Kramer and Soobum Lee in chapter 9 seek the meanings of the homeless, which may tell us very much about the society that gave to such a designation by using Kramer's theory of "Dimensional Accrual/Dissociation," which he expanded from Jean Gebser's work on comparative civilizations (Magic World, Mythic World, and Perspectival World). There are three types of homelessness, according to Kramer and Lee. The first kind is carefree heroes who drift around town to town in action adventure movies. They are homeless wanderers/vigilantes who articulate a militaristic version of the world and who make no domestic commitments. They are the ultimate modern individualists. The second type is the pathetic refugee. Unlike the hero drifter, this form of homeless person is powerless or moneyless. The third form rejects the habitat of normal social intercourse. This homeless type shuns all contact. In essence, the homeless communicates the absence of home, that which we take for granted and have come to understand as something that everyone should have. Homelessness, Kramer and Lee argue, comprises a state which occupies a space outside the realm of common sense to the point that portrayals of homeless people takes place within the context of culturally established meanings, meanings derived from place within the system. Television, for example, often reduces and equalizes the homeless to the status of signs, like everything else. We see the image and we are satisfied. The biggest threat, they argue, is nihilism and dissociation.

Finally, Richiko Ikeda and Eric Mark Kramer in chapter 12 examine the linguistic shift from *Furoosha* (bums) to *Hoomuresu* (homeless) in another highly advanced society, Japan, by using the theory of dissociation and Gebser's integral perspective in a postmodern sense. They suggest that the actions of the authorities as presented in the media and the shift in linguistic valence indicates a fundamental relationship between modern identity and economic status. They reveal the changing attitude of the Japanese people through the semiotic analysis of "bums" and "homeless," not merely as words, but as those people who are living in the shadows cast by the oft cited Japanese miracle. People have become dissociated from each other affecting the quality of community and interpersonal relationships. The homeless as "Others" is often dismissed as a meaningless object. Finally, they suggest the constitution of a qualitative relationship and Gebser's "systatic" relationship, which appreciate the differences that Others present and give us an enriched existence.

This collection of readings examines media and social discourses from the 1980s to present and addresses future prospects. It consciously strives to present the many viewpoints on images and language conflicts of those discourses on the homeless from scholarly and real world perspectives. It emphasizes that new issues are likely to emerge as the dialogue and debate. Materials in this collection include both published and unpublished items. Some of the materials are "classics" in the study of the media image of the homeless. These images provide a significant yet politically problematic perceptual framework for making sense of other social issues.

REFERENCES

Carey J. W. (1975). A cultural approach to communication. *Communication*, 2, 1–2.

Foucault, M. (1979). *Discipline and Punish: The Birth of the Prison* (A. Sheridan, Trans.). New York: Vintage Books. (Original work published 1975.)

Manhoff, R. K., Schudson, M. (1986). *Reading the News*. New York: Pantheon Books.

Newcomb, H. (1974). *TV: The Most Popular Art*. New York: Anchors Books.

Rossi, Peter H. (1994). Troubling families. *American Behavioral Scientist*, 37(3), 342–395.

Terzian, P. (January 6, 1999). Homelessness is out of fashion. *Providence Journal*.

Chapter 1

For Cultural Interpretation: A Study of the Culture of Homelessness

John Fiske

The role of interpretation in cultural and media studies is constantly debated. Through an interpretation of the culture of homelessness in the United States, this chapter attempts to demonstrate the value of conjunctural interpretive analysis. Such an analysis is multilevel (ranging from macrostructures to micropractices), multimodal (encompassing texts, practices, empirical data, mediations, organizations, and policy), and explicitly theoretical and political. The chapter also addresses some of the differences between a critical-structural analysis and analyses produced by other, more positivist epistemologies. This chapter presents an example of and an argument for cultural interpretation. It works with two interlinked definitions of culture—"a whole way of live" (Williams, 1958/1989) and "the generation and social circulation of meanings, pleasures and values" (Fiske, 1987). Its argument is framed by and helps to define critical-structural theory as a way of engaging in a materialist cultural studies. Within this perspective it addresses the related questions of what it is that the cultural analyst should study and how the process of interpretation might be validated. The case study upon which the argument is hung is an attempt to understand which meanings of homelessness are currently in circulation in the United States, how and from which social positions they are produced, and what is involved in interpreting and evaluating them. The movement of the chapter is from the micro to the macro, from data to theory, from practice to structure.

AN INSTANCE: READING TEXTS

In a church shelter for homeless men in Midtown, a small Midwestern city, some fifteen or twenty men are watching *Die Hard*.[1] It is early in the movie, and the villains have just invaded the Christmas party of the senior executives of the Nakatomi Corporation. Tagaki, the CEO, is taken to one side and shot after refusing to reveal the computer key to the vaults and the $64 million they contain.

At the moment of death the screen erupts in red, and the audience of homeless men erupts in cheers.

Later in the movie, the villains have gained control of the skyscraper and are holding the surviving executives hostage. Only the hero is beyond their control. The Los Angeles police, who have surrounded the building, bring up an armored vehicle equipped with a battering ram (the one used "in real life" by the LAPD to smash into suspected crack houses). The villains fire a rocket that disables it. From his hidden-vantage point, the hero sees them preparing to fire another; in voiceover he "silently" begs them not to. They do, and the camera shows in detail the tactically unnecessary destruction of the vehicle and the men inside it. More loud cheers from the audience of homeless men.

Of course, this is not an unlicensed reading: The text has consistently represented the LAPD unsympathetically, and I suspect that even the most socially conformist members of the audience will, while aligning themselves with the hero, gain some real if contradictory pleasure in the defeat of this police force. What is significant in this particular case is the unambiguity and enthusiasm of the men's reading. By rejecting the hero's position, they minimized the textual contradictions and aligned themselves univocally with the terrorists.

Most (if not all) of the men had seen the movie before.[2] They paid little attention to the screen until the attack on the skyscraper. They turned off the videotape long before the restoration of law and order at the end. The violence in the movie consistently represented power struggles between unequals—between a small (but well-organized and well-equipped) gang and a huge multinational corporation, between the villains and the lone, ill-equipped hero; between the lowly African-American cop and the white chief of police. The homeless men generated considerable pleasure in imaginatively aligning themselves with the weaker side of each violent conflict. As the movie progressed and the hero became more closely identified with the police outside, so they progressively lost interest in him.

The shelter could receive broadcast television (though not cable), but the men far preferred to watch movies, almost always violent ones, on the VCR. As one of them commented about scheduled TV, "There's nothing on there that interests me, I don't keep set hours, I'm not always around a TV and if I did watch a show and liked it then I'd miss it." The lounge in which the men watched the movie was supplied with "good" reading material: *Life, Time, People, Newsweek,* the local daily newspaper, and religious texts. The men smuggled in tabloids and soft pornography, which they read within the covers of the respectable magazines.

Aligning themselves with the terrorists against the hero's plea not to complete the unnecessary slaughter is reading against the social values embodied in that plea in much the same way as reading pornography within the covers of *Newsweek* is reading against the social values embedded in the rules of the shelter. Rejecting scheduled television is similarly the semiotic activity of distancing themselves from the norms of domesticity and family relationships, of work and leisure, of earning and spending money, which are all deeply inscribed in that schedule. In their reading and viewing practices the men systematically reject the social values that have rejected them. Homelessness is not just their material condition; it saturates their "whole way of life." In interpreting these cultural practices of the homeless I shall use a systematic model, not a positive one. It is their systematicity that makes these practices significant and worthy of interpretation, and it is their systematicity that is the final object of cultural interpretation. Despite—or rather, because of—their social marginality, they offer vital evidence of the working of the social system (that of Reaganomic capitalism). Their validity as an object of study is thus established quite differently than is that of the representative sample of positivism. The concluding section of this chapter will explore further those theoretical and political differences between positivism and critical-structural theory that are, at this stage of the argument, merely signaled.

THE MICRO-ENVIRONMENT

Identifying the relationships between material conditions (such as homelessness) and cultural practices (such as watching television) is not only beginning to clarify the, object of interpretation, it is beginning the interpretive process itself. But these cultural practices do not merely occur at the intersection of texts with socially situated readers; they occur in a specific environment that needs to be treated as a cultural site structured by the same social conditions as those structuring the intersection of text and reader, and the social production of both. This environment is as cultural as any text and any reading practice. The shelter is the spatial equivalent of the text of *Die Hard*; the practices of living within it are the equivalent of the reading practices by which the potential meanings of the text are made into the actualized meanings of the men. Like the text, the environment is produced by the socially central or dominant, but both become part of a way of life only when they are read or lived in by those who, in this case, are positioned quite differently in the social order. The practices of reading and dwelling involve the negotiation of social difference and the power inscribed within it.

This micro-environment[3] is, before the men enter it, already saturated with meanings, among which—as in the unread text of *Die Hard*—those of the socially central and marginal exist conflictually. There are two lounges in the shelter; smoking is allowed in one and not the other. Both contain a mixture of institutional furniture and items donated by, or rather cast off from, middle-class families. The "nicer" furniture is in the nonsmoking lounge; the men watch the violent movies in the "smoker." The rooms were decorated by volunteers from the church, and they look like someone's idea of what would be pleasant and comfortable for undifferentiated others certainly not for oneself. There is one couch in each lounge, but the rest of the chairs are hard and upright. At the back of the room are three tables for playing cards or reading. Just outside the lounges is the supervisor's office from which he can keep an eye on the men's behavior in them.

The shelter that houses the lounges is attached to, yet clearly separated from, a Protestant church. The door between the two is kept locked, and the men have no access to the key. The entrance to the shelter is in a back alley invisible from the entrance to the church; as "Bill," one of the homeless men, commented sardonically, "We can't offend the decent people who come to worship here." The physical features of the shelter and its contents comprise a site of semiotic struggle. For the homeless men, they are packed with meanings of social marginalization, of alienation and of being castoffs or outcasts. Their readings of the shelter are structurally related to their readings of *Die Hard*. But as *Die Hard* contained the meanings and values of the socially central, so too does the shelter. The socially privileged will read *Die Hard* differently and will make very different meanings out of the physical features of the shelter. The difference between the meanings of the socially central and the marginalized is not one of liberal pluralist tolerance but one of social and semiotic struggle. The men's meanings are made against the dominant ones; for them the social difference is part of their consciousness, and they frequently allude to it in their conversation and behavior. For the dominant, however, the sense of social conflict is more muted, if not extinguished; unlike the subordinated, they serve their social interests best by denying social conflict.

The micro-environment is not composed of physical bearers of meaning alone; the regulations and conventions of the shelter are just as powerful a part of its signification. We have seen how the rule banning pornography and the discouragement of tabloid papers have been subverted. Gambling, too, is forbidden, so the men have devised a system of tally—keeping whereby they can play cards with no visible sign of currency exchange; accounts are settled in secret later (usually in cigarettes or money). The men frequently express resentment, scorn, or just bafflement at the shelter's constant attempt to impose what they explicitly identify as irrelevantly middle-class standards upon their behavior. Nowhere is this more apparent than in the rule that they have to be out of the shelter between 8:00 A.M. and 5:00 P.M. These are the hours when "normal" men are out of the house working, and the men are expected to conform to these norms at least to the extent of looking for work. Panhandling, one of the ways in which they spend their days, may be the unemployed's equivalent of work, but it is not the intended outcome of the rule. The men "turn" the rule and the expectations it generates against the class in which it originates.

A similar "turning" of social norms occurs in their reversal of the meanings of night and day. For them, the night in the shelter is a time of warmth, comparative comfort, and social contact, so they do not waste it by sleeping. The day, however, is the opposite, and when not panhandling they try to find places to sleep. Another rule of the shelter limits any man's stay to thirty consecutive nights. For the socially privileged, this rule signifies the comfortable meaning that homelessness is a temporary condition, best met by helping a man get through it until he can get on his feet again. For the men, however, it signifies both the immense difference between their sense of homelessness and that of the charitable providers, and the class conflict inscribed in the difference.

There is a cultural continuum, then, between the micropractices involved in the encounters between text and reader and the immediate environment within which those encounters occur. The relationships among the cultural sites and practices along this continuum are not ones of determination but are mutually informing ones. Environments and texts are structures that contain or shape the practices of dwelling or reading, but the practices are essential to their environmentality or textuality. So, too, the practices are part of what structures the whole way of life, and neither can be said to determine the other. The relationships are constantly in process multidimensionally among practices, among structures, and between practices and structures. Cultural analysis involves "freezing" instances of its object in process (a text, a place, a practice) and extracting them from this constant play of meanings. But the interpretation of this analysis requires its reinsertion back into this multidimensional circulation of meanings that is systematic object of cultural interpretation. Cultural analysis and interpretation needs to move back and forth between sites, practices, and structures, for ultimately the culture of "a whole way of life" is to be sought in the connecting relationships that make life "whole" rather than in selectively privileged quotations from it.

THE MACRO-ENVIRONMENT

The micro-environment of the shelter did not develop in isolation. Just as the shelter-as-environment and the practices of the men living within it are continuous with each other, so, too, the shelter is continuous with the macro-environment. This macro-environment (which I might identify, after Campbell and Reeves, 1989, as "the common-sense of homelessness in the U.S. 1990") is too diffuse and ill-defined to be described exhaustively, but I think I can identify three of the main domains of its production. One domain comprises the aggregation of the numerous organizations, like this shelter, that are trying to cope with homeless people at the local level. Most of them are run by caring, well-intentioned members of the middle-classes, though, as we shall see later, they are being increasingly challenged by activist organizations run by the homeless themselves.

Another domain is that of the national policy toward the homeless. A policy has both a semiotic and a material dimension. In the semiotic one, meanings and evaluations of the homeless are put into circulation; in the material one, economic resources (whose extent is determined in part by the semiotic dimension) are distributed. Reagan's 1984 reference to those who lived on the streets "as you might say, by their own choice" works in the semiotic dimension of the policy whose economic dimension simultaneously increased homelessness and decreased the material resources devoted to it. On both dimensions, the policy of homelessness is related to national policy in general.

The third domain consists of all the uncountable encounters with homelessness that have become part of the daily experience of life in the contemporary United States. These encounters may be actual (passing the homeless in the streets, being panhandled by them), they may be mediated (reading about them in the press, talking about them), or they may be internalized (thinking about homelessness, trying to understand it).

These three domains of organizations, policy, and encounters do not exhaust the terrain in which the struggle for common sense is waged, but they are particularly salient in this example. In my attempt to sketch in broad outline some of their interrelationships, I shall focus on the semiotic dimension, but we cannot finally separate the semiotic from the economic. The circulations of meanings and of material resources are inextricably interdependent in capitalist democracies, and the struggle for one is always part of the struggle for the other. In the last instance, they are the same struggle.[4]

The first section of this chapter has described a specific organizational site. We will return to organizations later after considering the domain of national policy.

A SEMIOTIC AND ECONOMIC FRAMEWORK

Reaganism in the 1980s provided the semiotic and economic framework within which homelessness developed as both a concept and a social reality. Total numbers of the homeless are almost impossible to assess.[5] But for 1982 I found estimates ranging from 250,000 to 1,000,000 (*Editorial Research Reports II*, 1982), and for 1988 from 500,000 to 3,000,000 (*Star Tribune*, 1988). Not surprisingly, the lower figures tended to come from government sources and the higher from organizations working in the field, such as the National Coalition for the Homeless. (Statistics are as important a site of political struggle as any other mode of representation.) But all parties agree on the increase. Even the U.S. Department of Housing and Urban Development (HUD*) (National Survey of Shelters for the Homeless*, 1989) admits that the use of shelters for the homeless tripled between 1984 and 1988.

The increase in the numbers of the homeless has been accompanied by a decrease in government assistance. The funding for HUD shrank from $35.7 billion in 1980 to $14.2 billion in 1987 to $7 billion in 1989 (*Homelessness in Minnesota*, 1989). The number of housing units assisted by the federal government fell from 326,000 in 1978 to 95,000 in 1987 *(U.S. News and World Report,* 1987). Government tax policies under Reagan reduced the tax incentives for private investment in low-income housing and curtailed public housing authorities' ability to issue tax-exempt bonds. As a result, average metropolitan rents doubled, and low-income housing decreased by 30 percent. This loss of low-income housing accompanied a rise in the need for it. Poverty rose 36 percent between 1978 and 1983, the Aid for Families with Dependent Children (AFDC) monthly payments were reduced from a high of $520 in 1968 to $325 in 1985 (figures in 1985 dollars), and the economy as a whole lost approximately 16,000,000 jobs, most of them at the lower end of the wage scale (*Parenting,* 1987).

Homelessness is structural. The majority of the homeless are not personally inadequate. If the homeless population contains proportionately more of the mentally and physically dysfunctional than the population at large, it is because they are the most vulnerable to systematic deprivation. The combination of this structural deprivation with government refusal to accept responsibility caused a gap that only charity could fill—which it did. HUD (*National Survey of Shelters for the Homeless*, 1989) reports with satisfaction that the effort to help the homeless is "characterized by volunteerism." Such rhetoric, like the policy it serves, makes meanings of homelessness that work against the interests of the homeless themselves and in the interests of the advantaged, whether hawks or doves. For volunteerism, semiotically, works to disguise the structural dimension of homelessness by recasting it as a problem for those individuals concerned. The type of charity that works only to ameliorate the immediate problems of homeless people, valuable though such efforts are is finally complicit with the policy that has produced the condition.

In saying this, I intend a sharp distinction between the ethics and politics of the volunteers and donors (which are often benign) and those of the system itself (which are not). Most of the men in the Midtown shelter had good personal relationships with the supervisor and appreciated the efforts he made on their behalf. His Christianity baffled them somewhat, but they coped by interpreting it as a sign of his disconnection from real life. The point is that personal politics may differ from the national policies within which they are put into practice, and personal relationships may contradict the social relations that structure them: Personal relationships are practices, social relations are structural.

These homeless men are some of the flesh-and-blood meanings of a policy that minimizes the role of the state in social life and maximizes the roles of capital and the market. One of the most important functions of the state in capitalism is to preserve the institutions and individual rights of a civil society independently of party political interests on the one hand or of the unfettered market economy on the other. In Reaganomics, however, the linguistic category "civil rights" does not include housing and the means of sustenance. Constructing these semiotically not as civil rights but as the matter of charity to be given by the privileged to the deprived reconfigures homelessness. The relationship of the homeless to the social order becomes not one of citizens whose rights and welfare are the concern of their government, but of social castoffs waiting for one of Bush's "thousand points of light" to wink on them. The cultural dimension of volunteerism and charity circulates politically active meanings of citizenship and of social relations for both recipients and donors.

SOCIAL CONFLICT MADE EXPLICIT

When homelessness is semiotically deviant but economically structural, the social conflict between the privileged (the "normal") and the homeless (the "deviant") becomes explicit. These social conflicts can be traced at all levels, from the most micro (the homeless men's pleasures in *Die Hard*) to the macro level of national policy. A political economy of meanings and audiences extends that of industrial production and distribution, and, in its attempt to trace the mutually informed relationships between semiotics and economics, seeks to avoid the risks of econo-determinism, which are endemic in a theory of political economy that excludes semiosis.

Riot police sweep the homeless from Tompkins Square Park in Manhattan because of increasing social conflict with local residents. Local merchants have organized themselves to address the problem; their president says: "All of us are liberal people. We want to do something to re-establish a community presence in the park—not to kick the homeless out—to try to regulate it. I'm a victim of this. What happens to all the government programs? It all filters down to the community—all of us little people who are now forced to contribute our income, our time, our energy and money to finally do something. I guess that's what

Reagan wanted" (*Pacific News Service*, 1990). While deploring some of the economic effects of the policy (it makes local merchants spend their time and money), she aligns herself with its semiotics by using the word "community," to exclude the homeless. In this she is not alone: Dan Rather, on CBS News, uses language that "locates the homeless in the realm of the 'other,' the 'not us,' 'them'" (Campbell and Reeves, 1989, p. 27). The providers of the Midtown shelter, the Manhattan merchant, and the TV news anchor, all members of similar social formations, all put into circulation similar—"outcast" or "castoff" meanings of homelessness. In resistance, the Tompkins Square Park homeless have organized themselves into the Tent City Posse both to oppose the police and to politicize their condition by recasting it away from the charitable provision of shelter into the class-based condition of poverty.

In People's Park in Berkeley, the University of California also orders police action to clear out the homeless and has evicted People's Cafe's a soup kitchen run by the Catholic Worker. It is ironically significant that People's Park and Tompkins Square Park, both centers of love-ins and peace rallies in the 1960s should be centers of social conflict in the 1980s.

Similar conflictual social relations play themselves out in face-to-face encounters in the streets. Paradise, an African-American homeless man in Greenwich Village, wears cast-off preppy clothes that contradict the seashells woven into his dreadlocks. He shouts at a group of businessmen climbing into their Lincoln Continental, "Look, corporate criminals! Hello Mr. Executive, how you doing? You remember how to be human don't you. Come on, give me a dollar man, I bet you make $50,000 in 10 minutes." As the car moves off the driver winds down the window and says, "Get a job, will you." (*Pacific News Service*, 1990). I do not know if Paradise has ever seen *Die Hard*, but I think I could predict his reaction to the invasion of the executives' Christmas party.

Such explicit conflict is not confined to social encounters but is growing within organizations. Charity and volunteerism defy social privilege; so too, in a different way, does social welfare. All work to produce what has become known as "the dependency mentality" in which the homeless consent to the position that the dominant social order wishes them to occupy.

But in many cities the homeless are forming their own activist groups that aim to challenge this dependency mentality and the class control inherent in it; their attempt to increase the control of the homeless over their social conditions is an engagement in class conflict. As a member of the National Union for the Homeless says, "[The homeless] don't want shelters, they want houses, they don't want welfare, they want jobs. That's a profound threat to people who say they want to enable, but really want to control" (*City Pages*, 1990). Another 9 member of the union comments, "We've got a war here you've got the poor on one side and the rich and the movers and shakers on the other. The shelter providers are in the middle they grab crumbs from the powerful to keep us from really doing battle with the system" (*City Pages*, 1990).

A Minneapolis homeless activist group called Up and Out of Poverty (UOP) has engendered local criticism for its insistence that homelessness is a political problem in which the homeless themselves must have a voice. And the criticism comes mainly from the traditional service providers—the charitable organizations and welfare agencies whose services are seen by the homeless as ways of controlling them. An organizer of Community Campaign for Housing Now, for example, has criticized UOP "for victimizing vulnerable people by encouraging them to break the law in 91 housing squats and thus making them subject to arrest" (*City Pages*, 1990, p. 12).

The semiotic struggle over homelessness is part of a social struggle, and it is being waged in all the domains that go to make up the national common sense. Conflicts between organizations, street clashes between the police and the homeless, sidewalk confrontations between panhandlers and passersby, and the homeless men cheering in Midtown as the CEO is killed onscreen are all part of the social contestations for the meanings of homelessness. Their relationship to each other is not deterministic but systemic, multidimensional, and multidirectional. This systematicity is evidenced in the similarity of the cultural practices of Paradise in Manhattan, in his preppy suit, engaging in verbal class warfare with the corporate executives and Bill in Midtown, on his cast-off middle-class couch, aligning himself with the villains in their attack on the corporate headquarters. There is no direct connection between Paradise and Bill, but their practices are systemic instances of the social system developed over a decade of Reaganomics. So, too, the violence in *Die Hard* is not deterministically but conjuncturally related to the violence in the streets. It is not mere coincidence that representations of antisocial violence are popular at the same time as social inequalities have been exacerbated. The homeless men cheering the defeat of the police in *Die Hard* and activist homeless organizations clashing with the police in Minneapolis and Washington are part of the same conjuncture of social forces. Social movements take place in people's he ads and in the streets, in conversation and in the voting booth. Meanings circulate in multiple forms in multiple sites and are active in all modes of social experience.[6]

Although this multidirectional circulation of meanings cannot be reduced to deterministic models of cause and effect, I must emphasize that it does not occur freely, nor does it occur under conditions of equality. Macrostructural forces are at times modified by micropractices, but micropractices are always modified and shaped by macrostructures. The interactivity of this mutual structuration is not equal—the macro is more determinative than the micro. The macrostructural forces of Reaganomics constitute the powerfully determinative, but not totally deterministic, conditions within (and sometimes against which) micropractices are put into action. Yet despite this inequality, practices can, and often do take antagonistic stances to the structures that constrain them and in this antagonism can work to loosen the constraints and modify the structures.

The connections between Bill and Paradise and Reaganomics may never take a concrete form that can provide us with empirical evidence of their existence, but they are amenable to theoretical analysis, and their existence can be demonstrated by theoretically if not empirically. As the object of cultural analysis lies in, the movement between practices and structures, so the mode of cultural analysis must be able to move between empirical data and social theory, between the contextualized utterance and the discursive system. The sites and practices where the continual flux of meanings in process become visible can lead the cultural critic through their less visible interconnections to an under-standing of the sociocultural order in process at a specific historical conjuncture.

INTERPRETATION AND THEORY

I have been working with two linked definitions of culture: one is "a whole way of life," and the other is "the generation and social circulation of meanings, pleasures and values." The first is so all encompassing that it may seem daunting to the analyst, but its value lies in its insistence that no single manifestation of culture (text, reader-response, ideological moment, and so on) can be interpreted on its own. The second leads the analyst to seek out a number of sites where this social circulation is accessible to analysis.

In this study I have selected my sites of analysis according to two criteria. I wanted ones situated on different levels of social experience that spanned the continuum from the micro to the macro. I also looked for ones of different mo-dalities or moods, that is, of different relationships to a material reality. The conditional mood (the mood of the "as if") of the men's meanings of *Die Hard*, with its imaginary (but "really" imagined) world of reversed power relations, is analyzed in conjunction with the indicative mood (the mood of "what is") street encounters and the imperative mood (the mood of "what must be") of Reaganite policy and police. Cheering the killing of a corporate executive in a movie, having a request for a dollar rejected in the street, and being turned into an ob-ject of charity or police repression are modally different and geographically dis-persed, but they are structurally related. If our sites of analysis span a range of levels and modalities of cultural experience, we may have greater confidence that the theoretically produced relations among them are valid evidence of their systematicity, interpretation can never be objective but must always be theoreti-cal, and insofar as the choice of one theory requires the rejection of others, the-ory implies politics. (The one-time positivist belief that one theory is "truer" than another can no longer be tenable.) In a positivist epistemology, theorizing takes place after data have been observed and collected, and the theoretical un-derstanding of the social whole is achieved by fitting together the previously and independently acquired knowledge of its parts. The theory thus constructed is evaluated by its ability to account for the data that precede it and upon which it is dependent.

De Saussure (1974), however, reverses the relationship: "Far from it being the object which antedates the viewpoint, it would seem that it is the viewpoint which creates the object" (p. 8). In this view, theory construction precedes and determines the collection of data: Theory does not account for the already known but provides a way of conceptualizing both the reality that is to be inter-preted and the process of interpretation. Theory acknowledges that data have to be selected, for we can never analyze totality, they also have to be identified and separated from that totality. The processes of selection and separation are theo-retically driven, and different theories will produce different data. In one epis-temology, data exist in a pretheoretical universe; in the other they (can only) exist in a pretheorized one.

Bill's words, "We can't offend the decent people who come to worship here," can be produced as different data by different theories. My critical structuralist theory first selects his word "decent" as more significant than, say, the word "worship," and then generates the interpretation of it. A semiotic inflection of this theory produces, "decent" as an example of the multi-accentuality of the sign by which the social struggle is continued in the semiotic domain (Volosinov, 1973). Bill is, in this light, stealing the word from the discourse of those whom he describes ironically by it, and "turning" it. against them. He takes their word into his discourse and gives his meanings of it greater power than theirs; in doing this he does not deny "their" meanings but opposes them and, in the opposition, reverses the normal power relations. Macrosocial conflict between the privileged and the dispossessed is practiced in his use of the one word.[7] Bill is not unique in his linguistic trickery. Campbell and Reeves (1989) quote another homeless man turning the dominant discourse against itself on CBS News: "I am not mentally ill. I happen to be what you would call economically unstable" (p. 30).

The discursive discordance between "mentally ill" and "economically unstable" is an utterance of the social differences between "I" and "you." It is evidence of the competence of the subordinate to exploit multi-accentuality and engage in the struggle for meaning. When the scope of multi-accentuality is enlarged from sign to discourse, the concept is enlarged into that of heteroglossia. In heteroglossic discourse the voices of the subordinate refuse to be silenced, which is why heteroglossia is progressive and monoglossia reactionary (Bakhtin, 1981). The discourse of domination tends toward monoglossia and its signs toward uni-accentuality because domination requires only its own discourse and attempts to absorb the discourses of the subordinate into it (Barthes, 1973). The subordinate, however, need and develop competence in both dominant and subordinate discourses; the social and semiotic conditions of subordination are necessarily multi-accentual and heteroglossic. The competence to exploit multi-accentuality is therefore better developed in subordinate than in dominant social formations.

The theory of multi-accentuality does not stress the importance of the meaning of signs (in a definitional or referential sense) so much as the social relations that are reenacted in the struggle for those meanings. Multi-accentuality, heteroglossia, and polysemy are related concepts that characterize signs and texts not as an open multiplicity of meanings but as structured terrains whereon the struggle for meanings may be engaged. Texts do not have intrinsically preferred meanings against which oppositional or negotiated readings position themselves; rather, they contain structured sets of (often contradictory) values that may be conjuncturally related to the structured values of the social order. When the homeless men aligned themselves with the terrorists against the hero, they were not so much reading against the text (for the text gave ample license for the alignment) but were rather aligning themselves against the dominant social values embodied in the hero's words. They were engaging in social relations rather than making meanings that opposed those preferred by the textual structures of preference but rather that these structures of preference conjuncturally with social structures and need to be analyzed in terms of conjuncture which automati-

cally preferred meanings of a text may vary according to the social and historical conditions of its circulation.

The theory of multi-accentuality also requires us to rethink the notion of
subjectivity, particularly its inability to allow subjects their own "accents" by
which to speak their experience or to contest their subjection. Although these
men were materially subjected, there was considerable evidence that many of
them had not become subjects in ideology. Their consciousness remained
largely theirs, despite the material and semiotic deprivation they suffered.

There is a strong case for replacing the concept of subjectivity (however
split, contradictory, or nomadic) with that of "socially interested agency."[8] Late
capitalist societies are so elaborated and contradictory, power within them is
exerted in so many ways (not all of which endorse each other all of the time),
that they require of the people living within them a degree of agency by which
to negotiate the mundanities of their everyday lives. The conditions within
which this agency is exerted are always constrained; but nevertheless agency is
exerted, and its exertion can at times oppose and weaken the constraints that
seek to contain and limit it. The agents (i.e., the people who practice agency)
have a consciousness of their social conditions that is theirs and that therefore
operates in antagonistic relationship to any ideological consciousness, and that is
used, inter alia, by the agents to produce their own sense of their social interests
and of how these interests may be mobilized in their immediate social relations.
The concept of agency, then, entails the ability both to be aware of one's social
interests and to act to promote them.

Such socially interested agents are not subjects, though the forces of subjection determine in part both the conditions under which agency is practiced and
the resources available to perform it. Socially interested agents are not free
agents; enlightenment rationalism, freely available to all, is a categorically different theoretical construct. The ability to perceive and promote one's social
interests may indeed involve reason, but this reasoning is no more an ahistorical,
asocial rationality than is the agent a free-willed individual. While reason may
be involved in agency, it is never all that is involved. Reading pornography under the covers of *Newsweek* is a socially interested action, but it is rational only
up to a point, and its "reasonableness" is specific to the immediate conditions of
its performance. There are also other nonrational ways of knowing at work here,
which are ways of knowing and promoting one's social interests situationally
rather than understanding and planning them rationally. They produce localized,
embodied, constrained understandings that are appropriate to a situated agency,
for agency can be practiced only in historically and socially specific conditions
and as part of the interplay of power that is endemic in them.

If agency is never free, neither is it equal, for the social allegiances that constitute the power bloc are well aware of their social interests and how to promote
them, and the resources by which they can empower their agency are greater by
far than those available to the homeless men. But there is more to the men's
cheers at the destruction of the police and their vehicle than is revealed by interpreting the social relations in which they were engaging and their agency performed in that engagement. The cheers were loud, enthusiastic, and deeply felt;
they were evidence of an affective pleasure whose significance lay in its inten-

sity. We observed more emotional energy in the men's responses to *Die Hard* and similar movies than in any other aspect of their daily lives. Which meanings were being activated and put into circulation may be a matter of interpretive debate, but the affective intensity of the process is beyond question.

These scenes from *Die Hard* mattered to the men. In their popular culture there was a totality and animation that was lacking elsewhere in their daily lives. This may be an example of that invested energy identified by Grossberg (1988) as "affect," which is so important in popular culture, particularly the self-empowerment it offers in the construction and validation of a social identity from below, a space or moment that the dispossessed can possess and control as theirs. This is not a mere escape from the forces of domination but is a holding out against them that produces a form of power or confidence that can sustain our everyday struggles against them when we leave our textual "refuge" (movie, rock concert, book) and re-engage with those forces in their more material forms.

THEORETICAL CONSISTENCY

Interpretation is always a risky business and must always' retain an element of provisionality, which theory works to minimize by applying a number of methodological "checks." One such check is for theoretical consistency between different levels of analysis between, for example, the analysis of Bill's use of the word "decent" and the already theorized social reality of capitalism as a system of conflicting interests. Other consistency checks are made between data produced at different sites and of different ontological statuses. "Decent" and "economically unstable" were produced at different sites; "decent" and the men's cheers at *Die Hard* were from adjacent sites but differed ontologically. "Decent" was spoken to the investigator and (possibly) would not have existed outside of the investigation that produced it. But the cheers at the unnecessary destruction of the police and the vehicle in *Die Hard*, were, I believe, less directly affected by the process of investigation. Interpreting these pleasures as lying in their "turning" of the "decent" meanings of the incident (those preferred by the hero in the text and the dominant value system in society) is theoretically consistent, via multi-accentuality and across ontological difference, with the interpretation of Bill's words.

Multi-accentuality, as a concept within a critical structural theory, also proposes that the socially contextualized utterance has greater significance than the speech system that makes it possible. Both "decent" and the *Die Hard* scene have these meanings only in the specific social relations of their use. In the language system in the abstract, the multi-accentuality of "decent" is merely an unrealized potential that because of the interrelationship between the language system and the social system, is not open or equal but is structured in dominance to favor its socially central meanings. Bill's use of it, then, in this particular context, is oppositional. So, too, the multi-accentuality of the scene from *Die Hard* in the system of the text simultaneously favors the socially and semiotically dominant while exposing this dominance to contestation.

This interpretive cross-checking can be usefully extended to data that exist independently of the investigation such as the furniture of the lounge, and the placing of the shelter vis-à-vis the church and its rules and regulations. Their production as data is purely theoretical. But they, too, are multi-accentual; their quite different meanings for the providers and recipients of charity are part of the same sociosemiotic conflict, and their signifying potential is structured by the same social relations as are the uses of "decent" and *Die Hard*.

Although the furniture may preexist the investigation, it is produced as data only when taken up by theory and put into discourse; before that it is semiotically inert, unsignifying. Putting into discourse is a major transformation, not only changing the status of the object into a sign but as part of that process transposing it from the experiential world of the investigated into the theoretical world of the investigator. The differences between the discourses through which people experience their everyday lives and theoretical discourse of intepretation constitute a serious epistemological problem for the cultural analyst. Any solution to it must, I believe, involve a dialogic rather than an imperialist relation between the two. By this, I mean that the interpreter should not impose his or her discourse, already constituted as superior in explanatory power, upon the other, but should seek points of discursive congruence between the two, and in constructing these congruences should allow the interpreting discourse to be inflected by that of the interpreted. Putting the shelter's furniture into discourse by describing it as "cast-off" is, therefore, a crucial transformative movement, not only from the inert into the signifying, from object into datum, but also from an experiential discourse into an interpretive one. I believe that there are valid congruences between the two discourses, in that the men's resentment at the shelter's attempt to impose upon them norms that they see as inappropriately middle-class has led me to describe the furniture in terms of the class conflict between its point of origin and point of use. "Cast-off," as a descriptor, forms to a point of congruence between the experiential discourse of the men, the interpretive discourse of the analyst, and the larger theoretical discourse of critical-structural theory. It is, I would argue, theoretically consistent and therefore valid.

Describing the shelter's furniture or Paradise's suit as "donated," however, would be part of a liberal pluralist interpretation that might fit with the experiential discourse of the providers of charity but would be incongruent with that of its recipients. Such a liberal pluralist theory might readily interpret the policy of volunteerism, but it would be stretched to account satisfactorily for the men's pleasures in *Die Hard* and would find it almost impossible to account for the street clashes with the police and the law-breaking squats. I reject an interpretation of the furniture as "donated" first because of its noncongruence with the discourses that the homeless men use in their daily lives and second because of its inconsistency with a critical-structural theory of capitalist societies as unequal and conflictual. As a theoretical constant, this sense of social conflict can be found in the textuality of *Die Hard* and in the homeless men's reading of it. It can be found in the placement, furnishings, and regulations of the shelter vis-à-vis the men's practices of living within it. The back alley entrance, Paradise's dress, and the Manhattan merchant's exclusion of the homeless from the community all signify the social outcasting of the deviant by the central at the microlevel of sites and practices. It is this semiotic outcasting that produces the material cast-off furniture, cast-off clothing, and cast-off men.

At the macrolevel this same outcasting is interpreted as one significance of the economic policies of the 1980s, which have situated homelessness politically, economically, and semiotically within the domain of charity. In this domain the social relations between donor and recipient reproduce those between the dominant and the subordinate; making homelessness the concern of charity inserts it into the class struggle in a way that it would not be were it constructed as a matter of citizens' rights. The same class struggle that is waged semiotically in the shelter in Midtown is waged socially in Tompkins Square Park and People's Park. Interpreting the men's turning off the videotape before the police victory at the end of *Die Hard* requires a theoretically produced perception of the conjunctural relationships between specific police actions in New York and San Francisco, watching a movie in Midtown, and the political economy of the early 1990s. And all need to be theoretically consistent with a socially critical account of the history and internal structures of capitalist societies.

DISCOURSE ANALYSIS AND THE SYSTEMIC MODEL

The data that interact so crucially with theory in the interpretive model I am attempting to demonstrate are empirical but not empiricist and thus differ significantly from the data of positivism. Positivism, particularly in its quantitative form, insists that its data should be representative, that is, that they should constitute a proportionately accurate miniaturization of the larger social reality. In a critical structural theory, data are not representative but systemic. By this I mean that they are instances of a system in practice. The homeless men in Midtown are not representative of the homeless in general, they are, white, male, Midwestern, single, among others, but insofar as their experiences are systemic we can generalize from them, not to other homeless, but to the workings of the system (Reaganomic capitalism) within which these specific conditions of homelessness have developed. This process of generalization (from a practice to the system) differs categorically from generalizing in positivism (from the representative sample to the whole population).

The methodology underlying the systemic model is that of discourse analysis. No utterance is representative of other utterances, though of course it shares structural features with them; a discourse analyst studies utterances in order to understand how the potential of the linguistic system can be activated when it intersects at its moments of use with a social system. The utterance is an actualization in a historical relationship of the linguistic potential. So the cultural analyst studies utterances of culture in order to understand both the system that structures "the whole way of life" and the ways of living that people devise within it.

The study of the homeless men in Midtown was not an ethnography in the anthropological or social scientific sense of the term; it did not aim to attain a full or objective understanding of their whole way of life, for that would be impossible. Rather, it was an attempt to listen, to try to hear ways in which their speech was accented by them, not by the dominant. Robert Dawson, my colleague, spent many nights sitting patiently in the lounge, sharing cigarettes and conversation with those of the men who chose to approach him. He asked no prepared or directive questions and distributed no questionnaires; instead he tried to explain who he was and why he was there, and then waited to listen to what they wanted to tell him or observed what they allowed him to. The intention was for me to join him once he judged that I would be accepted; this point was never reached, so the data were gathered by him alone. The men generally considered the study somewhat silly and referred to Robert with good-humored disdain as "schoolboy," but some of them at least gradually came to accept (maybe because of its "silliness") that neither the study nor Robert were part of the system of deprivation and rejection. Of course, they never lost their sense of difference—Robert was never able to participate in their culture—but we believe that they did allow him, on their terms, some access to what they wanted him to hear from them.

We have attempted to ensure that our interpretations of their experiences have been informed, as far as possible, by their "accents"; we have tried to allow, as far as we could, their voices to accent our discourse, though of course we can never speak with their accents nor for their experiences. Our study was, therefore, in no way scientific, comprehensive, or objective. The glimpses it afforded us were partial, were less under our control than the men's; we "heard" only what they wanted to tell us. (We do, of course, consider that allowing us to observe their behavior was a way of telling, that behavior in the presence of an observer is a form of speech.) Consequently, the knowledge that we produced by transforming what we "heard" into our discourse took the form not of objective data but of critical and engaged understanding. Such a knowledge is not objective, detached, or distant, but is a socially engaged knowledge hoping to contribute to those social forces that are working to change the social order that is always the final object of its analysis.

The term "structure" or "structural" is common to both positivist and systemic models, but there are crucial differences in the ways in which each uses it. For positivism (e.g., content analysis), a structure is a coherent patterning of empirical data that is part of the larger social reality theoretically derived from the data. Such a structure may be related to more abstract, less empirically derived structures in that social reality (particularly value structures, as in Gerbner's cultivation theory). So a content analysis of gender portrayal on television revealing that women are portrayed less frequently than men and in a narrower range of occupations and settings may be convincingly related to the more abstract values of patriarchy. The tracing of such interstructural relationships is common to both systemic models and positivist ones, but the similarity ends there. Systemic theories of structure go further than do positivist ones, for systemic structures, such as language, are generative whereas positivist structures are descriptive. Systemic structures generate the practices by which they are used—and are, in their turn, modified by those practices. Positivist structures, however, have effects, not practices, and the relationship between structure and effect is one-way. In positivism, structures have no practice.

The structure of language, on the other hand, has a mutually informing relationship with the utterances that are its practices. The system is produced in part, at least, by its practices, as the practices are produced in part, at least, by the system. Systems and practices both structure each other and are structured by each other; structuration is a two-way process. Because positivism does not theorize structures in relationship to practice, it does not have a theory of either how they change or how they can act as agents of change. Bourdieu (1984) makes the point that theoretical methods are better able to account for social change than those of quantitative positivism, for these produce snapshots of a social system at a particular moment, and positivism therefore tends to model social differences as social stratification. Theory, however (and for Bourdieu the word seems to be a code for Marxist critical theory), is better able to trace social struggle, for that occurs over time as part of the dialectic of history; consequently, this type of theory models social differences not as stratification but as struggle.

When positivism models the differences in the social order as relatively stable and/or harmonious, its policies tend toward liberal pluralism; when it evacuates that social order from the research agenda altogether (as in much TV effects research), its politics shift toward the reactionary. Some of the differences between liberal pluralist positivism and critical-structural theory emerge in the debate around "the active audience." The "active audience" of uses and gratifications (a positivist theory) differs significantly from that of critical theory particularly in its claim that active uses of the media actually gratify needs. This is not the case in critical structural theory. Here the needs (for more material or symbolic resources, for more power and control) can be met only by social action; the activity of the media user is that of articulating those needs within the social relations that both produce and frustrate them and of establishing and validating a social identity that is a bottom-up product rather than a top-down one. Audience activity is an engagement in social relations across social inequality; the satisfaction in the process lies in control over the terms of that engagement, but there is no satisfaction of the needs generated by the inequality. In fact the reverse is the case—the activity of the audience articulates, confirms, and validates its social needs. The homeless men's use of *Die Hard* did nothing to change their conditions of—rejection and deprivation but clarified and confirmed their consciousness of them. The men's active viewing was gratifying only insofar as it enabled them to participate in producing a bottom-up culture of homelessness, alongside Paradise in Greenwich and the activist organizations in Minneapolis, Washington, and elsewhere.

Critical-structural theory and positivism also interpret television violence very differently. Critical theory assumes that certain violent actions, whether social or textual, can be embodiments of and engagement in social struggle. Interpreting violence as a performance of social relations inserts it into a categorically different epistemology from that of traditional effects research. The "effects" construction of violence as individualized behavior not only excludes the social system from the problem to be investigated but assumes that, in the event of a mismatch between the behavior of individuals and the social order, the desired "fit" must be achieved by changing the individual and not the society. It is a reactionary epistemology, and research within it has, unsurprisingly, been demanded by right-wing lobby groups and generously funded by government research grants.

In media studies, positivism has tended to produce a normative epistemology; critical-structural theory, however, does not. It does not assume that what is statistically most normal is therefore most significant. Instead, discourse analysts (like poets) often find that marginal and abnormal uses of language are highly significant because they reveal, in a way that more normal linguistic usages do not, the extremes of which a system is capable. Systems are often more susceptible to change or modification at their margins than at their centers; social change typically originates in marginalized or subordinated minorities and, as critical theory has a political stake in social change, it requires a model that allows the marginal, the deviant, and the abnormal to be always granted significance and at times major significance. History may show that the 29 percent of women who were not wives, stewardesses, or models may be more significant than the 71 percent who were (Dominick and Rauch, 1972). The choice of homeless men as an object of study was therefore a theoretical and political choice, and its objective was not just to understand their social conditions but rather through an interpretation of those conditions to shed some light upon the system at a point of extremity, a point where a movement for social change might originate.

THE NEED FOR CONJUNCTURAL ANALYSIS

In this chapter I have attempted to argue by example in favor of that sort of cultural interpretation which, following Gramsci and Hall (e.g., Hall, et al., 1978), I have called conjunctural, as opposed to organic. An organic analysis is appropriate to a social order at times of relative stability, and it seeks to understand the means by which such hegemonic stability is achieved. Conjunctural analysis, however, is appropriate to societies (or areas within them) at points of crisis, where they are more vulnerable to change. At such moments social struggle is most acute and most visible; it is therefore most readily accessible to a conjunctural analysis that seeks to understand the variety of social forces that come together and conflict at any one particular historical moment.

The form of cultural interpretation I am arguing for in this chapter is based upon a (partial and obviously incomplete) conjunctural analysis because I believe that homelessness may well constitute such a crisis point in U.S. society. Such interpretation is socially extensive, for it moves between macrohistorical factors and micropractices taking in texts, people, and objects along the way. Its extensiveness becomes the final object of the interpretation, for it is only in its extensiveness that cultural circulation matters. Individual sites, texts, and practices may afford us glimpses of this circulation, but their interpretation requires their re-insertion into the conjunctural relationships from which they are necessarily abstracted for detailed analysis. Conjunctural interpretation requires its theoretical dimension to be explicit, for the validity of the interpretation and the validity of the theory are interdependent. The potential circularity of the relationship between theory and interpretation is challenged by the multimodality of the data with which both have to cope, and their validity can be evaluated only comparatively, not in terms of absolute truth. The critical evaluation of theory involves a comparison between different theoretical perspectives, the data they produce as significant, and the consistency with which those data can be both interpreted and related to larger historical and social forces that can only be analyzed theoretically, not empirically. The potential of empirical data to be counterinterpreted within other theoretical frames is what enables them to challenge the theory that informs them.

The comparative evaluation of theories has also a historical dimension, for theories are as much products of their time as any other cultural phenomena. I believe, then, that the increasing consciousness of social conflict sharpened by the increasing material difference between the haves and the have-nots during the 1980s constitutes a powerful argument for the contemporary pertinence of critical structural theory. But the evaluation of a theory cannot be confined to its comprehensiveness, consistency, and historical pertinence; it must finally involve questions of ethics and politics. The knowledge a theory produces and the ways of knowing it promotes have social effects and therefore are imbricated in the values by which those who choose to work within it live within the social order that is the object of that knowledge. Any cultural interpretation acts upon the sociocultural order that it interprets, and such action will finally be evaluated by assessing which aspects of that order it works to endorse and which to criticize, and therefore which sees of social interests it aligns itself with and which against. Interpretations, theories, and politics are inescapably part of our academic culture; they are the prime means by which we contribute to the social circulation of meanings and values, and that is why debate about them matters.

NOTES

1. For a fuller account of the ethnographic work upon which this study is based see Dawson (1990) and Fiske and Dawson (in press). The second of these pieces treats more fully the important issues of gender and of the taste for representations of violence and the calls to regulate them. To focus my argument and to keep this chapter within reasonable bounds I have decided, reluctantly, not to address these issues here.

2. For those who have not seen the movie: The hero is a New York cop who travels to Los Angeles to spend Christmas with his estranged wife and their daughter. His wife left him to further her career as an executive. During the executives' Christmas party, terrorists take over the corporate headquarters and hold everyone for ransom. The plot involves the lone hero gradually killing the terrorists one by one and finally defeating them. In the process of restoring law and order he wins back his wife.

3. I call this environment "micro" to distinguish it from the "macro" environment of broader social and historical forces that I explore in the next section.

4. Campbell and Reeves (1989), in their detailed and insightful study of the representation of homelessness on TV, have shown how the growth in the numbers of the homeless in the 1980s was accompanied by the appearance of "homelessness" as a new semiotic category in both news discourse and in American "common sense," one that, incidentally, displaced the previous one of "vagrancy." Material changes and semiotic changes are always interlinked historically. The semiotics of the word "homeless" are equally worthy of analysis. The loss of home signifies, more or less invisibly, the loss of job, the loss of family, and the loss of a legitimate, normalized relationship to the social

order. "Home," one of the most meaning-saturated signs in the U.S. lexicon, is well able to meet the demands placed upon it here.

5. The absence of statistics with any claim to authority is an indicator of how little attention Reaganite policies pay to homelessness; compare, for instance, the statistical abundance granted to crime.

6. One of the more bizarre sites where meanings of homelessness may be found is the brochure of the fashion designer Christian Francis Roth for his spring show in New York in 1991. One of his "themes" is that of "hoboes" (a more anodyne word for the homeless even than "vagrant"), which entails covering his clothes with loud bright patches. He explains, "My hobo group is all about the idea of making clothes last. If a hobo has a suit with holes, he patches it up. If a woman gets a hole in her jacket, why shouldn't she patch it? Or get one from me, pre-patched?" A more offensive attempt to incorporate the signs of homelessness would be hard to imagine, but at least this example shows the extremes of class difference engaged in the struggle for meaning.

7. I could also draw upon Bakhtin (1968), whose theories are, unsurprisingly, consistent with those of Volosinov, to analyze in a similar way the social struggle practiced in the word "offend."

8. The work of Archer (1988), Bauman (1973), and Giddens (1979) is formative here.

REFERENCES

Archer, M. (1988). *Culture and agency: The place of culture in social theory.* Cambridge: Cambridge University Press.

Bakhtin, M. (1968). *Rabelais and his world.* Cambridge, MA: MIT Press.

Bakhtin, M. (1981). *The dialogic imagination.* Austin, TX: University of Texas Press.

Barthes, R. (1973). *Anthologies.* London: Paladin.

Bauman, Z. (1973). *Culture as praxis.* London: Routledge and Kegan Paul.

Bourdieu, P (1984). *Distinction: A social critique of the judgment of taste.* Cambridge, MA: Harvard University Press.

Campbell, R., and Reeves, J. (1989). Covering the homeless: The Joyce Brown story. *Critical Studies in Mass Communication,* 6, 21–42.

City Pages (August 1, 1990). Minneapolis, MN, p. 12.

Dawson, R. (July 16–20, 1990). Culture and deprivation: Ethnography and everyday life. Paper presented at the *International Communication Association Conference,* Dublin.

De Saussure, F. (1974). *Course in general linguistics.* London: Fontana.

Dominick, J. R., and Rauch, G. E. (1972). The image of women in network TV commercials. *Journal of Broadcasting,* 16, 259–265.

Editorial Research Reports II (16). (1982).

Fiske, J. (1987). British cultural studies and television. In R. Allen (Ed.), *Channels of discourse* (pp. 254–289). Chapel Hill: University of North Carolina.

Fiske, J., and Dawson, R. (in press). Audiencing violence. In L. Grossberg and E. Wartella (Eds.), *Towards a comprehensive theory of the audience.* Champaign: University of Illinois Press.

Giddens, A. (1979). *Central problems in social theory.* London: Macmillan.

Grossberg, L. (1988). Postmodernity and affect: All dressed up, with no place to go. *Communication,* 10, 271–293.

Hall, S., Critcher, C., Jefferson, T., Clarke, J., and Roberts, B. (1978). *Policing the crisis: Mugging, the state, and law and order.* London: Macmillan.

Homelessness in Minnesota (February, 1989). Report by the Minnesota State Planning Agency.

National survey of shelters for the homeless (March, 1989). Washington, DC: U.S. Department of Housing and Urban Development.

Pacific News Service (April 16, 1990). Minneapolis.

Parenting (March, 1987).

Star Tribune (November 4, 1988). Minneapolis,

U.S. News and World Report, (August 7, 1987).

Volosinov, V. (1973). *Marxism and the philosophy of language.* New York: Seminar Press.

Williams, R. (1989). Culture is ordinary. In R. Williams, *Resources of hope.* London: Verso. (Original work published 1958.)

Chapter 2

Covering the Homeless:
The Joyce Brown Story

Richard Campbell and Jimmie L. Reeves

Mainstream American journalism "discovered" the homeless in the early 1980s. Those investigating homelessness contend that shortly after 1980 the phenomenon "moved from the margins of public awareness to center stage" (Redburn and Buss 1986, p. 113). Indeed, one indicator of this movement to the center is a striking semantic shift in the world of news. Throughout the 1970s, *The New York Times* Index provided no "homeless persons" category, listing instead scattered articles under "vagrancy" or "housing." In 1981 and 1982, only five articles were indexed under homeless while in each of these years, sixty-one and ninety-nine articles turned up under vagrancy. In 1983, the language dramatically changed as homeless persons displaced vagrancy as a classification. That year, eighty-two news articles and editorials appeared under homeless persons; only five articles appeared under vagrancy. By 1984, a total of 159 stories turned up under homeless; two under vagrancy. And in 1985, the number swelled to 235, none under vagrancy.

Why the semantic shift from vagrancy to homelessness? The modification in part represented changes in both the socioeconomic structure and in the numbers and types of homeless persons. Vagrancy conjures up bygone images of tramps and hobos, of drifters who choose to wander and live on the margins of society. Being without home, however, speaks much more to a severe rupture in the fabric of Middle America—to the lack of individual choice. Homelessness signifies being without those centrist virtues "home" connotes: safety, stability, family, warmth, neighborhood, community (see Watson and Austerberry, 1986). Being without home transports a person, often violently and unwillingly, from mainstream to margin.

Certainly homelessness is not a 1980s phenomenon. Most studies trace its roots as a serious social problem to the industrialization and urbanization of the nineteenth century (Watson and Austerberry, 1986, p. 26). Still, it is 1980s news, and it became so in much the same fashion as war protests became news in the 1960s or ecology in the 1970s. Just as staged draft card burnings or Earth

Day put antiwar activism and ecology on the media map, homeless activism, such as Mitch Snyder's hunger protests, gave journalism a news frame (and a character) for its dramas. "Today, homelessness has been rediscovered as a social problem distinct from the broader problems of persistent poverty, unemployment, and social deviance," note Redburn and Buss (1986, p. 2). In fact, it was not until 1984 that HUD reported the first national "systematic research" on homelessness since the Depression (Redburn and Buss, 1986; U.S. Department of Housing and Urban Development, 1984).

Several factors contributed not only to modified word usage but to a genuine rise in homelessness in the 1980s. A common perception of the homeless often fostered by startling news images of incoherent street people, is that most are mentally ill (Kozol, 1988). However, while the deinstitutionalization of mental hospital patients in the 1970s triggered the start of a new generation of homeless, most current studies consider the mentally ill to account only for 20 to 25 percent of the total homeless population, with some estimates as low as 16 percent (Kozol, 1988; Marion, 1987; Redburn and Buss, 1986).

Current research argues instead that homelessness is an economic problem rooted in three areas. First, the recession of the early 1980s continues to siphon off 2 million industrial jobs a year; many then lose homes and find the street (Kozol, 1988; Redburn and Buss, 1986). Second, the lack of affordable homes and federal cutbacks for low-income housing subsidies (which dropped during the Reagan Administration from $30 billion in 1980 to $7.5 billion by 1988) also account for increases, especially in the number of homeless families and children (Kozol, 1988). Third, "the gentrification of the cities" saw entrepreneurs reclaim cheap flophouses and skid row districts where marginal communities sought solace and invisibility (Kozol, 1988; Redburn and Buss, 1986; U.S. Department of Housing and Urban Development, 1984). As Marion (1987, p. 44) puts it, "Doorways, alleys, abandoned buildings, vacant lots—these holes in the cityscape, these gaps in public consciousness, became real estate. The homeless, who had been there all the time, were overtaken by economic progress, and they became intruders." Add increased drug and alcohol abuse to these basic factors, and an alarming portrait of an expanding homeless problem, certainly much more rooted in economy than in madness, emerges. Estimates of the number of American homeless range from 250,000 to 3 million (Kozol, 1988; Marin, 1987; Redburn and Buss, 1986; U.S. Department of Housing and Urban Development, 1984). And in trying to account for the large disparity in these numbers, one study laments, "Counting invisible people is difficult" (Redburn and Buss, 1986, p. 16).

In late 1987 and early 1988, however, one homeless person became highly visible. Her name was Joyce Brown, but she sometimes used the aliases Ann Smith or Billy Boggs. Joyce Brown first became newsworthy when the City of New York whisked her from the street and committed her to psychiatric care. In telling her story, three network news packages, aired between November 5 and 10, 1987, followed the lead of a November 3 *New York Times* story that began, "Lawyers and psychiatrists clashed in a, courtroom at the Bellevue Hospital Center yesterday over whether New York City had the right to take a homeless woman from the streets and treat her against her will in a psychiatric ward." The television stories then presented a battle pitting New York's Project Help, a plan to aid people who cannot help themselves, against the constitutionality of committing homeless people without their consent. In the ABC, CBS, and NBC news packages and in a subsequent "60 Minutes" version, narrative battlelines are drawn between competing experts, between personal rights and social obligations, and between normal (common sense) and deviant (nonsense) behavior.

In the television treatment of her homelessness, Joyce Brown would become an icon for homeless people throughout the United States. The center of a controversy that Morley Safer of "60 Minutes" would call "an urban fable for our time," Brown animated a clash of contradictory meanings and competing values that strike at the very heart of the American ideal of "liberty and justice for all." Her story, we argue, also explores the limits of government, freedom, compassion, individualism, and the boundaries of common sense itself.

In the analysis and interpretation that follow, we first lay the groundwork for regarding news as a form of common sense knowledge. Part of the task of journalism requires the translation of experience into common sense news reports. In this process, reporters must make sense of the voices that reside outside the traditional bounds of common sense, such as those that speak expert knowledge and nonsense. Next, our discussion moves to a specific textual analysis of how network news makes sense of the homeless. Here we interpret three conventional network news narratives and a "60 Minutes" story about Joyce Brown. We describe how the networks frame and narrate the problem of homelessness through four distinct stages of the routine news package. We then interpret how the anchors and reporters, and well-informed citizens who manage the discourse about the homeless, divide common sense from expert knowledge. and nonsense. Finally, we look at a dramatic rewriting of the Joyce Brown story by "60 Minutes"; here Joyce Brown moves from being a mere artist's sketch in the conventional stories to the spirited heroine of a "60 Minutes" social drama. In our examination of how television news marks boundaries between the marginal and the mainstream, we argue that the major socioeconomic problem of homelessness which requires collective participation for resolution often plays out in the news as isolated personal problems demanding individual correction.

THE SOCIAL STOCK OF KNOWLEDGE

News and Common Sense

During the 1988 vice-presidential debate, Republican candidate Dan Quayle aligned his Midwestern values, his grandmother's advice, and his party with "common sense," a virtue, in Quayle's view, sadly lacking among liberals. On the other hand, Democrats and news columns for months criticized the youthful Quayle's placement on the GOP ticket as a decision also sadly lacking in common sense. The borders of common sense then are precious but contested spaces. While it is identified politically as a solid Middle American virtue, slippery footing marks the definitional terrain of common sense.

Nevertheless, borrowing from the sociology of knowledge (Berger and Luckmann, 1966; Park, 1940; Schutz and Luckmann, 1973), from cultural anthropology (Geertz, 1983), and from ideological and cultural studies (Gramsci, 1971; Hall, et al., 1978), we refer to the consensual, taken-for-granted knowledge served by, the news as common sense. The term connotes "conventional wisdom"; it has a natural, "that's the way things are" quality about it. Geertz

(1983, pp. 85–91) discusses its aura as "matter-of-fact," "down-to-earth," "colloquial wisdom." He defines common sense as five major features: naturalness ("of coarseness"), practicalness ("materially useful"), thinness ("simpleness" or "literalness"), immethodicalness ("unapologetically ad hoc"), and accessibleness ("open to all solid citizens," "anti-expert," "anti-intellectual"). Common sense "represents the world as a familiar world, one everyone can, and should, recognize and within which everyone stands, or should, on his (or her) own two feet" (p. 91).

Common sense both resists and accommodates the dominant or elite values of a particular culture (see Lears, 1985). Dependent groups operate contradictorily, identifying with the dominate value system while simultaneously resisting centrist values. As resistance, common sense celebrates "primary experience, unmediated by theory, reflection, speculation, argument"; this "empirical experience" is regarded as more "real" than other kinds of knowledge or experience (Hall et al., 1978, p. 152). Common sense, for example, allows an Iowa farmer, often represented in news stories as a prime representative of common sense, to admonish the "impractical" rhetoric of the politician. That admonition may become an act of resistance when the farmer refuses to vote. As accommodation, common sense repels self-scrutiny. Opposed to logical coherency, common sense contains no abstract strategies for critiquing elite or competing points of view and therefore certifies class divisions as natural and given.

A major distinguishing feature of common sense is its dexterity in withstanding definition and analysis. Because of its transparency, any "ordinary" person should instinctively recognize common sense; it is "what anyone with common sense" already knows. But Geertz (1983, p. 76) notes that despite its transparency, like myth, painting, religion, television, and news, common sense is also a ritualized "cultural system": "It can be questioned, disputed,—affirmed, developed, formalized, contemplated, even taught, and it can vary dramatically from one people to—the next." Although common sense presents itself as timeless, this kind of knowledge is not static or impervious to the rhythm of history. Instead, common sense is—a product of history, constantly changing, full of contradictions, subject to revision and revitalization. Common sense, as Hall and his colleagues (1978, p. 155) warn, is contradictory, fragmentary, and inconsistent "precisely because what is common about it is that it is not subject to tests of internal coherence and logical consistency." Coherence and consistency belong to another realm of knowledge, the domain of expert knowledge.

Expert Knowledge and the Well-Informed Reporter

Robert Park (1940, p. 672), who made one of the earliest connections between news and common sense, follows the lead of William James and distinguishes common sense from "knowledge about," which is "formal, rational, and systematic." Park (pp. 669–670) defines common sense instead as "acquaintance with," or "the sort of knowledge one inevitably acquires in the course of one's personal and firsthand encounters with everyday experience." Gramsci (1971, pp. 323–325) makes a similar distinction between common sense (the set of values and assumptions held in common by a society, characterized by incoherency and transparency) and good sense (systematic and empirical knowledge, characterized by the coherence of "intellectual-order").

From a journalist's viewpoint, "knowledge about" resides in contemporary culture in the realm of experts, whom Hall and his colleagues (1978) call "primary definers": those institutional leaders who dominate news stories as expert sources and establish the initial definitions or "ordinary interpretations" of news topics. Often at the edges of common sense, specialized "knowledge about" is typically possessed by highly trained practitioners in a variety of professions (music, law, education, medicine, among others) and inscribed in their expert jargon.

According to Schutz and Luckmann (1973, p. 331), the progressive division of labor in modern, technological societies has led to a "growing gap between expertness and the lack of it, and the growing, almost continuous dependency of the layman on the expert." A privileged few of us may function from time to time as experts. More commonly, however, we are lay persons, participants in, and practitioners of commonsense. We often confront the limits of our own knowledge in reminders that we do not, and cannot, know all that is known. And one especially significant consequence of the high-tech anxieties of "not knowing" is the emergence of a new social type peculiar to modern societies. Calling this new manner of being the well informed, Schutz and Luckmann (p. 331) contrast this social type with both the lay person and the expert:

This type is differentiated from the layman above all by the fact that he is not ready unreflectively to accept dependence on the judgment of the expert; on the other hand he is differentiated from the expert by the absence of specific explicit knowledge in the area in question.

Possessing access to special realms of knowledge, the well informed command a strategic symbolic station in modern cultures, a station located on the vistas between "expertness and the lack of it."

The television journalist is perhaps the exemplar of the well-informed type (see Schutz, 1964). Acting as an agent for the mass audience, the broadcast journalist fashions a news story that is "addressed" to common sense. And a primary mission of the well-informed reporter is to take specialized knowledge and transform it into common sense. The journalistic convention of the quote in print or the sound bite in broadcasting often locates "knowledge about" within the context of "acquaintance with." Once within this common sense frame, reporters may defend their stories as natural as the way things are, thereby rendering them transparent and no longer subject to critical inquiry that questions reportorial assumptions and conventions.

Making Sense of Nonsense

Another part of the well-informed reporter's cultural mission involves repairing internal cracks in common sense itself, contradictions that can disrupt the always provisional coherence of everyday life. Those internal cracks are especially conspicuous in news stories about America's homeless. In the incoherent snatches of language that are often a part of their television news images, the homeless present another type of knowledge that is represented as outside the bounds of both expert knowledge and common sense. This is the realm of nonsense. In contrast to common sense, nonsense resides in the domain of superstition, of condemned or absurd ideas, of obsolete knowledge that is no longer an element of consensus (see Silverstone, 1981, pp. 79–82). In news images, the social types who transmit those ideas—the condemned, the criminal, the mad—offer a marked contrast to the homeless. Our analysis of these experts the well informed, or voices of accounts treats both common sense and common sense.

The boundaries of nonsense and obsolete knowledge are fragile and subject to the rhythms of history. Foucault (1965), for instance, traces changes in how madness and the madman in literature—King Lear and Don Quixote are two examples—lost their association with sacred forms of special insight they had enjoyed during the Renaissance and were redefined in direct opposition to reason during the Enlightenment. Often center stage as the guardian of truth during the sixteenth century, madness is banished over the next two centuries: "By a strange act of force, the classical age was to reduce to silence the madness whose voices the Renaissance had just liberated" (p. 38). During the Enlightenment, as efficiency and work ethic both central to contemporary notions of common sense achieved new dominance in the social order, the mad characterized by their inability to work and their disturbance of the social order increasingly were viewed as outside the realm of reason, and certainly outside the borders of common sense.

Because it resides beyond the realms of expert knowledge and common sense, nonsense presents a difficult problem for journalists who must make sense of the apparently senseless. In the case of Joyce Brown, television news stories explore the boundaries of common sense, grappling with disparate views and virtues along a continuum of knowledge: at one end, the expert voices of doctors, lawyers, and politicians; at the other end, the troubled and often garbled voices of the homeless. Reporters try to make sense of the clashing voices to offer viewers at home a common sense position along the continuum that mediates between the privilege of experts and the affliction of news as cultural rituals, rituals that contribute to the production, maintenance repair, and transformation of social consensus (see Carey, 1975; 1988; Eason, 1984; 1986; Fiske, 1987; Hall et al., 1978; Said, 1981; Schudson, 1978; Tuchman, 1978). We propose that both common sense and news are processes "of signification giving social meaning to events." Both constitute "society as a 'consensus.' Both assume that we share a common stock of knowledge and that "we have access to similar mass of meaning" (Hall et al., 1978, p. 55). Our interpretation of the Joyce Brown coverage investigates the relationship between news narration and the social distribution of knowledge.

THE PACKAGING OF JOYCE BROWN

News Packages and the Public Idiom

In the journalistic ordering of expert knowledge, common sense, and nonsense, experience is translated into what Hall and his colleagues (1978) call the language of "the public idiom." Journalism institutions construct versions of "the language of the public" based on what they agree is "the rhetoric, imagery and underlying common stock of knowledge" (p. 62). This reportorial language, whether the inverted pyramid print news lead or the television news reporter package, carries shared assumptions about common sense. Ultimately, this language translates "into a public idiom the statement and viewpoints of the primary definers" or expert sources (p. 61). Eason (1981, p. 125) suggests that the public idiom is the story form; reporters, after all, have no expert jargon or "special language for reporting their findings. They make sense out of events by telling stories about them." For Hall and his colleagues (1978, p. 62), the public idiom sets the news agenda by inserting "the language of everyday communication back into the consensus," back into the common sense world of the familiar news narrative. The definitions and interpretations of powerful sources become part of the taken-for-granted reality of public discourse.

In the case of the homeless the powerful include the primary definers of the issue: the expert politicians, city officials, doctors, social workers, ministers, lawyers, and the well-informed citizens network anchors and television reporters who offer the primary interpretations of the homeless in the language of character, setting, plot, conflict, problem, and resolution.

Framing the Package

Literally a showcase for individual news stories, the regular evening newscast is dominated by the familiar performance of the network's star anchor. Located in studio settings and appearing live in most parts of the country, news anchors provide a grand narration of the news, a narration that gives the most scattered and diverse subject matter the semblance of continuity and coherence. As star moderators of the medium, they are masters of electronic eye contact who specialize in engaging the audience with the "Hi Mom" intimacy of direct address. Following in the footsteps of Edward R. Murrow and Walter Cronkite, they achieve star status by individualizing the well-informed type.[1] In other words, the anchor gives both bodily form and personal identity to the ideal of professionalism.

In setting the stage for the Joyce Brown story, all three anchors deliver what amounts to the lead paragraph of a newspaper report. On CBS and NBC, the studio shots include remarkably similar topic boxes (graphic situated over the right shoulders of the anchors) that display still photographs of destitute people. Electronic captions reading "The Homeless" underscore the photos on both networks. Whereas ABC's Peter Jennings and NBC's Tom Brokaw speak in the more detached third person, CBS's Dan Rather adopts the personal first person plural point of view:

> *Rather*: We pass them everyday. It is estimated that there may be as many as 3 million of them on the main streets and side streets of communities across the country. We call them the homeless. They call the streets their home. Now a new program to help these people in trouble is already in trouble itself. Harold Dow reports.

Rather's language has two significant consequences. By using the intimate pronoun "we," Rather enhances audience identification with this controversial star of the evening news, a technique that enables him to speak both *to* and *for* his viewers. However, Rather's narration also marks off the homeless as being outside his inner circle—the circle of common sense. Rather's language locates the homeless in the realm of the "other," the "not us," "them": "We call *them* the homeless. *They* call the streets *their* home." This tendency also appears in Jennings's lead-in, although it is concealed by his use of third person point of view. Jennings segues into the lead by first reporting winter-like weather in New York City and then connecting those conditions to the theme of homelessness: "There was even a momentary snow shower (dramatic pause) which often makes people notice the homeless." Again the anchor sorts out the homeless from the domain of people. This, Jennings like Rather, suggests that the homeless reside outside the bounds of what it means to be person in our society.

Narrating the Package

We describe her major similarities and differences regarding the narration use to package the Joyce Brow controversy.[2]

Despite being named in lead-ins and again in sign-offs, the reporters who narrate the Joyce Brown packages all fall into the generic category "television reporter." Except for Potter's fleeting stand-up in the middle of the ABC package their presence is only expressed in voiceover narration. CBS Harold Dow and NBC's Cassandra Clayton are reporters without faces. But, strangely enough, the anonymity of their narration enhances the authority of their accounts by contributing to the illusion of journalistic distance. As uncelebrated journalists the reporters sustain the impersonal posture of omniscient and dispassionate observers—harbingers of "the facts."

Reporter narration dominates the aural dimension of the news packages, both in terms of time and meaning. Nearly 70 percent of the sound track features reporter voiceovers and develops according to a storytelling strategy known in broadcast journalism textbooks as the "tie continuity model" (Hewitt, 1988). This model takes shape in our stages by (1) locating the story in present time and place; (2) taking viewers briefly to the past by providing context an background; (3) returning to the present by developing central narrative and dramatic tensions; and (4) pointing to future implications and actions.

In addition to the public idiom of reporter narration, the language of these reports also features sound bites. In all three stories, the sound bites animate a dialogue that operates along two axes horizontally between officials and experts and vertically between those with power and knowledge (people with governmental and/or professional identities) and those without power and knowledge (the homeless who are rarely identified an speak nonsense).[3] Our analysis examines each production stage and the reporters' role in mediating both, dialogic axes in constructing common sense.

Stage 1: The Present

Both ABC and NBC focus their openings on the activities of health officials patrolling the streets in blue city vans. Cassandra Clayton's NBC package begins with two traveling shots of a van synchronized with the voiceover: "Each day four city vans search the streets of New York. Inside, a social worker, a nurse, and a psychiatrist." A bearded male professional asks an apparently homeless man, "How have you been taking care of yourself?" A disturbing series of shots follows to provide a horrifying portrait of life and madness on the streets: an elderly man drinking from a discarded beer bottle; a modern-day Icarus flapping his army blanket wings in a stationary flight; a wild-eyed drunken man in a gutter, enraged and ranting; a man, holding a liquor bottle, screaming incoherently from across a busy street. Clayton's accompanying voiceover explains, "With questions and repeated visits, they determine which of the city's homeless are mentally ill and potentially dangerous to themselves or others. The teams are taking the most deranged off the streets, whether they want to go or not." Clayton then punctuates Stage 1 of the NBC story with two related sound bites: one extracted from a press conference with New York Mayor Edward Koch and the other from an interview segment with Norman Siegel of the ACLU:

> *Koch*: (an American flag in the background): These people, uh, are now in the hands of people who want to help them—who will help them. And the opponents, they ought to be ashamed of themselves.
> *Siegel*: You can't go for the quick fix. You can't adopt a program that's going to round people up so that they're not seen any more.

In joining these two bites, Clayton abdicates a dialogue between competing views of the city's program; Siegel's objections appear as a direct response to Koch's words.

ABC's introduction also shows the city health teams at work. But it concludes Stage 1 by showing a man identified as attorney George McDonald warning people, in Ned Potter's words, "against taking the city's help," obviously, characterizing the roundup as "help" places the city's program in a favorable light. Whereas Koch performs a leading role in the other packages Potter leaves the mayor out of the fray and instead orchestrates the controversy as a dispute between well-meaning experts: humanitarian psychiatrists versus activist lawyers. In contrast to Clayton's piece, ABCs' Potter ends his review of the current situation with ambient sound of another ACLU lawyer talking on an indigent black man:

> *Lawyer*: They're going around picking up homeless people and saying that they're crazy and holding them against their will.
> *Unidentified black man*: Oh.
> *Lawyer*: Do you understand what I mean?
> *Black man*: Yeah.

Where the other packages start with voiceover visual, CBS Harold Dow uses a "cold open" a short, dramatic sound bite. Dow here spotlights the voce of nonsense as spoken by a disoriented black man: "If I knew where to go, I'd know where to come. If I knew where to come, I'd know where to go." The interview sound then fades as Dow's voiceover begins: "Sometimes he calls himself John. Sometimes, Henry. This man is homeless. He's also mentally ill. There are 20,000 like him in New York City." It is not clear whether Dow means that there were 20,000 homeless people in New York City or 20,000 mentally ill homeless people or whether all homeless people are mentally ill. In fact, on conservative estimate puts the New York homeless population at 30,000 with 16 to 25 percent counted as mentally ill (Kozol, 1988; Redburn and Buss, 1986).

Dow then narrates a montage of general misery untangle similar to the images featured in NBC's opening. The montage rides in on the ambient sound of two uniformed policemen apprehending a man who intones: "Leave me alone. Leave me alone." Two shots of poverty stricken women follow, including a nightmarish view of an elderly "ballad" who expresses her contempt for the world by walloping the sidewalk with her cane. Whereas Clayton observes that the health teams are determining "which of the city's homeless are mentally ill and potentially dangerous to themselves or others," Dow asserts, "Many of the growing numbers of homeless in New York and other American cities are mentally ill or sometimes dangerous to themselves and others." Despite the difference between observation and assertion, both Clayton and Dow coordinate unsavory scenes of vagrancy with words that characterize the homeless as dangerous to others. In this case, ironically, the they are us. According to the boundaries drawn by the network news, "they" (the homeless) represent a danger to "us" because after all, "we pass them everyday." The network narration, along with the visual images, reinforces a view that the homeless are mad and deflects attention from economic factors.

Stage 2: The Past

In the time continuity model, this stage of the television package briefly sets the present against a larger social backdrop. The clearest shift to a consideration of the past appears in CBS voiceover when Harold Dow suddenly switches into the past tense: "New York decided to do something about it." Dow, unlike the other reporters, saves his discussion of the city's program or the second stage of his story. In filling in the background of the Brown controversy, Dow, like NBC's Clayton, presents an excerpt from a mayoral press conference where Koch confesses, "I'm mad at myself. I'm sorry that I didn't have the energy and the courage five years ago to do hat we did now." Shots follow of a city van, its occupants shedding their faces from the relentless eye of the news camera. Dow acknowledges this avoidance of scrutiny, suggesting, contrary to Koch's protests, a sinister side to the city's designs on the homeless: "Shunning cameras, psychiatrists and social workers are now cruising the streets with a list of wanted homeless people judged to be in need of hospitalization. New York's homeless feel afraid, defenseless." The last sentence accompanies a dramatic shot of a man staggering down the street and glancing nervously behind him.

The second stage of Dow's package ends dramatically in a second interview segment with a homeless person appeared and apparently drunken with man who slurs, "I am not mentally ill. I happen to be what you would call economically [sic] unstable." And, here, Dow works a twist on the familiar man-on-the-street interview. Whereas the typical street interview denotes the outlook of common sense, Dow's man-living-in-the-street interviews give a voice to nonsense. Such interviews are, in fact, a distinguishing attribute of Dow's work: the homeless do not merit interview bites in the other packages. Even so, Dow's package does not give this homeless man the same treatment accorded people appearing in other interview segments. Simply put, the man is not identified. Shots of Ed Koch, ACLU lawyers, psychiatrists, and other experts always feature, regardless of network's electronic captions with the person's name and credentials (e.g., "Noman Siegel, ACLU attorney"). In contrast, this homeless man, unlike John/Henry in the cold opening, is not named in the narration—a subtle, but powerful way of conveying his marginality, his relative lack of power, of sense, of individual identity.

Although brief, the second stage of NBC's package is the only one of attempt to put the story into historical context that extends beyond the specifics of the Joyce Brown controversy. Visually, NBC opens this stage with a wide establishing shot of an inner-city traffic jam. The camera tilts down and zooms in to reveal amid the hustle of modern city life, a destitute man engaged in a primordial struggle; he stands next to a trash can fire, firing off the cold like his prehistoric ancestors. This image undercuts the activism simultaneously described in Clayton's voiceover: "Civil libertarians are concerned that the new program is an infringement on these people's rights and a step backward toward returning them to institutions." The screen then displays three shots of black and white archival footage from a mental ward: two wide establishing shots of the ward accentuated by passive patients and patrolling nurses and a final close-up of a despairing elderly female invalid, her face buried in her hands. The black-and-white images lend a sense of verisimilitude to Clayton's two sentence history lesson: "In the early 1960s, a policy began to get them out of hospitals, give them more freedom. But many mental patients eventually ended up on the streets." (On ABC, background information focuses on Joyce Brown's past, so there is a blurring of boundaries between that network's second and third stage).

Stage 3: The Controversy

Joyce Brown's case is the organizing principle of this stage in all three packages. Consequently, this segment varies the least from package to package. And the most profound resemblance involves the use of courtroom sketches. Composed by three different artists, to untrained eyes the sketches are indistinguishable from one another. All three networks use zooms and close-ups to make the static composites more visually compelling. One voiceover paraphrases another:

> *Clayton* (NBC): One of the first people picked up is challenging the program in court. City psychiatrists say Joyce Brown is schizophrenic, that she often defecated on the sidewalk. But calls herself a professional homeless person. Brown lived the past 18 months beside a heating grate of an ice cream store.
> *Dow* (CBS): The first person committed to a psychiatric ward is challenging the city's action. Ann Smith says she's not mentally ill even though city officials say she has been living a filthy, incoherent life, shouting obscenities from this street corner.

The most complicated use of the sketches, though, appears in the ABC package. The courtroom sketches bracket three segments that together make up the heart of Ned Potter's report: an interview segment with a lawyer, a conflicting interview with a psychiatrist, and a short stand-up by Potter taped beside the heating vent where Joyce Brown lives. During the leading shot of the sketch, the camera zooms out from a close-up of Brown to a full view of the courtroom as Potter explains, "A homeless patient who called herself Billie Boggs agreed to let civil liberties lawyers take the city to court." Contradictory interviews from Norman Siegel and Dr. Luis Marcos, a city health official, follow:

Siegel: If we throw individual freedom and individual liberty for homeless people out the window today, in 1987, who's next?
Marcos: I believe that, uh, to be psychotic, to be mentally ill, deteriorating in the streets, when there is treatment available, is not freedom. It's the worst kind of imprisonment.

Potter then pursues this contrasting expert testimony with the only stand-up to appear in the three packages. From a close-up of the heating vent, the camera tilts up and zooms out to reveal Potter standing in a casual pose (his hands in his pockets) and speaking directly to the viewer: "If Billie Boggs had any home, it was this heating vent on Second Avenue. Her real name was Joyce Brown. After she was picked up, a city psychiatrist said she was paranoid schizophrenic. Sometimes perfectly normal. Other times violent and suicidal." A dissolve to the trailing shot of the courtroom sketch follows the stand-up. As the camera zooms from a medium to a close-up of Brown's portrait, Potter reports, "She told the court she's sane and would rather be in the cold than locked up in a hospital."

CBS, which provides the longest report, follows its sketch sequence by introducing the woman who Dow identifies as Ann Smith; and after the brief glimpse of her street corner, the package contains an interview with Ron Levy of the ACLU who delivers the staccato pronouncement about Brown: "She is lucid. She is articulate. She knows where she is. She knows what's happening to her. She knows what her rights are." Levy's credibility is undermined by numerous countervailing examples of homeless people who are not lucid or articulate who do not know what is happening to them or what their rights are. Levy's sound bite, though is followed by images of homeless people who are apparently concerned with securing their rights. Gathered outside Bellevue hospital, they appear holding "Free Ann Smith" banners and yelling, in unison, "Stop the roundup. Koch is crazy." However, this demonstration of support is also qualified by a segment that marks the end of this phase of Dow's package and severely damages the ACLU's position in the story. The segment organizes around weird shot that begins with a tight close-up of the back of a woman's head, her golden earring gleaming in the sunlight. A zoom out discloses that she is one of three well-dressed black women standing with their backs to the camera as they address a large group of reporters. During his shot, Dow explains, "As support was building for her release, Smith's family stepped in, refusing to face cameras, but pleading with authorities to give her the treatment they say she desperately needs." This voiceover is then substantiated with a sound bite from one of Brown's sisters that captures the thrust for all three network packages: "She's a danger to herself and others." CBS is the only network to use sound bites from Brown's family, and this dialogue functions here as a person-on the-street interviews voice for common sense and support for the city's program.

Stage 4: The Future

In this final phase of the time continuity model, all three networks paint bleak portraits regarding the future. CBS's Harold Dow illustrates his grim one—sentence wrap up with two shots of the city van suceeded by yet two more bleak images of homeless people: "Whatever the outcome, New York City is pressing forward with the pilot program certain to be the focus of national debate about what to do about these people who are disturbed and homeless."

ABC also uses the vans in its closing. But, in keeping with the psychiatrist/lawyer dialectic of this story, ABC cuts from the vans to ACLU's George McDonald talking to another homeless black man. Commenting on the futility of this situation, Ned Potter's voce takes on a melancholy tone: "Meanwhile, the city vans continue to search and George McDonald continues, too." The sound bit of Potter's package then documents McDonald's words to the man: "If they come after you, O.K. you call us and we'll help you." Potter's package provides three final visions of desperation on the street as he reaches his gloomy conclusion: A terrible problem. A troublesome solution severely challenged by one test case.

Just as NBC's package is the only one to furnish historical context that reaches back beyond the immediate past, it is also the only one to explore the future in detail. Against scenes of a health care worker taking a man's blood pressure, Clayton reports that after homeless people are released from hospitals, "there are few outpatient programs like this one to provide housing and support." An interview segment with the Reverend John McVean of St. Francis Shelter then reinforces Clayton's point:

It's one thing to bring someone into the hospital and then get them stabilized. But, then, what are you going to do with them at that point? And I think that's the dilemma that the mayor and other government officials are now facing.

After briefly showing an ACLU lawyer warning another homeless blackman about "a new plan that the mayor adopted," NBC also ends the package with more shots of disoriented homeless people in dire circumstances. During these closing shots, Clayton's voiceover continues the pattern of depersonalizing the homeless by placing them outside the boundary of society: "Across the country, other cities are watching the program's effect, as they confront the issue of protecting society while also protecting the right of the mentally ill homeless."

A HIERARCHY OF DISCOURSE

While no network offers easy narrative resolution and closure, they all relocate the problem of homelessness mainly in the domain of madness. Kozol (1988, pp. 154–155) argues that such a strategy provides shelter from confronting the broader social conditions that produce the homeless:

The notion that the homeless are largely psychotics who belong in institutions, rather than victims of displacement at the hands of enterprising Realtors, spares us from the need to offer realistic solutions to the fact of deep and widening extremes on wealth and poverty in the United States. It also enables us to tell ourselves that the despair of homeless people bears no intimate connection to the privileged existence we enjoy when, for example, we rent or purchase one of those restored townhouses that once provided shelter for people now huddled in the street.

This vision of the homeless as mad more closely supports a common sense view aligned with dominant values; this view interprets homelessness as a marginal problem outside the mainstream. After all, most of the homeless episode portrayed in these packages speak nonsense, that is, the lack the common sense to dig themselves out of their under-class hole. They even lack the "sense" to hide from the scrutiny of the television camera, as would many "invisible" homeless who feel the burden of shame and failure that goes with living on the margins.

Despite their differences, then all three packages share a similar orientation toward the homeless: they are not like us; they are a "danger to themselves an others." And, because of this orientation, the city's side of the controversy is slightly favored "troubling solution, but help nonetheless." By default, placing the city's program—in the well-meaning "help" column converts ACLU activism into a misguided "hindrance."

What also emerges in all three packages is a similar hierarchy of discourse. In representing the voices and views of the well informed, reporters incorporate contradictory versions of the world into a dialogic definition of the situation. Put another way, in attempting to maintain a neutral stance, the reporters present the current situation as a dynamic dialogue that operates along vertical and horizontal axes. It is in the ordering of the vertical dialogue that the hierarchy takes shape.

The discourse of the well informed orchestrate this hierarchy by governing two planes of narration: the grand narration of the anchors and the story narration of the generic reporters. Setting the stage for the package, the anchors draw preliminary boundaries, marking off the homeless as outside the domain of common sense, as some thing that we notice when the weather turns cold. The repeaters then color in the boundaries with bleak images of the city the street, and the gutter.

Implicitly, reporter narration caries the next level of discourse the plane of common sense. Explicitly, the voice of common sense is represented in the familiar person-on-the-street interview. Someone, selected not for expertise but for ordinariness, is asked to voice an opinion about a newsworthy event or issue. When presented in the context of a new package, such interviews take in the aura of consensus. Consequently, in stories presenting controversies, a lone interview of sound bite often determines which—of the competing definition of the situation is perceived as "correct." Although common sense is ordinarily animated by the woman or man on the street (but not of the street), in the CBS package it is expressed in the words of one of Joyce Brown's concerned relatives: "She's a danger to herself and others."

The discourse that dominates the net level in the hierarchy is the horizontal dialogue of governmental power and expert knowledge. Operating as well informed professionals, the reporters seek out appropriate experts who provide enough conflict to sustain the story. On the one hand, NBC and CBS emphasize Mayor Koch's role by framing the controversy as a fight between city government and a liberal special interest group. ABC, on the other hand, portrays the controversy as a futile struggle between psychiatrists and lawyers.

The dehumanized discourse of the unidentified homeless is near the bottom of the hierarchy. In all the packages, this discourse appears in two situations: footage showing the homeless suffering on the streets and ambient sound bites of homeless, people interacting with lawyers from the ACLU. NBC's package also includes ambient sound of a health team examining a homeless person, and BS includes interview segments with two disoriented homeless males. Although in every instance the. homeless appear in dire need of help, their situations also seem the result of personal deficiencies associated with drunkenness and/or madness. Once again, they are distanced from us and larger social and economic considerations. Mediated by the narration of the well informed and the dialogue between experts, the homeless re rendered as "a danger to the selves and others," as transients without fixed names, addresses, occupations, or identities. Situated outside the bounds of society, they give a wretched form and a garbled voice to the dark side of common sense—the irrational realm of nonsense.

But one person's discourse is even of lower status: Joyce Brown/Ann Smith/Billie Boggs. In all the packages, she is an abstraction—a sketch, a street corner, a heating grate, a protest banner, a test case. Her words only appear secondhand and in the context of what she said at her commitment hearing. According to these attributions, Joyce Brown stated hat she was not mentally ill, she was a professional homeless person, she was happy on the sidewalk and able to care or herself, and that she preferred the cold to a hospital. But in every case, Brown's claims re then placed in dialogue with counterclaims: that she is a paranoid schizophrenic, that she shouts obscenities, and that she defecates on the sidewalk. And these counterclaims are given considerable credence by the non-sense discourse of the unidentified homeless for none of the networks show even one homeless person who conforms to Brown's self-described professionalized homelessness.

Therefore, Joyce Brown's discourse finds the bottom of the hierarchy of discourse. As a menacing abstraction, this level is filtered and informed by the other levels: by the narration of the well informed, by the common sense of her family, by the horizontal dialogue of government officials and experts, and finally, by the gripping images of the unidentified homeless. However, Joyce Brown assumes a dramatically different status in the "60 Minutes" rewrites of the network stories. In this narrative, which aired two months after the packages, 60 minutes frames the story as a personal drama pitting Joyce Brown against Mayor Koch. In this morality play, Joyce Brown climbs the hierarchy of discourse, ascending from the banished realm of nonsense; here she is recast as the spirited heroine of a "60 Minutes" social drama. No longer a murky abstraction or sketch, Brown comes to life, holding her own with experts and speaking with the authority of common sense.

REWRITING JOYCE BROWN

At the top of most "60 Minutes" segments, the screen displays a giant mockup of a glossy magazine spread. On January 24, 1988, the mock-up that launches Morley Safer's report features the large blue words "Brown vs. Koch." The sketch that displays the spread, though, is by far the most significant unit of analysis. Like the artwork in the three network packages, the spread shows an artist's sketch of Joyce Brown. But where the news packages show profile views of Brown surrounded by white professionals in a courtroom, the "60 Minutes" sketch depicts Brown from a head-on perspective, her eyes cutting defiantly to the right of the screen, the edges of her mouth drooping, but more in cynicism than despair. As in the sketches in the news packages, Brown's image is positioned between two white male professionals—and they are not her lawyers. In front and behind her image are the men who play leading roles in this dramatization of the Brown controversy. Ed Koch, her antagonist, is sketched in behind

Brown in the familiar magazine mockup. In the foreground, Morley after (her ally and co-protagonist) addresses the audience as he delivers his own lead-in.

The composition of this framing shot signals the scope of "60 Minutes" radical rewriting of the controversy. First, in displacing the grand narration of the network anchor, the "60 Minutes" reporter assumes a much higher profile than those faceless voices who narrate the news packages. Second, instead of emphasizing conflict between psychiatrists and lawyers, or between government officials and activists, "60 Minutes" transforms the story into a more traditional social drama, a dispute between a heroic individual and a meddling autocrat. Third, Brown's status in the "60 Minutes" treatment rises in the prominent placement of her sketch in relation to Koch's, a clear indication of her climb up the ladder of discourse.

Arbitrating Dramatic Tension

The late Buton Benjamin (1987), former executive producer of the CBS Evening News, argued that "60 Minutes" distinguishes itself from regular evening newscasts because reporters become "Participants in their stories, players in the drama." So, in contrast to the tree network versions of the Brown story, Morley Safer becomes a central character in "Brown vs. Koch." Safer's larger role is demonstrated by the sheer number of on-camera shots starring the reporter. Whereas the generic reporters of the evening news packages only appear in one out of a cumulative total of 78 shots in the 14-minute, 45-second "Brown vs. Koch" episode, Safer tuns up in 36 of 121 shots. In fact, he appears more, both in terms of shots and time, than either Koch or Brown.

In "60 Minutes," dramatic confrontations build story conflict by pitting individual against institution, nature against culture, tradition against change,—honesty against deception, humanity against technology (Campbell, 1987). While conventional news stories develop these same themes, "60 Minutes" takes a more explicit stand by abandoning allegiance to the conventional referee posture of routine news reports. In his lead-in, Safer expertly guides or reading of the program's rewriting of these themes: "Brown versus Koch is but one of the thousands of stories that break every day in New York City." Such explicit acknowledgment of the episodes dramatic structure as story, as "urban fable," is a motif on "60 Minutes." And framing experience as narrative allows Safer to introduce the major characters, their social class positions, and the hierarchy of discourse in linear fashion. First, we meet Safer; he then introduces Joyce Brown, victim of the story and voice of common sense. Next, we meet Koch, official leader of New York City government. Shots follow of unidentified homeless, representatives of the world of nonsense who, unlike Safer, Brown, and Koch, do not speak in this story.

In the three network packages, narrative conflict resides amid competing experts, amid personal and social realms, and amid normalcy and deviance. "60 Minutes" also exploits these tensions but adds additional layers of conflict. First of all, in the opening to Safer's edited report Joyce Brown moves suddenly from a sketched abstraction to a powerful presence defending individualism in the battle against institutionalization: "I am an adult, a 40-year-old intelligent woman. And I don't need Mayor Koch or Bellevue to tell me where I can live." This opening statement effectively sets up a confrontation with autocracy and bureaucracy. Secondly, a class battle takes shape between the homeless under-class and, in Safer's words, "the rich people on the upper East Side." At different points in the story, Safer argues that the city's Project Help commits homeless people to Bellevue because they trespass into "high rise, high life territory where you can spend $50 a week to have your dog walked or $450 a month to have your car parked." Safer skillfully plugs Koch into this class war: "He also lives on the upper East Side in this gracious home just off Gracie Square, barely a mile away from Joyce Brown's spot." That spot Safer tells us, is "literally the pavement" over a hot air vent.

After setting up Koch as a member of the elite, "60 Minutes" then conducts an interview in which Brown claims to be a "political prisoner" with a Koch interview in which the mayor smugly but emotionally responds, "Please, this is not the Soviet Union where she's a political prisoner. Is anyone suggesting that Joyce Brown is a political prisoner?" Safer now has his villain. He points to Koch, firmly shakes his finger, and says, "Joyce Brown Joyce Brown is."

As institutional representative, Koch makes his case against Joyce Brown, insisting over and over that Brown, her position, and her supporter are "bizarre," "ridiculous," and "outrageous." But Safer carefully places his arguments in the context of a battle over whether Brown speaks with the voice of common sense or nonsense. In one of the tight close-ups which put her individuality under cramped scrutiny, Brown defends her "right" to be homeless by affirming personal freedom, a sacred tenet of individualism: "This is the United States of America, the Constitution, freedom of choice. If that's the way a person wants to live their life, and they're an adult, who am I to say they can't do that?"

In sensible tones, she explains her bizarre behavior. She prefers the streets to living in a shelter. "Shelters are very dangerous. I've been in one before. The people that you're there with, you don't know, uh, why they're there, what brought them there. Some are insane. Some are criminals. They are very dangerous people. And they're not kept up good." Notice that Brown, in vindicating herself, adopts the same view of the homeless population that dominates the three network packages. They, after all, are very dangerous people. And Brown makes it clear that she does not consider herself to be one of them.

She also calmly explains why she defaced in the streets: "As far as using the pavement as a toilet, I didn't have access to a bathroom. There were times when I would go to restaurants and ask them "Could I use their bathroom? and they would say, No, you can't. Even if I offered to buy something." Lastly, when Safer confronts her with the charge that she burned money, she provides another rational response:

Brown: I only needed $7 to eat per day. I never kept any more than $10 per day because I was on the street and I could be mugged.
Safer: Is that reason to burn up the money?
Brown: It depended on the manner in which they gave it to me whether or not I burned.
Safer: How do you mean?
Brown: Well, sometimes they would throw money at me. Just ball it up an throw it at me. Now that's not the way you give people money. Everyone doesn't want to live on the street. But if that's what they want to do, let them do it.

Her testimonial to individualism is interact with reactions from a sympathetic Safer. And, immediately following this polite interchange, "60 Minutes" punctuates the preferred interpretation of her explanations with a sound bite from one of her lawyers:

Ley: Joyce Brown is rational, coherent, articulate, today, just a she was when she was on the street. She has a track record of living on the street for over year, keeping herself warm, providing food for herself, entering the hospital in good physical condition. A person like that simply doesn't meet the civil commitment standards, under the Constitution or under existing law.

Her seemingly sane responses to the most outrageous charges undermine Koch, his experts (five city psychiatrists who diagnosed her as paranoid schizophrenic), and their position that she inhabits a world of nonsense. Thus, Joyce Brown seems to win the war of sound bites with Koch, emerging as, in the words, of the lawyer, "rational, coherent, articulate" a dyed-in-the wool civil libertarian who really knows what she wants and who could pass for a "board member of the American Civil Liberties Union."

In advocating Brown's side of the controversy, "60 Minutes" calculated choices about what to include and exclude from the narrative. Although its nearly 15-minute version offers a personal interview with Joyce Brown which is absent from the November 1987 packages, "60 Minutes" excludes documentation from Brown's own relatives ("She's a danger to herself and others") supporting the mayor's position. This documentation is included in the earlier CBS package—and in earlier New York Times stories from November 5 and 7—which "60 Minutes" had access to. Perhaps this inclusion may have complicated the clear individual-institution, under-upper class tensions that give coherence to the narrative. This rewriting of CBS own package strengthens the case of Joyce Brown as representative of common sense at the same time her exclusion weakens Koch's expert stance and reinforces his role as autocratic villain.

Reconstituting the Social Order

In part, television news offers reassurance and order in a world where experiences sometimes refuse to cohere. However, in seducing us with compelling narratives which display a reconstituted moral order, television news—like its print counterpart—does not draw us actively into bearing a responsibility for the reconstitution. Like the conventional reporter, we—the audience—are too often detached, comforted by the familiarity of the story and its ability to insulate us from actual experience.

An example of this reassuring reconstitution occurs in the first update of "Brown vs. Koch," which aired February 21, 1988. Harry Reasoner says that Brown has been released by the city. In part because of the "60 Minutes" story, she now has an apartment, a part-time job, and "a half dozen book and movie offers to sort through." And last week she lectured at Harvard Law School. The subject, "The Homeless Crisis: A View from the Street." Here, Joyce Brown takes on trappings of middle and upper-class success by gaining social credentials. Not only has her name been restored, but she has a job and a "real" address. As she climbs from silent abstraction to a level above officials and experts in the hierarchy of discourse, her sudden rise in status works to reconcile the residue of contradictions regarding her former underclass standing. In supporting centrist virtues, "60 Minutes" once again prizes the discourse of common sense over the discourse of experts and officialdom.[4]

But in reclaiming Brown from the domain of nonsense, "60 Minutes" does not, in any way, also bring the unidentified homeless into the fold. In Brown's ascent up the hierarchy of knowledge, in becoming an "expert" lecturer on homelessness, she leapfrogs over the discourse of the unidentified homeless leaving them in the nether region of "the other." In this respect, Safer's story does not significantly rewrite the dominant meaning of homelessness embraced by the three network packages. They still represent a danger to us—a meaning that, as Safer reported, is even shared by Joyce Brown at the beginning of the "60 Minutes" story when she responds to her status as a test case for New York's Project Help:

> Brown (interview bite): I was definitely the wrong one that they did pick on. (she smiles and laughs).
> Safer (off screen and laughing): How do you mean that?
> Brown: Because I'm sane. I'm not insane. And there are thousands out there they could have used for a model. I'm the wrong one.

Her endearing laughter helps establish her as a protagonist in this drama, and her words help sustain the "thousands" of unidentified homeless out there as part of a lunatic fringe existing beyond the outskirts of common sense.

CONCLUSION

Herman Gray (1988) has argued that new seldom accounts for the economic inequalities, social prejudices, and technological upheavals that contribute to the historically determined formation of the under class. Gray has found that, rather than examine these generative mechanisms, the news typically emphasizes intellectual, mental, and moral deficiencies of individual members of the update of "Brown vs. Koch" in June is advantaged. In this symbolic operation, social problems demanding collective engagement are reduced to personal problems requiring private remedies.

In all the news accounts of the Brown controversy, homelessness is primarily attributed to personal deficiencies, drunkenness, and mental illness. Kozol (1988 pp. 1–58) notes that "the label of mental illness places the destitute outside the sphere of ordinary life. It personalizes an anguish that is public in its genesis; it individualizes a misery that is both general in cause and general in application." The few moments that implicate the general economic system in the misery are contained in interview sound bites by Joyce Brown, her lawyers, and the unidentified homeless man who drunkenly declared he was "economically [sic] unstable." Neither CBS's Dow, or NBC's Clayton, nor ABC's Potter amplify, or even acknowledge, these moments in their anonymous narration.

Only "60 Minutes" frames the controversy in terms of a class conflict, but even then the conflict is personalized as a dispute between Brown the individualist and Koch the elitist. As do all reporters, Safer leaves references to his own class status, to his CBS salary, and to his own New York living arrangements out of the narrative. And, as we have suggested, the drama of class conflict is generally resolved by celebrating, not condemning, the social order—order that often identifies those who progress economically as portraits in the triumph of ingenuity and those who regress as sketches in personal failure.

In the "60 Minutes" rewrite, Joyce Brown's personal triumph suggests in part that American individualism works. In fact, "60 Minutes" aired a second update of "Brown vs. Koch" in June 1988 and reported that Ronald Reagan had appropriated the story as both a representative example of rugged individualism and "the care with which America deals with its homeless."[5] But as a representative of individualism and the homeless, Joyce Brown is not at all representative. If she is mentally ill, as the city of New York claim, she probably represents less than 20 percent of the homeless. If she is homeless by choice, as her lawyers and Reagan claim, she represents less than 6 percent of the homeless (Redburn and Buss, 1986, p. 56).

But what has made Joyce Brown the icon of homelessness from news and especially "60 Minutes" is her ability to articulate common sense position which makes her plight less threatening and which ultimately extols heartland individualism. Through the Joyce Brown stories, the news—which often operates to reaffirm basic centrist virtues—places the apparent deviancy of homelessness "back into the consensus" by "translating the unfamiliar into the familiar world" of the narrative (Hall et al., 1978, p. 62). As Marin (1987, p. 44) reminds us, "the homeless, simply because they are homeless, are strangers, aliens—and therefore a threat. Their presence, in itself, comes to constitute a kin of violence; it deprives us of our sense of safety." The three network news packages restore safety and distance by marking of the homeless as marginal. The "60 Minutes" story restores safety and normalcy as Joyce Brown, this alien representative from another world, reenters and reaffirms our world.

In the process of transforming the troubling experiences of homelessness into familiar news packages and stories television news polices the border between the marginal and the mainstream. Television as an intimate medium sits in the comfort of our kitchens, living rooms, and bedroom's our homes. At the same time television peeks at the plight of those without homes, it also imposes distance. The medium lets us see the homeless, identify briefly with their predicament, yet, in the end, it sustains the fragile boundaries that mark off the intruders. As Kozol (1988, p. 155) contends, "Terming economic victims 'psychotic' or 'disordered' helps to place them at distance. It says that they aren't quite like us—and, more important, that we could not be like them." Redburn and Buss (1986, p. 76) note in their study of American homelessness that between those "who see homelessness as institutional failure and those who see it as manifesting individual weakness, there stretches a jumbled landscape of conflicting information and interpretations." This is the world we share. And, in a broad sense, journalism's problem is our problem.

NOTES

1. This view of the media star as an individualized social type is derived from Dyer's work on film stardom (1979, pp. 108–113; see also Reeves 1988).

2. We would like to thank the Vanderbilt Television News Archive in Nashville for providing videotape access to the three network packages. The Archives Television News

Index was also a valuable tool in originally locating the homeless packages. CBS aired a 160-second report on November 5, ABC a 111-second report on November 6, and NBC a 28-second report on November 10.

3. Our dialogic view of news narration is derived from theories of language associated with the Russian philosopher Bakhtin (1981; see also Clark and Holoquis, 1984; Newcomb, 1984; Todorov, 1984; Voloshinov, 1973).

4. The most recent news updates on Joyce Brown state that in the spring of 1988 she was back on the street, although she was living in a city shelter at night. In September 1998, news stories reported that she had been arrested for drug possession.

5. At a press conference held during the 1988 Moscow Summit, Reagan defended the nation's treatment of the homeless by citing the Brown case: "A young lady living on the sidewalks of New York, living out there on the sidewalk, winter and summer, and so for her own sake, the police picked her up to bring her to where she could be paced in a shelter and she took her case to court and won her case in court that she should be allowed to go back and sleep on the sidewalk, where she had been because that's what she preferred to do." ("Critics Say," 1988, p A1 4). The same account reported that Brown, when asked to respond to Reagan's remarks, said, "Although I have my freedom, I still do not have adequate housing. Why doesn't the President assist me in getting permanent housing?"

REFERENCES

Bakhtin, M. (1981). *The dialogic imagination: Four essays* (C. Emerson and M. Holoquist, Trans.). Austin: University of Texas Press.

Benjamin, B. (October 29, 1987). (Interview conducted through the Hoard R. Marsh Visiting Lecturer program, Department of Communication, University of Michigan, Ann Arbor).

Berger, P. L., and Luckann, T. (1966). *The social construction of reality: A treatise in the sociology of knowledge.* Garden City, NY: Anchor-Double.

Campbell, R. (1987). Securing the middle ground: Report formulas in "60 Minutes." *Critical Studies in Mass Communication,* 4, 325–350.

Carey, J. W. (1975). A cultural approach to communication. *Communication,* 2, 1–2.

Carey, J. (Ed.). (1988). *Media, myths, and narratives: Television and the press.* Beverly Hills: Sage.

Clark, K., and Holoquist, M. (1984). *Mikhail Bakhtin.* Cambridge, MA: Belkna Press.

Critics say Reagan misstates plight of homeless. (June 2, 1988). *Detroit Free Press,* A1–4.

Dyer, R. (1979). *Stars.* London: British Film Institute.

Eason, D. L. (1981). Telling stories and making sense. *Journal of Popular Culture,* 15, 125–130.

Eason, D. L. (1984). The new journalism and the image-world: Two modes of organizing experience. *Critical Studies in Mass Communication,* 1, 51–65.

Eason D. L. (1986). On journalistic authority: The Janet Cooke scandal. *Critical Studies in Mass Communication,* 3, 429–447.

Fiske, J. (1987). *Television culture.* London: Methuen.

Foucault, M. (1965). *Madness and civilization* (R. Howard, Trans.). New York: Vintage.

Geertz, C. (1983). *Common sense as a cultural system in local knowledge* (pp. 73–93). New York: Basic Books.

Gramci, A. (1971). *Selections from the prison notebooks* (Q. Hoare and G. N. Smith, Trans.). London: Lawrence and Wishart.

Gray, H. (March 18,1988). Interview conducted during Howard R. Marsh Visiting Lecturer Program, Department of Communication, University of Michigan, Ann Arbor.

Hall, S, Critcher, C., Jefferson, T., Clark, J., and Roberts, B. (1978). *Policing the crisis: Mugging, the state, and law and order.* London: Macmillan.

Hewitt, J. (1988). *Air words: Writing for broadcast news.* Mountain View, CA: Mayfield Publishing Company.

Kozol, J. (1988). Distancing the homeless. *The Yale Review,* 77, 153–167. (A shortened and different version of this article, titled "Are the homeless crazy?" appeared in *Harper's,* September 1988, pp. 17–19).

Lears, T. J. J. (1985). The concept of cultural hegemony: Problems and possibilities. *The American Historical Review,* 90, 567–593.

Marion, P. (January, 1987). Helping and hanging the homeless: The struggle of the margins of America. *Harper's,* pp. 39–49.

Newcomb, H. (1984). On the dialogic aspects of as communication. *Critical Studies in Mass Communication,* 1, 4–50.

Park, R. (1940). News as form of knowledge: A chapter in the sociology of knowledge. *American Journal of Sociology,* 45, 669–686.

Redburn, F. S., and Buss T. (1986). *Responding to America's homeless: Public policy alternatives.* New York: Praeger.

Reeves, J. (1988). Television stardom: A ritual of social typification and individualization. In J. Carey (Ed.), *Media, myth, and narratives: Television and the press* (pp. 146–160). Beverly Hills: Sage.

Said, E. W. (1981). *Covering Islam: How the media and the experts determine how we see the rest of the world.* New York: Pantheon.

Schudson, M (1978). *Discovering the new: A social history of American newspapers.* New York: Basic Book.

Schudson, M. (1982). The politics of narrative form: The emergence of news conventions in print and television. *Daedelus,* 91–111.

Schutz, A. (1964) The well-informed citizen. In *Collected papers II. Studies in social theory* (pp. 121–134). The Hague: Martinus Nijhoff.

Schutz, A., and Luckmann, T. (1973) *The structures of the life-word* (R. M. Zaner and H. T. Engelhadt Jr., Trans.). Evanston, IL: Northwestern University Press.

Silverstone, R. (1981). The message of television: Myth and narrative in contemporary culture. London: Heinemann.

Todorov T. (1984). Mikhail Bakhtin: the dialogical principle. Minneapolis: University of Minnesota Press.

Tuchman, G. (1978). *Making news—A study in the construction of reality.* New York: Free Press.

U.S. Department of Housing and Urban Development (1984*). A report to the secretary on the homeless and emergency shelters.* Washington, DC: Office of Policy Development and Research

Voloshinov, V. (1973). *Marxism and the philosophy of language* (L. Mateka and I. R. Titunik, trans.). New York: Seminar Press

Watson, S., and Austerberry, H. (1986). *Housing and homelessness: A feminist perspective.* London: Routledge and Kegan Paul.

Chapter 3

Re-Covering the Homeless: Hindsights on the Joyce Brown Story

Jimmie L. Reeves

Near the end of the Reagan era, one homeless person named Joyce Brown was accorded newsworthiness when the City of New York removed her from a haunt above a heating vent on Second Avenue and committed her, against her will, to a psychiatric ward in Bellevue Hospital. An analysis of news coverage devoted to the Brown affair (included in this book) marked my first collaboration with Richard Campbell.[1] For us, the Joyce Brown story provided a limited set of texts that addressed an expansive set of cultural, theoretical, and interpretive issues. In dividing up the work, I teased out the similarities and differences among three network news packages broadcast between November 5 and 10, 1987, that depicted a heart-rendering struggle in which the seemingly humanitarian efforts of New York City's Project Help, a plan designed to aid people who could not help themselves, came into conflict with the constitutionality of hospitalizing itinerant people without their consent. Campbell took the comparative analysis to another level by demonstrating how "60 Minutes'" subsequent rewriting of the Brown saga in Morley Safer's "Brown vs. Koch" segment embodied many of the narrative conventions and mythic tensions of the most celebrated and popular news magazine in the history of American television.[2] Ultimately, we argued that this news coverage explored the limits of government, freedom, compassion, individualism, and the boundaries of common sense itself.

In this reconsideration of the Joyce Brown story, I take the comparative analysis to still another level by drawing on insights gained and lessons learned during a later collaboration with Campbell—*Cracked Coverage*, a book-length study of the 1980's drug news.[3] In *Cracked Coverage*, we conceived of over 200 news reports broadcast between 1981 and 1988 as the Reagan-era "cocaine narrative." Here, I deploy a similar strategy in treating the Joyce Brown affair as a significant moment in the flow of 246 television news reports broadcast between 1981 and 1988 that, collectively, gave expression to the Reagan-era "homeless narrative." In this macrolevel critical analysis, I approach the 246 news stories as a kind of grand mosaic that took shape around the economic instabilities, cultural conflicts, and political rivalries of the day. My preliminary findings suggest that although there were distinct similarities in the cocaine and homeless news coverage of the 1980s there were also striking differences. By placing these two competing and compelling news narratives in dialogue, I intend not only to document the continuities and disruptions of what it meant to be homeless in 1980s America, but I also hope to enrich our understanding of how the network news operated as a mechanism for covering the radical inequities of the Reagan decade.

THE REAGAN-ERA HOMELESS NARRATIVE

Slicing through the Coverage

Following a method applied in *Cracked Coverage*,[4] I submitted "homeless" as a key word to search the computerized data base that is now accessible on the internet of the *Vanderbilt Television News Index and Archive*.[5] Next, I screened the list of stories generated by the search to eliminate those items that did not deal directly with homelessness as a domestic social problem. For instance, the search of the 1987 data base included stories on homelessness in South Africa, Mexico, and the USSR. Of the 270 items generated by the initial search, 24 were not considered relevant to this study.

Table 3.1
The Homeless Narrative

Year	1981	1982	1983	1984	1985	1986	1987	1988
Stories	2	8	16	25	30	53	45	67

Table 3.1 indicates how the remaining stories were distributed over time—the yearly number of homeless stories rose dramatically during the decade until 1986; in 1987, the coverage dwindled; however, homelessness reached its highest point of coverage during the following presidential election year. As Table 3.2 illustrates, the shape of this coverage is hauntingly similar to the distribution of the 228 network news packages that dealt with cocaine as a domestic social problem during the same period.[6]

Table 3.2
The Cocaine Narrative

Year	1981	1982	1983	1984	1985	1986	1987	1988
Stories	1	19	14	19	27	77	32	39

Using abstracts published in the *Vanderbilt News Index* which are also available on the internet, I then conducted a preliminary narrative analysis of the major trends of coverage. Drawing on narrative theory[7] to analyze these abstracts, I made a distinction between two kinds of events: *Kernels* and *Satellites*. Kernels are those crucial events that actively contribute to the story's progression.[8] The Joyce Brown affair, for instance, is one such occurrence. Satellite events, in contrast, are less significant moments that are more routine and not as central to the cause-effect chain of the unfolding narrative. The obligatory Thanksgiving Day reports of the hungry being fed turkey dinners by the Salvation Army, as well as the familiar reports of the homeless suffering from winter weather conditions, are prime examples of satellite stories. As these examples suggest, the routine coverage of homelessness exhibits a clear and consistent temporal pattern. Indeed, William K. Bunis, Angela Yancik, and David A. Snow have demonstrated that the monthly distributions of the coverage of homelessness in the *New York Times,* the *Los Angeles Times*, and on the "CBS Evening News" are remarkably similar—coverage increases in November, peaks in December, and declines in January.[9]

Table 3.3
Monthly Coverage, 1981–1988

Month	Homeless Stories	Cocaine Stories
April	7	22
May	23	27
June	5	35
July	7	26
August	10	24
September	12	25
October	15	25
November	38	9
December	62	12
January	31	8
February	21	5
March	15	10

My own charting of the monthly coverage of homelessness by the three networks during the Reagan era, depicted in Table 3.3, reveals the same distribution of coverage. Interestingly, Table 3.3 also indicates that the monthly distribution of the cocaine coverage between 1981 and 1988 is almost diametrically opposed to the arc of the homeless coverage; peaking in June, the cocaine coverage falls off dramatically in November and December, dips to a low in February, and begins to rise again in April.

The differences in these distribution patterns may simply be a matter of visibility. On the one hand, the homeless could be more visible, more noticeable, in the winter when their suffering from harsh weather conditions is difficult to ignore. On the other hand, the use of illegal drugs could be more visible in the summer months when the warm weather permits drug transactions to be conducted on the street. But Bunis, Yancik, and Snow come to a more complicated conclusion. In considering and rejecting the weather hypothesis, Bunis and his colleagues document that when the homeless coverage drops off in January and February, the weather conditions in most parts of the country are even more severe. In New York City, for instance, the average minimum temperatures for November, December, January, and February are, respectively, 40, 29, 26, and 25. So what does account for the coverage pattern? According to Bunis et al., the holiday season bracketted by Thanksgiving and Christmas provide the news media with an opportunity to "temporarily widen the span of sympathy."[10] In this ritualized display of compassion, the routine homeless news of the satellite stories may be one highly conventionalized way of managing collective sentiments by encouraging society to confront itself in a "moral communion" that exorcises collective guilt and restores collective strength. Of course, this explanation does little to elucidate the counter-patterning of the cocaine coverage—unless the summer season somehow prompts a ritualized display of antipathy in which victim blaming and chemical scapegoating abound.

While the notion of spans of sympathy connected to the holiday season may account for the monthly variation in homeless coverage, it is, nevertheless, an ahistorical hypothesis that evades the historically specific economic transformations and political formations that, together, generated the 1980s homeless narrative. In other words, in accounting for stable patterns of coverage, it fails to address how the meaning of homelessness has shifted and mutated since it first emerged as a recognizable social problem in the early 1980s. The following analysis of the kernel events of the 1980s homeless narrative takes a very different angle on the news coverage of homelessness. Venturing into history, this analysis places news coverage of homelessness in two interlocking contexts: the demise of Fordism and the triumph of Reaganism.

Historicizing the Coverage[11]

Named for Henry Ford, Fordism was the economic order that sustained the general prosperity of the United States during its much celebrated postwar boom. The name pays tribute to Henry Ford's fame as one of the first industrialists to recognize that mass marketing involved much more than the economies of scale associated with producing products on an assembly line. Ford also understood that mass marketing required the perpetual fostering of consumer demand. First and foremost, an ideological project promoting mass consumption was not simply a matter of convincing people to buy new appliances, (paraphrasing Garry Wills) it was also about creating "a desire for the kind of life that craves such appliances."[12] Interestingly, Fordism's consumerist version of the American Dream was hawked by Ronald Reagan in the 1950s. Working for General Electric, Reagan appeared with his second wife in magazine ads as GE's model couple relaxing in their model "GE all-electric home."[13] The family ideal represented by the young Reagans was precisely the all-consuming kind of life that GE was devoted to electrifying.

According to David Harvey, the key to the extended success of Fordism, and its ultimate failure, was its rigidity.[14] As a system whereby mass production drove mass consumption and vice versa, Fordism relied on the stabilization of reciprocal relations among big labor, big capital, and big government. However, the rigidities of this order—including long-term and large-scale fixed capital investments, collective bargaining for long-term contracts, and long-term state commitment to entitlement programs—were sustainable only as long as there was stable economic growth. From 1945 to 1973 the rigidities of the system basically succeeded in stimulating heavily regulated growth to the general benefit of most U.S. workers. However, social barriers in the workplace, school, and housing market still excluded many from the Fordist dream of employment security, upward mobility through education, and home ownership. Under Fordism, the labor market was divided into a heavily unionized "monopoly sector" made up of "affluent workers," and a low-wage "competitive sector" made up of what Michael Harrington termed the "other America."[15] In Harvey's estimation, the inequities of this divided labor market "produced serious tensions and strong social movements on the part of the excluded—movements that were compounded by the way in which race, gender, and ethnicity often determined who had access to privileged employment and who did not."[16] In the 1960s, the government tried to contain this discontent with Great Society measures including welfare, job training, and educational programs.

The loose monetary policies and the escalating wartime economy of the 1960s allowed the Fordist order to absorb, for a short time, the expenses of these new social programs. However, throughout the 1970s the rigidities of Fordism would be destabilized by a series of traumatic developments. The greatest shock to the system came in 1973 when the shift to a peacetime economy and the oil embargo thrust the nation into a sharp recession. The hard times that followed were marked not only by deindustrialization, high inflation, high unemployment, and high taxes, but by a steady decline in the power of organized labor, a steady erosion of public support for the expensive social programs instituted by Great Society containment, and a steady failure to restore enduring economic growth. As the reciprocal relations among big labor, big government, and big capital were progressively undermined, a new economic order emerged—an order that Harvey calls "flexible accumulation."[17]

As the name implies, flexible accumulation departs drastically from the rigidities of the Fordist order. Displacing the long-term stabilities of Fordism with the instabilities of short-term engagement, flexible accumulation promoted a fundamental shift in collective norms and beliefs toward the values of an entrepreneurial culture based on old-fashioned competitive individualism. These values oriented on windfall profits, hit-and-run marketing, and "paper entrepreneurialism," emphasized, in Harvey's words, "the new, the fleeting, the ephemeral, the fugitive, and the contingent in modern life, rather than the more solid values implanted under Fordism."[18] On the supply side, flexible accumulation has been marked by expansions of the service sector (most notably, in the private health—care, banking, real estate, fast-food, and entertainment industries), accelerations in the pace of product innovation, reductions in turnover time, and explorations of highly specialized market niches. On the demand side, it has entailed what Davis terms "overconsumptionism."[19]

The radical restructuring of the labor market under flexible accumulation would not only diminish the power of the unions, but it would also have a devastating impact on the non-unionized working poor, especially those isolated in America's inner cities. In fact, the job migrations, deregulation, and deindustrialization of the new order allowed employers to exert even more pressures of control on the work force—and provided much more flexibility in controlling labor costs. Characterized by a move away from regular employment, a surge in service employment, a reliance on part-time or temporary work arrangements, the labor market of the new order is organized into a franchised core group and fragmented peripheral groups. The core, a steadily shrinking job market, is the laboring aristocracy that still basically enjoys the good life of the Fordist affluent worker, with one major difference—under the new order, the core worker is expected to be "adaptable, flexible, and, if necessary, geographically mobile."[20] The peripheral job market essentially represents an explosive elaboration of the Fordist competitive sector. Under this split-level configuration, the new labor market takes on a bottom-heavy shape—some high-wage jobs, many low-wage service jobs, and a "missing middle."[21] Where, under Fordism, General Motors was the nation's largest private employer, under flexible accumulation the temporary service Manpower now holds that distinction. The widespread economic insecurities, status anxieties, and competitive tensions accompanying the polarizations of this flexible labor market certainly contributed to the antifeminist and antisocial—welfare backlash of the 1970s, 1980s, and 1990s. As always, when times are tough, scapegoats abound.

Reagan, like Thatcher, was able to colonize these insecurities, anxieties, and tensions by demonizing the old Fordist regime while sanctifying the new entrepreneurial order of flexible accumulation. Reaganism condemned both big government and big labor as symbols of a thoroughly discredited liberal establishment. Paraphrasing Stuart Hall's analysis of Thatcherism, the discourse of Reaganism condensed at the negative pole statism, bureaucracy, big labor, and liberal Democrats. Against this rhetorical construction of the "power bloc," Reaganism "counterposed various condensations" of possessive individualism, personal initiative, privatization, and freedom from government restraints as the positive pole. In this way, Reaganism was able to represent big labor as "part of the big battalions, ranged against the 'little man' (and his family)"—part of an oppressive system of high taxes, high inflation, and intrusive government regulations. Thus, in opposing this power bloc, Reagan was portrayed as "out there struggling with little people" and the labor unions were depicted as just another special interest seeking special treatment at "our" expense.[22]

In many profound ways this sanctification of the new order is a nostalgic rewriting of the late nineteenth-century utopian myth of Horatio Alger. In Alger's capitalist utopia, the ideal society is a meritocracy in which brains, initiative, and hard work earn their just rewards. According to Robert Reich (who was to become a top economic advisor to President Bill Clinton), the Alger cosmology endorsed large disparities in wealth, since riches were the award for applying yourself, saving your money and trading shrewdly. The key virtue was self-reliance; "the admirable man was the self-made man; the goal was to be your own boss rather than to work for someone else."[23] Indeed, along with the cocaine and homeless narratives, one of the ideological hallmarks of 1980s America was the resurrection of celebratory tales of the heroic entrepreneur. Lee Iacocca, Peter Ueberroth, Donald Trump, and Ted Turner were all canonized as folk heroes who gave visible form to the American ethic of capitalistic success. Their recognition and fame not only inspired a generation of young business school graduates (as well as drug dealers), but such regard lent credibility to an individualist and elitist historiography that was the basis of Reagan's economic policies: the "great man" theory of history. Founded on "the belief that history is made by inspired acts of outstanding individuals, whose genius transcends the normal constraints of historical context,"[24] this view is generally discredited by contemporary historians, although it is still the way that common sense—and journalists as custodians of common sense—comprehend the world and its often incomprehensible complexity.[25]

Reaganism's great man theory of economic progress is expressed in its starkest terms by the conservative economist George Gilder in these passages from *The Spirit of Enterprise*:

All of us are dependent for our livelihood and progress not on a vast and predictable machine, but on the creativity and courage of the particular men who accept the risks which generate our riches.[26] The key to growth is quite simple: creative men with money. The cause of stagnation is similarly clear: depriving creative individuals of financial power.[27]

Implicit in this patriarchal and individualistic spin on the operation of the domestic economy are two categories of productive activity: the entrepreneur and the drone. According to Reich, "in the popular mind, people were not fated for one or the other category":

In the popular mind the distinction had nothing to do with class. Almost anyone could become an entrepreneur with enough drive and daring. The economy needed both, of course—creative entrepreneurs to formulate the Big Ideas that would find their way into new products and production techniques, and the drones to undertake the routine chores involved in realizing these ideas. But for the economy to grow and prosper, it was presumed necessary to reward people who opted to become entrepreneurs and discipline those who remained drones.[28]

In Reaganomics, this presumption that economic growth was simply a matter of stimulating the entrepreneurial realm with economic rewards would justify the reverse Robin Hoodism of slashing taxes on the wealthy while eliminating social programs aiding the poor.

Reverse Robin Hoodism, of course, exemplifies the shadow side Reaganism's upbeat economic message. The "again" in the campaign slogan—"It's morning again in America"—voiced a conservative egalitarianism that, in Greil Marcus's phrasing "promised everything to anyone with the grace to leave the damned behind."[29] Although a superficially "inclusive" message, the "morning again" slogan expressed an ideology that according to Thomas Byrne Edsall and Mary D. Edsall, "used opposition to federal tax burdens to unite the rich and working class, as opposed to the use of federal spending to unite the poor and the middle class, an ideology purged of overt bias, tinged-in the wake of unprecedented social change—with nostalgia, and with an implicit but stern admonition to life's losers."[30] Or, put another way, the nostalgic orthodoxy of Reaganism vowed to take back America in a double sense. On the one hand, as an orthodoxy of inclusion, it promised to take all of America back to the gilded age of a pre-Fordist, Horatio Alger enterprise culture; on the other hand, as an orthodoxy of exclusion, it promised to take America back from the color—and gender coded special interest groups of the Keynesian welfare state.

Just as Gilder justified the sunny side of Reaganism's orthodoxy of nostalgia, the shadow side was justified by another one of the most reactionary and influential studies of the Reagan Era: Charles Murray's *Losing Ground: American Social Policy, 1950–1980*.[31] Providing seemingly objective research, Murray managed to gloss over the collapse of the Keynesian-Fordist economic order by blaming Great Society initiatives for the rising poverty rate in the late 1970s. Attacking welfare dependency for undermining self reliance, the work ethic, and family values, Murray's book was virtually a rewriting of anticharity sentiments popular during the First Gilded Age (mid-1870s to mid-1890s). As Stephanie Coontz observed, Murray's work represented nothing less than a return to the social Darwinism of the First Gilded Age: "Social Darwinism preached that millionaires exemplified the 'survival of the fittest.'" The poor were labeled "unfit," a drag on the race. To preserve the unfit in any way was to court disaster. "Nature's cure for most social and political diseases is better than man's," argued the president of Columbia University, as did his successors in the 1970s and 1980s, George Gilder and Charles Murray.[32] Advocating for elimination of all social programs aimed at the poor (with the exception of unemployment insurance for the working-age population), Murray replaced the "benign neglect" of the Nixon era with a much more malignant, Reaganesque animosity toward the suffering of those in poverty.

Thus, in a strange symbolic inversion, Murray, Gilder, and other New Right intellectuals converted the great man theory's radically individualistic outlook on economic prosperity into a "poor man" theory of personal/familial failure. In its application to Reaganism's revision of the meaning of the Great Society, the economic turmoil and family instability accompanying the shift from a manufacturing to a service economy was understood as simply the consequences of cultural pathologies driven by individual immorality. In Craig Reinarman and Harry Levine's phrasing:

Unemployment, poverty, urban decay, school crises, crime, and all their attendant forms of human troubles were spoken of and acted upon as if they were the result of *individual* deviance, immorality, and weakness. The aperture of attribution for America's ills was constricted. People *in* trouble were reconceptualized as people who *make* trouble; social control replaced social welfare as the organizing principle of state policy.[33]

Again, just as Reaganism's individualistic historiography embraced the idea that entrepreneurs must be rewarded, it proposed that the mob of unruly drones must be disciplined.

This shift in state policy from a commitment to social welfare to an infatuation with social control is perhaps best captured by the meteoric rise in two related sets of numbers: the federal drug control budget and the U.S. incarceration rate. In 1981, $1.5 billion was devoted to domestic enforcement, international and border control, and demand reduction. Under Reagan's leadership, the drug budget more than quadrupled ($6.6 billion spent in 1989) at a time of drastic cuts in many other government programs.[34] During this same period, the U.S. prison population nearly doubled (from 329,821 in 1980 to 627,402 in 1989)[35] as the number of drug arrests nationwide increased from 471,000 in 1980 to

1,247,000 in 1989.[36] By 1990, the United States had the highest incarceration rate in the world (426 per 100,000 compared to 333 per 100,000 in South Africa, its closest competitor).[37] In that same year when about half the inmates in federal prisons were there on drug offenses[38] African Americans made up almost half the U.S. prison population, and about one in four young black males in their twenties were either in jail, on parole, or on probation (compared to only 6 percent for white males).[39]

These ballooning numbers, when considered in conjunction with the tax cuts, budget cuts, deregulation, union busting, and privatization of the Reagan era, provide empirical testimony to the inequities of a decade in which the ruling bloc embarked on a highly self-conscious program to loosen governmental restraints on the rich and tighten "margins of illegality" on the poor. Reagan's war on drugs was absolutely central to enabling the incongruities of this cynical political agenda; it succeeded in redefining social problems grounded on global transformations in late capitalism (deinstrialization, job migration, the vanishing family wage of a vanishing manufacturing economy, the flexible exploitation of fragmented labor markets in a burgeoning service economy, the rise of transnational corporations, and so on) as individual moral problems that could be resolved by way of voluntary therapeutic treatment, compulsory drug testing, mandatory prison sentences, even the penalty of death. As we demonstrate in *Cracked Coverage*, in constructing and reaffirming cocaine use as a moral disease or a criminal pathology, the network news adopted a "support the troops" mentality that facilitated the staging and legitimating of Reagan's war on drugs as a major political spectacle.[40]

But, where Reagan and his allies in the drug control establishment are properly considered co-authors of the cocaine news narrative, the 1980s homeless narrative was promoted by a very different set of political agents. In the following analysis, I hope to demonstrate that the homeless coverage operated as something of an oppositional narrative, one that challenged the social agenda of Reaganism and was primarily authored, at least initially, by Reagan's rivals in Washington—the so-called liberal establishment. Therefore, from this radically historical interpretive perspective that treats the social construction of homelessness as a response to the shadowy side of Reaganism, I am now prepared to propose, with some confidence, that the 1980s homeless narrative developed according to the characteristic stages of what Victor Turner terms a "social drama": breach, crisis, redress, and reintegration or separation.[41]

The Breach Stage (1981–1982)

This interpretation of the homeless narrative as a social drama is heavily influenced by James S. Ettema's application of Turner's work to the study of news as ritual. According to Ettema, the breach stage of a social drama is a moment of rupture "in which some norm, law, or custom is violated in a public setting and in a way that challenges entrenched authority."[42] In the case of the homeless narrative, the "violation" that initiated the drama was Reagan's cutting of funding for social programs at a time of high unemployment and a deepening recession—an action that represented a break with the social welfare orientation that had guided state policy since the New Deal. Reagan's opponents in congress provided the setting for publicizing the breach.

According to my key word search, the very first stories of the Reagan era to use the word "homeless" appeared on March 11, 1981. On that day, two news packages, one on ABC, the other on NBC, covered Housing and Human Services Secretary Richard Schweiker's early efforts to sell Reagan's budget cuts to House Democrats. The ABC package featured hostile responses to Schweiker's lobbying by Representatives Shirley Chisholm, Peter Stark, Patricia Schroeder, George Danielson, and Tip O'Neill, all of whom criticized the budget's impact on the poor. For instance, Schroeder and Danielson claimed that under Reagan's proposed economic plan "the rich will get richer and the poor, poorer." The NBC package also featured Chisholm—but an even more significant figure to appear in both reports was an advocate for the poor named Jane Russell who spoke on behalf of a program for homeless orphans. Russell's description of the abandoned children as homeless evidently introduced the anti-Reagan inflection of the term "homeless" in 1980s network news discourse.

However, this initial moment in the homeless narrative would not immediately rewrite the news framing and naming of this newly promoted social problem. In the ABC package, the name of the activist organization that protested cuts in the food stamps program was the National Antihunger Coalition. Almost exactly ten months later, on January 12, 1982, a CBS story by Bernard Goldberg still applied the term "street people" to destitute folks suffering from freezing weather conditions in New York City. Homelessness would not arrive as part of the "common sense" language of television journalism until twenty-one months after the initial stories when a series of five reports used the term in connection with the difficulties experienced by the urban unemployed. The first of these reports appeared on December 11, 1982; the last, on Christmas Day. But the three middle reports, all broadcast on December 15, 1982, are the ones that together constitute a kernel event in the homeless narrative.

All three of the packages cover a hearing by the House subcommittee on housing investigating the increasing number of what was called the unemployed homeless. The subcommittee members heard testimony from several people in dire straits who described what was termed as their "plight" (George Andrews, Mary Long, Frank Detorie, and Pauline Pegues)—testimony that was excerpted in the ABC and CBS packages. The same sound bite from Salvation Army spokesperson Major Paul Kelly appeared in the CBS and NBC reports (according to Kelly, the organization's clothing deposit boxes were being used for shelter). The ABC story featured Salt Lake City Mayor Ted Wilson who described homelessness as "a national tragedy"—a sentiment echoed on NBC by New York City's Mayor Edward Koch. But perhaps the most significant figure to surface in this early moment in the homeless narrative was a man identified as a spokesperson for the Center for Creative Nonviolence, Mitch Snyder. Appearing in both the ABC and CBS packages, Snyder commented on the extent of the problem and accused Congress of being insensitive.

At the outset, then, this emergent way of describing the consequences of poverty was framed in terms of the discourse of victimization. The word "plight" would be permanently linked to "homelessness"—a word that speaks of unfairly enduring a brutal predicament that is beyond one's control. Homelessness was connected to unemployment, to the scarcity of affordable housing, to the worsening economic conditions associated with the economic recession. Perhaps even more importantly, the homeless were explicitly defined as casualties of Reaganomics.

The Crisis Stage (1983–May 1986)

As Ettema observes, in the crisis stage of the social drama, "antagonisms become visible and factions form along enduring social fault lines."[43] During this crisis period, the antagonisms made visible in the coverage of homelessness would place Reagan and his minions on one side of the line, and Reagan's detractors on the other. As might be expected, the latter faction promoted homelessness as a national disgrace for which Reagan was responsible. The first kernel event of this stage was a national day for the homeless scheduled for January 25, 1983, the day of Reagan's State of the Union Address. Featuring demonstrations on Capitol Hill, the timing of what some might term the pseudo-event was obviously meant to undercut the President's message to Congress. Significantly, CBS, in a news package that described the homeless as "victims of the recession," was the only network to cover these demonstrations Again, significantly, CBS was the only network to cover the other major staged protest of this period—a hunger strike by Mitch Snyder in 1984. A kind of "pre-text" to Morley Safer's "Brown vs. Koch" segment on "60 Minutes" in 1988, Snyder's activism was also the subject of a "60 Minutes" segment in 1984.

On the other side of the fault line was the Reagan camp, which sought to challenge and dismiss the reality of the homeless problem. In this regard, the most noteworthy event during the crisis stage was a statement by Edwin Meese implying that hunger not only didn't exist in a serious sense in the U.S. but that those taking advantage of soup kitchens do so because the food is free rather than because they're destitute. Again, CBS was the only network to report the Meese statement. Airing on December 9, 1983, the CBS package included responses by prominent Democrats, Gary Hart and Tip O'Neill.

CBS's willingness to report events staged by activist organizations and to jump on meanspirited statements by the Reagan Administration validates its institutional identity as a crumbling bastion of old-time liberalism. This evidence of CBS's antagonism toward Reagan is also concordant with our findings in *Cracked Coverage*. In its reporting of the futilities of the war on drugs, CBS's coverage was, in fact, distinguished by a consistently anti-Reagan spin.[44] Even so, coverage on all three networks, including CBS, periodically encouraged such strong identification with police action that it was little more than propaganda for the expansion of state power in the surveillance and repression of visible and vulnerable populations in America's inner cities.

Another crucial linkage between the homeless and cocaine narratives is the significance of death in the advancing storylines. The deaths of John Belushi, David Kennedy, Don Rogers, and, especially, Len Bias were all kernel events in the cocaine narrative.[45] During the crisis stage in the homeless narrative, the deaths of Jesse Carpenter, Lou Ellen "Lulu" Couch, and Jimmy Woods would also attract national attention. Carpenter's death was, by far, the most embarrassing to the Reagan Administration. Carpenter froze on the day after Christmas in Lafayette Park across from the White House. According to ABC's reporting of this tragedy, Carpenter died because he stayed with his wheelchair-bound homeless friend, John Lamb. But what made matters even worse for the Reagan Administration was that Carpenter won the Bronze Star in World War II and it was reported that plans were underway to bury his body at Arlington National Cemetery. Jimmy Woods, too, was a veteran, but his icy demise occurred on a Boston street after Woods refused a place to sleep in the Kingston Shelter. Lulu Couch's death was newsworthy because she had been featured in the documentary *Streetwise*. Unlike Carpenter and Woods, Couch was murdered during a street fracas.

These deaths helped generate something of a moral panic around the homeless issue and a pattern of escalating coverage that is normally associated with crime wave coverage. Just as Len Bias's death performed a pivotal role in authenticating news coverage of the 1986 crack crisis, the deaths of Carpenter, Woods, and Couch proclaimed that homelessness was really a problem happening now—that people were actually dying on the streets. In other words, the deaths, especially Carpenter's, corroborated the claims by Reagan's partisan and activist opponents regarding the seriousness and reality of the homeless problem.[46]

But another development during this stage of coverage would muddy the meaning of homelessness in a way that worked in favor of the Reagan camp: a series of reports on the mental health of the homeless. The first was broadcast by CBS on November 20, 1983, and reported on the "plight of the homeless mentally ill." This report was significant, not only because it anticipated the Joyce Brown affair, but also because it was the first to apply the term homeless to people who were not portrayed explicitly as victims of the recession or victims of Reagan's budget cuts. Instead, the mentally ill homeless were depicted as victims of a well-meaning program of de-institutionalization that, apparently, had gone desperately wrong. This inflection on the homeless narrative and broadening of the term to include the "abandoned mentally ill" foreshadowed how the meaning of homelessness would shift over the course of the decade.

The Redress Stage (May 1986)

According the Ettema, in the redress stage, "adjustive mechanisms ranging from personal advice to formal juridical procedures to rituals of sacrifice are invoked."[47] This analysis compresses the redress stage to one month, May 1986. May 25, 1986, was the day that a promoter named Ken Kragen orchestrated a grand pseudo-event called Hands Across America. Unlike the demonstrations, protests, and hunger strikes by Mitch Snyder and other homeless activists, Hands Across America attracted a great deal of coverage on all three networks. Like Live Aid and FarmAid, Hands Across America provided an opportunity for celebrities (among them, the performer then known as Prince, Glenn Close, and Lionel Richie) to indulge in a conspicuous display of compassion. In addition to celebrity endorsement, Hands Across America also received corporate sponsorship by Coca-Cola, Citibank, American Express, and other corporations implicated in the economic transformations that generated this problem called homelessness in the first place. Corporate public relations trickery is akin to the tobacco and alcohol industries contributing to the Partnership for a Drug Free America while aggressively test-marketing products like Uptown cigarettes. (R.J. Reynolds Tobacco Company) and PowerMaster malt liquor (G. Heileman) intended primarily for the black consumer market. At any rate, because of such "legitimate" backing for Hands Across America, no less than a dozen news packages were devoted to coverage of the event. This intense coverage not only accounts for the May spike in Table 3.3, but also explains the jump in coverage in 1986 depicted in Table 3.1.

There is ample reason, then, to treat Hands Across America as the single most important kernel event of the 1980s homeless narrative. But its importance is not simply a matter of the sheer number of stories devoted to the event. Instead, its significance is also bound up in the absurdity of the Reagans participating in the event. After all, how could President Reagan join hands in this affair when he was unwilling to acknowledge the reality of homelessness?

In fact, Reagan had initially refused to participate. On May 21, just four days prior to the event, Reagan created a stir when he stated that the "hungry starve due to their own ignorance." This classic example of Reaganesque victim-blaming was not well received by a public primed to turn out for Hands Across America. By May 23, wife Nancy and daughter Maureen had convinced Reagan to reverse his decision and take part in the event—but he had a lot of explaining to do. In a radio address, Reagan stated that his about face on Hands Across America was due to his admiration for the work of private volunteer groups such as the Christmas in April organization. However, several news packages covering the farce provided less flattering explanations for Reagan's begrudging support of Hands Across America. For instance, Democratic pollster Peter Hart, in a report on CBS, noted Reagan's consistently low ratings in the area of compassion and speculated that the support of the event was aimed at improving his public image.

On May 30, 1986, the "ABC Evening News" named Ken Kragen its "Person of the Week." A show business manager and promoter, Kragen's volunteerism stands in stark contrast to Mitch Snyder's activism. Although both might be accurately described as "moral entrepreneurs"[48] in the homeless narrative, the very fact that Kragen welcomed Reagan's participation in the event screams of the shallowness of his understanding of the problem. There can be no doubt that Hands Across America was a rousing success as a feel-good moment. Like Thanksgiving and Christmas, it provided the news media with an opportunity to temporarily widen the span of sympathy. Accordingly, Hands Across America was also probably successful as a mechanism for relieving some of the collective guilt generated by the homeless narrative. While it is perhaps unfair to fault the sentiments motivating the organizers of the event, the lasting impact of Hands Across America was not to provide significant relief to the homeless but to redefine the solution to homelessness in terms that were consistent with Reaganism—that is, in terms of private, individual volunteerism rather than public, collective struggle. In hindsight, Hands Across America was a moment of redress when Reaganism was able to yank the teeth out of the homeless drama. Thanks to the Reagans' highly publicized and hypocritical support of the event, Kragen's media spectacle was transformed from an expression of widespread compassion for the less fortunate into a celebration of volunteerism. In that transformation, Hands Across America became a travesty.

Considering the homeless narrative in isolation only tells a part of the story. In fact, the fifth month of 1986 was also an equally important moment in the cocaine narrative. According to the *New York Times's* Peter Kerr, a "turning point" in the coverage of the crack crisis occurred on May 18, just one week before the staging of Hands Across America.[49] On that momentous Sunday, three of New York City's newspapers (the *New York Times, Daily News*, and *Newsday*) published lengthy articles on the crack trend. Within ten days the three national networks followed suit: NBC's Dennis Murphy filed his copycat crack story on Friday, May 23 (the day the Reagans announced their decision to participate in Hands Across America); ABC's John McKenzie and CBS's Harold Dow filed their reports on the following Tuesday, May 27 (two days after Hands Across America). In June, July, and August of 1986, as the homeless narrative went into its traditional summer hiatus, the American public would witness what quantitative researchers term an "intermedia convergence" on the crack issue.[50] Not surprisingly, the "seismic jump"[51] in drug stories was accompanied by a parallel jolt in measurements of public opinion. In April 1986, only 2 percent of the respondents to a *New York Times/CBS News* Poll picked drugs as the nation's most important problem. By early September 1986 another survey by the same authority found drugs now topped the list of perceived ills with 13 percent of 1,210 adults interviewed choosing drugs as the nation's most important problem.[52] The results were matched by an ABC News poll, also released in September, that found that 80 percent of those responding believed that America was caught up in a national drug crisis. In the same poll, however, 62 percent also reported that drugs were not a major problem in their own hometowns. Clearly, in the battle for the hearts, minds, and votes of the American public, the cocaine narrative and its promoters had triumphed over the homeless narrative and its promoters—a triumph that would win widespread support for Reaganism's abandonment of social welfare and adoption of social control as the organizing principle of state policy.

The Reintegration or Separation Stage (June 1986–1988)

Which brings me to a reconsideration of the meaning and power of the Joyce Brown affair news coverage. Although the Joyce Brown story is not in the same category as Hands Across America, it does rank as the most significant kernel event of the concluding stage of the Reagan-era homeless drama. According to Ettema, in the final stage of the social drama "the attempts at redress are seen as either to succeed or fail and ceremonies may be enacted to mark reconciliation or else permanent cleavage."[53] The three network news packages devoted to covering the Brown controversy treated one highly visible manifestation of homelessness as the part that stands in for the whole. This generalization of the worst-case scenario in this type of trend reporting is a standard feature of mainstream news discourse. In personalizing social problems, such reporting often treats the most extreme and disturbing instances of a phenomenon (the crack mother, for example) as paradigmatic of the whole problem.[54] Conflating the whole of the problem to the mentally ill fragment, the news packages marked off the homeless as people whose suffering results from personal deficiencies associated with chemical dependency and/or madness. As put in 1989:

Mediated by the narration of the well informed reporters and the dialogue between experts, the homeless are rendered in all three network packages as "a danger to themselves and others," as transients without fixed names, addresses, occupations, or identities. Situated outside the bounds of society, they give a wretched form and a garbled voice to the dark side of common sense—the irrational realm of nonsense.[55]

The meaning of the homeless as victims of Reaganomics established in the breach and crisis stages of the homeless narrative had undergone a dramatic revision that, like the cocaine narrative, provided legitimation for the social control orientation of Reagan's domestic policies.

The "60 Minutes" rewriting of the Joyce Brown story (although it would rescue Brown from the realm of nonsense and make her a celebrity) did not significantly depart from the dominant meaning of homelessness embraced by the three network packages. *They* (the homeless) still represented a danger to *Us*—a meaning even shared by Brown who confided to Safer that Project Help made a terrible mistake in selecting her as a test case "because I'm sane: I'm not insane. And there are thousands out there they could have used for a model. I'm the wrong one." Furthermore, in validating Brown's claims of being a "professional homeless person" and celebrating Brown's "right" to be homeless, Safer and "60 Minutes" helped authenticate the Reaganite view that being poor is, after all, a matter of choice. However, perhaps the most damaging outcome of the news coverage of the Brown affair was the way it discredited Mayor Koch who had played an important role in earlier stages of the homeless narrative as an outspoken critic of Reaganomics. In this discrediting of Koch and Project Help, the coverage painted governmental solutions to this troubling problem as exercises in futility. Pitting social welfare operatives against the ACLU, and Mayor Koch against a woman who claimed to be homeless by choice, the Brown affair, ultimately, let Reaganism off the hook.

CONCLUSION

In Turner's words, a social drama operates as a cultural vehicle for "manifesting ourselves to ourselves and, of declaring where power and meaning lie and how they are distributed. As society complexifies, as the division of labor produces more and more specialized and professionalized modalities of sociocultural action, so do the means of assigning meaning to social dramas multiply—but the drama remains to the last simple and ineradicable, a fact of everyone's social experience, and a significant node in the development cycle of all groups that aspire to continuance."[56] In this brief treatment of the 1980s homeless narrative as a social drama, I have glossed over many kernel events in the evolution of what it meant to be homeless in 1980s America. Obviously, the thrust of this analysis has been to provide a new way of conceiving of the significance of the Joyce Brown affair. In the intervening years since Campbell and I first analyzed the Brown coverage, Joyce Brown has joined Jane Russell, Jesse Carpenter, Lulu Couch, Ken Kragen, April Savino, and Joseph Mauri on the list of forgotten people who once played a prominent role in the Reagan-era news coverage of homelessness. The last time that Joyce Brown appeared on the network evening news was on February 19, 1988, in a CBS package that reported on her celebrity status. However, though Joyce Brown vanished from the network news after her moment of celebrity, her story was still a crucial moment in the final stage of the Reagan-era homeless narrative.

This analysis suggests that Brown's story took on its power and meaning, not in isolation, but in dialogue with other related conflicts and struggles. One way of thinking about this dialogue is to conceive of the Brown affair as a kernel event within the larger social drama of the homeless narrative within the larger antagonisms of the politics of rich and poor in post-Fordist America. By the end of the Reagan era, in part because of the Brown controversy, the homeless had been redefined in the network news as a "danger to themselves and others"—as a policing problem, a personal problem, or a problem for private volunteer organizations—but not an economic problem. In hindsight, it is no wonder that by June 1988 Reagan had appropriated the Joyce Brown story into his repertoire of anecdotes as both a representative example of rugged individualism and "the care with which America deals with its homeless."[57] It is also no wonder that, although homelessness would emerge a major Democratic issue in the 1988 presidential campaign, the Republican's mobilization of the cocaine narrative would carry the election as responsibility for Americans in poverty was surrendered to the fickle mercy and flexible compassion of George Bush's mythical thousand points of light.

NOTES

1. Richard Campbell and Jimmie L. Reeves, "Covering the Homeless: The Joyce Brown Story," *Critical Studies in Mass Communication* 6, no. 1 (March 1989): 21–42.

2. This division of labor made sense at the time because Campbell was in the final stages of converting his dissertation on *60 Minutes* into a book. See Campbell, *60 Minutes and the News: A Mythology for Middle America* (Urbana: University of Illinois Press, 1991).

3. See Jimmie L. Reeves and Richard Campbell, *Cracked Coverage: Television News, the Anti-Cocaine Crusade, and the Reagan Legacy* (Durham: Duke University Press, 1994).

4. Reeves and Campbell, *Cracked Coverage*, pp. 16–18.

5. I am grateful to Kathryn Quilliam for her assistance during this phase of the research.

6. There were actually 528 items listed by the search for the key word "cocaine"—but, after eliminating all the "foreign intrigue" stories that dealt chiefly with international drug trafficking, we were left with 228 items.

7. Sarah Ruth Kozloff provides an excellent overview of narrative theory for media scholars in "Narrative Theory and Television," in Robert C. Allen, ed., *Channels of Discourse: Television and Contemporary Criticism* (Chapel Hill: University of North Caro-

lina Press, 1987), pp. 42–73. Also see Shlomith Rimmon-Kenan, *Narrative Fiction: Contemporary Poetics* (London: Metheun, 1983), p. 15.

8. Kozloff, "Narrative Theory," pp. 45–46. Also see Tzvetan Todorov, "The Grammar of Narrative," in *The Poetics of Prose*, trans. Richard Howard (Ithaca: Cornell University Press, 1977), p. 111.

9. William K. Bunis, Angela Yancik, and David A Snow, "The Cultural Patterning of Sympathy Toward the Homeless and Other Victims of Misfortune," *Social Problems* 43, no. 4 (November 1996): 387–402.

10. Ibid.

11. This subsection is derived from numerous passages scattered across several chapters of *Cracked Coverage* that have been reconfigured and reaccentuated to make them relevant to the homeless narrative.

12. See *Reagan's America: Innocents at Home* (New York: Doubleday, 1987), pp. 279–80.

13. See illustration 1.10 in Michael Rogin, *Ronald Reagan, the Movie and Other Essays in Political Demonology* (Berkeley: University of California Press, 1987).

14. See David Harvey, *The Condition of Postmodernity: An Enquiry into the Origins of Cultural Change* (Oxford: Basil Blackwell, 1989), pp. 132–33.

15. See Michael Harrington, *The Other America: Poverty in the United States* (New York: Macmillan, 1962).

16. Harvey, *The Condition of Postmodernity*, p. 138.

17. Ibid. pp. 141–72. This new economic order also has been called "post-Fordism," "overconsumptionism," and "flexible specialization." See also Mike Davis, *Prisoners of the American Dream: Politics and Economy in the History of the U.S. Working Class* (London: Verso, 1986), p. 206, and Stuart Hall, *The Hard Road to Renewal: Thatcherism and the Crisis on the Left* (London: Verso, 1988), pp. 275–76.

18. Harvey, *The Condition of Postmodernity*, p. 171.

19. Davis, *Prisoners of the American Dream*, p. 206; see also Harvey, *The Condition of Postmodernity*, p. 156.

20. Harvey, *The Condition of Postmodernity*, p. 150.

21. Davis, *Prisoners of the American Dream*, p. 220. Also see Barry Bluestone and Bennett Harrison, *The Deindustialization of America: Plant Closings, Community Abandonment, and the Dismantling of Basic Industry* (New York: Basic Books, 1982), p. 95.

22. Hall, *The Hard Road to Renewal*, p. 142.

23. Robert B. Reich, *Tales of a New America: The Anxious Liberal's Guide to the Future* (New York: Vintage Books, 1988), pp. 106–7.

24. See Robert C. Allen and Douglas Gomery, *Film History: Theory and Practice* (New York: Knopf, 1985), p. 53.

25. For instance, the news coverage of U.S. involvement in the Persian Gulf after the Iraqi invasion of Kuwait began by trying to place the Bush intervention in the messy context of neocolonialism, the regional politics of rich and poor, the control of the global economy, the long-standing U.S. alliance with Israel, the threat of Islamic fundamentalism, and the rise of Arab nationalism. But, by the time the United States launched it air war on January 16, 1991, this complexity had largely been simplified and personalized as a "showdown" (a CBS news promotion slogan) between two great men: Saddam Hussein, a great villain on the order of Hitler—and George Bush, a great statesman on the order of Churchill. The same pattern of "great man" simplification was also apparent in news coverage of the U.S. invasion of Panama in which the CIA's role in drug smuggling operations to support the Contras in Nicaragua was lost in the journalistic infatuation with vilifying Manuel Noriega.

26. George Gilder, *The Spirit of Enterprise* (New York: Simon and Schuster, 1985), p. 147.

27. Ibid., p. 290.

28. Reich, *Tales of New America*, p. 108.

29. Greil Marcus, *Lipstick Traces: A Secret History of the Twentieth Century* (Cambridge, MA: Harvard University Press, 1989), p. 135–36.

30. Thomas Byrne Edsall and Mary D. Edsall, *Chain Reaction: The Impact of Race, Rights, and Taxes on American Politics* (New York: W. W. Norton, 1991), p. 178.

31. Charles Murray, *Losing Ground: American Social Policy, 1950–1980* (New York: Basic Books, 1984).

32. Stephanie Coontz, *The Way We Never Were: American Families and the Nostalgia Trap* (New York: Basic Books, 1992), p. 103.

33. Craig Reinarman and Harry G. Levine, "The Crack Attack: Politics and Media in America's Latest Drug Scare," in Joel Best, ed., *Images of Issues: Typifying Contemporary Social Problems* (New York: Aldine de Gruyter, 1989), p. 127.

34. These numbers are derived from a graphic presented by Mathea Falco, "Foreign Drugs, Foreign Wars," *Daedalus* 121, no. 3 (Summer 1992): 6.

35. See Clarence Lusane, *Pipe Dream Blues: Racism and the War on Drugs* (Boston: South End Press, 1991), p. 44; "Prisoners in 1988," *Bureau of Justice Statistics Bulletin* (Washington, DC: U.S. Department of Justice), April 1989; "Profile of State Prison Inmates, 1986," *Special Report, Bureau of Justice Statistics* (Washington, DC: U.S. Department of Justice), January 1988.

36. Michael Massing, "What Ever Happened to the 'War on Drugs'?" *New York Review of Books* 39 (June 11, 1992), 45.

37. Sharon LaFraniere, "U.S. Has Most Prisoners Per Capita in the World," *Washington Post* (January 5, 1991), pp. A3.

38. Massing, "What Ever Happened," p. 45.

39. Ron Harris, "Blacks Feel Brunt of Drug War," *Los Angeles Times* (April 22, 1990), p. A1.

40. See Reeves and Campbell, *Cracked Coverage*, p. 38.

41. See Victor Turner, "Social Dramas and Stories About Them," in W. J. T. Mitchell, ed., *On Narrative* (New York: Praeger, 1989).

42. James S. Ettema, "Press Rites and Race Relations: A Study of Mass Mediated Ritual," *Critical Studies in Mass Communication* 7, no. 4 (December 1990): 309–31.

43. Ibid., p. 311.

44. Reeves and Campbell, *Cracked Coverage*, pp. 180–83.

45. Ibid., pp. 136–50.

46. See Mark Fishman, "Crime Waves as Ideology," in Stanley Cohen and Jock Young, eds., *The Manufacture of News: Social Problems, Deviance and the Mass Media*, rev. ed. (Beverly Hills: Sage, 1981), p. 98.

47. Ettema, "Press Rites," p. 511.

48. See Howard S. Becker's classic discussion of "moral entrepreneurs" in *Outsiders: Studies in the Sociology of Deviance* (London: Collier-Macmillan, 1963), p. 157.

49. Peter Kerr, "Anatomy of the Drug Issue: How, After Years, It Erupted," *New York Times* (November 17, 1986), pp. A1, 12.

50. Stephen D. Reese and Lucig H. Danielian, "Intermedia Influence and the Drug Issue: Converging on Cocaine," in Pamela J. Shoemaker, ed., *Communication Campaigns About Drugs: Government, Media, and the Public* (Hillsdale, NJ: Lawrence Erlbaum Associates, 1989) pp. 29–45.

51. This metaphor is borrowed from Representative Charles Shumer who was quoted in the *New York Times* as having some second thoughts about the $1.7 billion Omnibus Drug Bill that was passed into law in October 1986. Quoting Shumer: "Maybe we had the wrong solutions but not the wrong problem.... What happens is that this occurs in one seismic jump instead of a rational buildup. The down side is that you come up with poli-

cies too quickly and that the policies are aimed at looking good rather than solving problems." See Kerr, "Anatomy of the Drug Issue," p. A12.

52. See Adam Clymer, "Public Found Ready to Sacrifice in Drug Fight," *New York Times* (September 2, 1986), pp. A1, D16.

53. Ettema, "Press Rites," p. 511.

54. Reeves and Campbell, *Cracked Coverage*, pp. 207–16.

55. Campbell and Reeves, "Covering the Homeless," p. 34.

56. Turner, "Social Dramas," p. 154.

57. Reagan's appropriation of the Brown controversy was reported by "60 Minutes" when it aired a second update of "Brown vs. Koch" in June 1988.

Chapter 4

Media Image and the Culture of Homelessness: Possibilities for Identification

Gerald Power

Recently, I was at a fast food stand in south central Los Angeles. There was a man sitting on a bench nearby, disheveled and hungry-looking. As I passed him, I casually asked, "how you doin'." He looked me straight in the eye and answered, "how does it look like I'm doin,' niggers never do well." I could find nothing to say in response, partly because what he said was both true and untrue, but more importantly because I felt I could not identify with his life circumstances and with him as a person. I have no direct experience of extreme poverty or homelessness and I am not black. How could I know what it was like to be in his shoes. Perhaps, I could know a little more if I had seen this man or people like him on television, perhaps, and if I had what difference would it make to my life or to this man? This encounter begs for a cultural interpretation, because of the layers of signification involved for both parties. On the other hand, such cultural explanations for poverty like Wilson's (1991) use of culture to explain the plight of the "ghetto poor" are too narrow to capture the complexity of this phenomenon. They limit culture to an understanding of people in their own terms and ignore the other layers and processes of culture which contribute in a major way to understandings and definitions of poor people's existence to begin with.

Culture is manifested in many forms on many levels with multiple ramifications for those least in control of those definitions and terms despite isolated and occasional outbursts of sub-cultural resistance (Hall and Jefferson, 1975; Hebdidge, 1979). Jennie Livingston's (1991) movie *Paris Is Burning* makes this point frighteningly clear. Rather than treating culture as some homogeneous entity, what is needed is an acknowledgement of what Kenneth Thompson (1986) calls an "archaeology of culture." In a post industrial society, this archaeology of culture must include television as a major source of interpretations and meanings, in order to recognize in Thompson's words, "how appropriated elements of mass media culture have become lodged in the common consciousness" (1986, p. 99). This approach makes it possible to see connections between cultural layers and processes and social and political strata. In other words, this approach to culture would incorporate both an explanation of my inability to respond to the reality of this man's plight as well as his own clear understanding of his dilemma. Television is particularly influential when the connections involve issues and phenomena that most people have no direct experience of, where there is no clear definition of the situation. Poverty and homelessness are two such experiences.

This chapter presents the preliminary results of a research project designed to explore the relationship between television portrayals of homeless people and people's identification and interpretations of homelessness based on these portrayals. It is hypothesized that identification will vary as a function of two variables, attribution and stigmatization. The findings suggest that the role that culture plays in societal definitions of poverty goes beyond the characteristics of the environment within which poor people live. Rather, culture raises its ugly head in television's and consequently viewer's inability to go beyond individual explanations for homelessness. Yet television can generate meanings and understandings which are very much tied to a larger culture where poverty is understood in terms of lack of individual effort and achievement, explanations consistent with Lewis' (1978) culture of inequality. "In its hegemony," the individual-as-central sensibility, "permeates everyday discourse and shapes the conventional wisdom on the meaning of failure and success in American life" (p. 14).

Where individual effort and individual achievement has primacy, it is only possible to understand the lack of individual effort or achievement as bad luck, a temporary downturn or some chance occurrence. Success constitutes the basis of comparison, such that any aberration can only be interpreted as abnormal and uncharacteristic (Lewis, 1978). To the extent that the "culture of inequality" framework is valid, it suggests that we should find evidence of this process operating both in media portrayals of homelessness and in viewer responses to those portrayals.

CULTURE—THE EXPLANATORY VARIABLE

Recent theory and research on urban poverty has advanced the notion that "culture" plays a large part in the perpetuation of the problem (Wilson, 1991). In an attempt to define the cultural part of the explanation for inner-city social dislocations, Wilson (1991) described poverty as follows:

Poverty like other aspects of class inequality is a consequence not only of differential distribution of economic and political privileges and resources, but of differential access to culture as well. (p. 1)

Drawing on Bandura's (1986) social learning theory, Wilson defines this cultural component of the poverty equation as "the extent to which individuals follow their inclinations as they have been developed by learning or influence from other members of the community" (p. 10). I would like to suggest that a large part of the "collective efficacy" (Bandura, 1982) of the ghetto poor (Wilson, 1991) is derived not only from the immediate neighborhood culture but rather from the larger media culture wherein messages, particularly for poor people, are extremely conflicting. To the extent that the media provides information likely to satisfy goals of social and self understanding (Ball-Rokeach and Readon, 1988), then the media contributes to people's understandings of what it means to be poor or homeless for poor people themselves as well as for other: These conflicting messages may constitute a major part of the motivation for poor people to engage in "alternative income-generating activities" in the absence of stable and legitimate employment (Wilson, 1991).

Culture cannot be used as a theoretical explanation of social outcomes without taking into account mass mediated images and messages (Rosengren, 1986; Williams, 1976). Explanations of action or lack of action based on meaning construction processes in the culture can no longer drop the media variable from the equation. The media, and television, in particular, constitutes a major source of cultural meanings and interpretations in this society. It reinforces our notions of what is right and wrong, moral and immoral (Cohen, 1980), normal and abnormal (Cohen and Young, 1973; Hall, 1982), and most importantly what is made to appear as common sense (Hall, 1986b; Gramsci, 1971). Because of this potential, television is capable of generating alternative cultural interpretations and meanings to explain outcomes in a certain way (Tuchman, 1978) and thus plays a major role in connecting the various layers and processes in the archaeology of culture (Thompson, 1986).

In an attempt to document the extent to which television news frames poverty as an individual or societal problem, Iyengar and Lenart (1989) conducted a content analysis of all network news stories broadcast between 1973 and 1986. Stories were selected which made reference to poverty, welfare, hunger, the homeless, housing, food stamps and other key words. The authors conclude that, "between 1981 and 1986 viewers of network news would have been almost twice as likely to see news stories covering individual victims of poverty as a collective or societal phenomenon" (p. 31).

Through such news values as personalization, events are attributed to the actions of individuals as opposed to structures, institutions or social arrangements (Galtung and Ruge, 1973; McLeod, Brown, Becker and Zieke, 1977). Portrayals vary, therefore on whether the attribution of causality for the individuals homelessness lies with the individual (dispositional) or with society (situational) (Kluegel and Smith, 1981; Pettigrew, 1985, 1979; Shaver, 1985). Culturally, the understanding of poverty or homelessness as being attributed to individual characteristics is more likely to cue people to think of individuals as guilty for their situation as opposed to being victims of a systemic problem (Bennett, 1988; Hartley, 1982). In addition to attributing the problem of homelessness to individuals, the characterization of homeless people on television has also been subject to stigmatization (Goffman, 1963; Stafford and Scott, 1986). The stigma prevails not only by the absence of work and private property, but more seriously, by the focus on personal problems like chemical abuse and mental illness. A study conducted by Campbell and Reeves (1989) analyzed three conventional network news narratives and a "60 Minutes" story about Joyce Brown, a homeless woman who was institutionalized by the city of New York, against her will. The narrative is analyzed using the notions of "common sense," "expert knowledge" and "nonsense." The general conclusion of the authors is that the news accounts of the Joyce Brown story attribute homelessness primarily to such stigmatized characteristics as personal deficiency, drunkenness and mental illness. These portrayals contribute to cultural understandings about the causes of homelessness individual rather than social (Gray, 1989), and of homeless people as being stigmatized.

IDENTIFICATION

However, for those people who have no direct experience of poverty of homelessness, the major vehicle whereby people develop cultural understandings of situations beyond their immediate environment is through identification with other people living in those environments. "Identification with," is a term used in common parlance to describe how people make sense of and relate to both fictional and nonfictional portrayals of television characters. Identification has been defined as equivalent to the "act of imagining oneself to be in the place of another person" (Rosengren and Windahl, 1979 p. 172). It has, therefore, far reaching possibilities for engendering alternative readings of television and consequently, facilitating a range of outcomes with regard to how people make sense of television content. Whether identification results in attitudes, values or behaviors which are anti or pro-social, the capacity for viewers to relate to television content because of its personal salience or absence thereof, has a wealth of theoretical and empirical potential in the quest to understand "media effects."

IDENTIFICATION AND MEDIA

The concept of identification has been applied in a number of different ways to a variety of mass communication situations. It has been argued that identification is one of three processes of social influence, the others being compliance and internalization (Kelman, 1961). Identification occurs "when an individual adopts behavior derived from another person or a group because this behavior is associated with a satisfying self-defining relation to this-person or group" (p. 65). In a review of literature on processes of socialization, Gecas (1982) distinguishes between "identification of", as the establishment of identities, that is the determination of who one is and who the others are in the situation, as opposed to "identification with," which refers to the emotional and psychological attachment that one has with some person or group (p. 166). Meyrowitz (1985) focuses on the ways in which mass media draws new lines to define one's group identity. Building specifically on Turner's (1985) work on social identity, the cues necessary for respondents to identify with one group rather than another in their expression of public opinion issues have also been examined.

Identification has also been addressed in interviews with working class and non-working class women to see the differences in the ways they identify with television drama characters (Press, 1989). She found that working class women were more likely to notice the middle class material world depicted in the television shows and to judge this world to be representative of the real world. In addition, Press (1989) found that many interpretations of "The Cosby Show" reflected a belief that material success was achieved through individual effort and was unrelated to race, a finding corroborated by Jhally and Lewis (1992) in their recently published study of viewers interpretations of "The Cosby Show."

Research has also been conducted seeking to connect viewer's identification and their relationships with characters in the soap opera, Dallas (Livingstone,

1990). She employed an index of identification consisting of three items: "How much are you at all like XI?" "Think of the people you know such as your family and friends." "Do you know anybody at all like X?" "Who and how much do you like XI?" Livingstone (1990) suggests that "viewers may identify with particular characters, seeing themselves, as in the character's shoes; they may regard a character as a role model, imitating some of that character's behavior in order to gain some of the rewards which the character is shown to enjoy; or they may recognize aspects of a character as similar to a significant person in their own lives, engaging in what Horton and Wohl (1956) term parasocial interaction, watching the action as if playing opposite the character, as if the character were interacting with them directly" (p. 22). Identification was also employed by Liebes and Katz (1990) in their crossnational study of characters in Dallas. Three measures of identification were used: "I am like him, I am not like him"; "I want to be like him, I don't want to be like him"; "I like him, I dislike him" (p. 98). The findings suggest two types of identification. First, viewers imagine themselves as being one of the characters or as being associated with a character in a counter role. Second, viewers take on different roles, either knowingly or unknowingly and shift back and forth between various positions.

DEFINING IDENTIFICATION

One of the problems addressing the notion of identification is committing to an appropriate definition. It has been suggested that interaction and identification are relations that exist between human beings and individuals in the mass media world (Rosengren and Windahl, 1979). These two relations are combined to constitute a typology between the audience and actors of the mass media: interaction without identification would constitute parasocial interaction (Horton and Wohl, 1956); interaction combined with identification is conceived to be an accurate measure of involvement.

Identification can develop for a variety of reasons: membership in the same social unit—same race, same sex, same social organization or same religion; possession of similar characteristics, beliefs, or attitudes; the existence of common goals or mutual threats (Raven and Rubin, 1976, p. 115). Applying this framework to how individuals experience media characters begs the questions: who or what is the individual comparing and contrasting the media character to? Who or what is the referent? I suggest that, perhaps, identification is facilitated by a number of different channels simultaneously.

For example, individuals may respond to media characters on the primal level of emotions, queuing Mead's (1934) "I," rather than the "me." For example, a response like, "I know the way she feels," where identification is facilitated on the emotional level. On the other hand, identification may be characterized by a greater sensitivity to social factors, a notion consistent with Festinger's (1954) social comparison drawing the distinction between me and them (Aydin, 1987; Ball-Rokeach and Reardon, 1988). An example of this type of identification is illustrated by the response, "I used to be like that when I was first married." Finally, identification may manifest itself on a higher level of analysis similar to Sherif and Sherif's (1956) in-groups and out-groups punctuating the distinction between "us" and "them." For example, "all people in California think that life is easy."

THEORETICAL FRAMEWORK

This research is an attempt to move forward in a theoretical and empirical way to understanding what role identification plays in how people make sense of television characters in this culture. The research has a number of related objectives: (1) to identify characteristics of portrayals which one could reasonably expect that identification would vary; (2) to construct a measure of identification, in this case, with non-fictional television portrayals; and (3) to contextualize and make greater sense of the measured responses of identification.

HYPOTHESIS

The expectation is that viewer identification with individuals in media portrayals will be greater where the life circumstances of homeless people are attributed to social factors rather than to the individual. Individuals are more likely to identify with television characters that they perceive to be similar to themselves in the sense that they are subject to the same social circumstances. Second, viewer identification with individuals in media portrayals will be greater where homeless people are not stigmatized rather than stigmatized. In other words, people are more likely to identify with characters who are portrayed as superior in terms of morality or competence and therefore, non-stigmatized. Further, it is hypothesized that there will be an interaction effect where identification is lowest among those individuals exposed to media portrayals where homeless people are both stigmatized and the life circumstances are attributed to individual factors.

The reverse, however, does not hold, that is, the highest level of identification is not expected to occur where the portrayal focuses on social attribution and nonstigmatization. Rather, it is expected that identification is highest among those individuals exposed to portrayals where homeless people are not stigmatized and where life circumstances are attributed to the individual. This expectation is based partly on what is termed the fundamental attribution error (Ross, 1977), the tendency to overestimate dispositional factors and underestimate situational factors, but more importantly on the inability of media portrayals to invite readings/interpretations that go beyond individual explanations of outcomes.

MEASURE OF IDENTIFICATION

Maximizing the existing theoretical foundation for what constitutes identification, a six-item measure of identification was designed. Identification was measured by six 5-point Likert agreement–disagreement response scales presented below, that ranged from strongly disagree (1) to strongly agree (5). Three items are stated negatively and three are stated positively.

1. Nothing about me is similar to the individual/s portrayed in the news segment.
2. My life is very different from the life of the person in the news segment.
3. I could never imagine myself being the individual/s portrayed in the news segment.
4. I have the same goals as the individual/s portrayed in the news segment.
5. It is easy for me to understand the feelings of the individual portrayed in the news segment.

6. There is very little difference between the individual portrayed in the news segment and the rest of us.

METHOD

A subset of 14 segments were extracted by the researcher from 124 network news segments of homeless people from 1982 to 1988 which were assumed to vary on the relevant dimensions of attribution and stigmatization. Four pairs of coders viewed the subset of fourteen segments and were instructed to place each of the fourteen segments in one of the cells of a 4 x 2 matrix. This required coders to make the following judgements: (1) Individuals was/were stigmatized or not stigmatized; (2) the situation was improved and/or fairly good and/or not improved and/or fairly bad; and (3) the homeless individuals situation was either attributed to the individual or to other agents.

Stigmatization was defined as the discrediting of the individual based on their physical appearance (blemishes and deformities); character (mental disorder, imprisonment, addiction, homosexuality, unemployment, suicidal attempts, radical political behavior); or membership in specific groups. Situation was defined as the mental and/or emotional state of the individuals day-to-day life and was specific to each individual segment. Attribution was defines as the process of locating or identifying the cause or responsibility for the outcome. The outcome of interest was the individuals life situation.

Combining the coder judgments, eight ideal portrayal types were selected, based on the highest across-coder consensus. Each segment varied on three dimensions: the individuals portrayed in the news segment were either stigmatized or not stigmatized, their life circumstances were either bad/not improved or good/improved, and were either attributed to the individuals themselves or to other factors (See Table 4.1).

Table 4.1
Segment Number and Cell for Each of the Eight News Segments
(Good Total = 120; Bad Total = 164)

Attribution	Stigmatized	Non-Stigmatized
Good Individual Situation	Segment 7 (n = 22)	Segment 2 (n = 32)
Bad Social Situation	Segment 6 (n = 33)	Segment 3 (n = 32)
Bad Individual Situation	Segment 4 (n = 33)	Segment 8 (n = 26)
Bad Social Situation	Segment 5 (n = 42)	Segment (n = 63)

SAMPLE

The subjects recruited were parents of incoming students attending a University Orientation Program. A total of 284 adults participated, 176 females (62%) and 106 males (37.3%) and 2 missing cases. There were 37 Asian/ Pacific islanders (13%), 11 Blacks (3.9%), 23 Latinos (8.1%), 204 Whites (71.8%), 5 others (1.8) and 4 missing cases. The age of research participants ranged from 21–30 (1.1%, N = 3), 31–40 (5.3%, N = 15), 41–50 (73.9%, N = 210), 51–60 (15.8%, N = 45), 61–70 (1.8%, N = 5), and 6 missing cases. Finally, a small majority of these subjects identified themselves as being Republican (51.1%, N

= 145), 26.1% (N = 74) Democrats, 13.4% (N = 38) Independents, and 5.6% (N = 16) other.

The experiment was introduced to the participants by the Dean of Student Life as an opportunity to participate in ongoing research at the university. During the Orientation Program, a flyer was distributed to all of the parents which explained that the purpose of the research was to investigate the ways in which people understand television. The flyer also included a statement to the effect that participants would view a short network television news segment, about which they would be asked a few brief survey questions. Participation was voluntary. Participants were randomly divided into two groups and then escorted accordingly to two separate auditoria where they saw one of two preselected news segments. Survey instruments were administered by the researcher and an assistant. After viewing their assigned segment, subjects completed the survey instrument and returned the completed surveys. Two of the eight news segments were shown during each session thus obtaining the number of respondents for each cell as identified in Table 4.1. Subjects were also asked a general open-ended identification question: which asked respondents to "explain what it was about the individuals in the news segment that made it easy or difficult for you to identify with them." The final section included demographic items on sex, race/ethnicity, age, occupation, political affiliation, experience with homeless people and experience with homelessness. The last question asked respondents: "If your only exposure to homeless people had been the news segment you just saw, what would be your impression of homeless people?" I turn now to a discussion of the results generated from this part of the study.

RESULTS

The discussion of the results is divided into three sections. First, I discuss the measure of identification and how viewers, levels of identification varied according to the hypothesized relationships with portrayals distinguished by attribution and stigmatization. Second, I present results based on a coding of open ended responses to examine their relationship to the levels of identification for specific segments. Finally, I explore the open-ended responses in more detail in order to extend the understanding of the quantitative measures already discussed.

Results—Measure of Identification

An experimental design was employed to test the research hypotheses concerning the conditions of audience member identification (or lack thereof) with homeless people portrayed in the preselected and precoded news segments. The research participants (N = 284) viewed one of the eight segments. Differences in degree of identification were hypothesized to be a joint function of two variables, attribution and stigmatization (See Table 4.2). The six item identification scale yielded a Cronbach's alpha reliability coefficient of .70. This alpha level decreases if any one of the six items are dropped from the analysis (See Table 4.3). The inter item correlations range from moderate to low. The only inter item correlation higher than .50 is that between item (1) "nothing about me is similar to the individual/s portrayed in the news segment," and (2) "My life is very different from the life of the person/s in the news segment" (See Table 4.4).

Table 4.2
Hypothesized Levels of Identification as a Function of Attribution and Stigmatization (1 = Low; 4 = High)

Attribution	Individual Attribution	Social Attribution
Stigmatization	Low Identification (1)	Identification (2)
Non-Stigmatization	High Identification (4)	Identification (3)

Table 4.3
Degrees of Agreement or Disagreement (N = 284)

Statements (1-6)	Strongly Disagree	Strongly Agree
Mean/St. Div.	Mean	Standard Deviation
S1	2.14	1.17
S2	1.49	0.84
S3	2.76	1.49
S4	3.54	1.21
S5	2.29	1.37
S6	2.67	1.35

S1. Nothing about me is similar to the individual(s) portrayed in the news segment.
S2. My life is very different from the life of the person(s) in the news segment.
S3. I have the same goals as the individual/s portrayed in the news segment.
S4. It is easy for me to understand the feelings of the individual portrayed in the news segment.
S5. I could never imagine myself being the individuals portrayed in the news segment.
S6. There is very little difference between the individual portrayed in the news segment and the rest of us.

Table 4.4
Identification Items: Inter Item Correlations

Items	1	2	3	4	5	6
1	1.0000					
2	.5222	1.0000				
3	.4082	.3264	1.0000			
4	.2049	.1690	.2990	1.0000		
5	.2860	.2101	.2404	.4700	1.0000	
6 ·	.2532	.2370	.3219	.2393	.2763	1.0000

Items (Alpha Reliability if Item Deleted)
1. Nothing about me is similar to the individual(s) portrayed in the news segment (.6551).
2. My life is very different from the life of the person(s) in the news segment (.6786).
3. I have the same goals as the individual/s portrayed in the news segment (.6532).
4. It is easy for me to understand the feelings of the individual portrayed in the news segment (6772).
5. I could never imagine myself being the individuals portrayed in the news segment (.6599).
6. There is very little difference between the individual portrayed in the news segment and the rest of us (.6832).

As indicated by one-way analysis of variance, identification varies significantly across the eight segments ($F = 8.9643$, $df = 7$, $p = .0000$, Sig 0.05). Table 4.5 indicates that five pairs of segments are significantly different at the .05 significance level. Namely, segment 4 is significantly different in mean level of identification from segments 5, 6, 2, 1 and 8. This analysis employed the Scheffe multiple comparison test which is a conservative method for pairwise comparison of means, since it requires larger differences between means for significance than many other methods (Norusis, 1986).

Table 4.5
Means, Standard Deviation, and N for Identification Across the 8 Segments

Mean	SD	N	Segment	Segment 4
1.6823	.4507	32	4	
2.3333	.6983	19	7	
2.3659	.9115	41	5	*
2.3793	.7954	29	3	
2.5430	.5773	31	6	*
2.6022	.8646	31	2	*
2.8122	.6623	63	1	*
2.8846	.7699	26	8	*

*Denotes pairs of groups significantly different at 0.05 (Scheffe)
** The lower the mean, the lower the identification.
$F = 8.9643$, $p = .0000$, D.F = 7

IDENTIFICATION AND ATTRIBUTION

First, I hypothesized that "viewer identification with individuals in media portrayals will be greater where the life circumstances of homeless people are attributed to social factors than to the individual."

The results (ANOVA) indicate that levels of identification are significantly higher among individuals exposed to content where the specific life circumstances portrayed in a segment are attributed to social factors as opposed to those exposed to individual factors ($F = 5.1181$, $df = 271$, $p = .0245$, Sig 0.05). Higher means represent higher levels of identification. (See Table 4.6.) The first hypothesis, therefore, was supported.

Table 4.6
One-way Analysis of Variance Means and SD of Identification by Level of Attribution

Level of Attribution	N	Identification Mean	Standard Deviation
Individual	108	2.3503	.8423
Structural	164	2.5723	.7619

$F = 5.1181$, $p = .0245$, D. F. = 271

IDENTIFICATION AND STIGMATIZATION

Second, I hypothesized that "viewer identification with individuals in media portrayals will be greater where homeless people are not stigmatized rather than stigmatized." An ANOVA test indicates that levels of identification are higher among individuals exposed to media portrayals in which homeless people are not stigmatized as opposed to stigmatized ($F = 25.1886$, $df = 271$, $p = .0000$, Sig 0.05). (See Table 4.7.) This hypothesis, therefore, receives rather clear support.

Table 4.7
One-way Analysis of Variance Means and SD of Identification by Stigmatization

Stigmatization	N	Identification Mean	SD
Yes	123	2.2276	.7677
No	149	2.6969	.7672

F = 25.1886. p = .0000, D. F. = 271

IDENTIFICATION, STIGMATIZATION AND ATTRIBUTION

Third, I hypothesized that "viewer identification will be lowest among those individuals exposed to media portrayals where homeless people are stigmatized and where life circumstance are attributed to the individual." Finally, I hypothesized that "identification will be highest among those individuals exposed to portrayals where homeless people are not stigmatized and where life circumstances are attributed to the individual." These hypotheses, then, take into account effects of stigmatization and the attribution mode combined.

A 2 (Stigmatized vs. Non-stigmatized) x 2 (Individual attribution vs. Structural attribution) ANOVA was conducted to test for the interaction effects predicted in the third and fourth hypothesis. The two-way interaction of stigmatization and attribution was significant (F = 9.403, d.f = 1, p < .005). See Tables 4.8 and 4.9 for interaction effects and the relevant means, respectively.

Table 4.8
Two-way Analysis of Variance Main Effects and Two-way Interactions of Stigmatization and Level of Attribution on Identification

	SS	DF	Mean Square	F	P Square
Main Effects	17.636	2	8.818	15.658	.000
Stigmatization	14.402	1	14.402	25.574	.000
Level of Attribution	2.801	1	2.801	4.974	

Two-way Interactions

Stig. Level Attrib.	5.295	1	5.295	9.403	.002
Explained	22.931	3	7.644	13.573	.000
Residual	150.922	268	.563		
Total	173.853	271	.642		

The mean level of identification was lowest among those individuals exposed to media portrayals where homeless people were stigmatized and where their life circumstances were attributed to the individual. The mean level of identification among this group was lower than could be expected by combining the means of the groups (stigmatized and individual attribution) separately. (See Table 4.9.) The fourth hypothesis was, therefore, also supported by this result.

The mean level of identification was highest among those individuals exposed to media portrayals where homeless people were not stigmatized and where their life circumstances were attributed to the individuals. The mean level of identification among this group was higher than could be expected by combining the means of the groups (non-stigmatized and individual attribution) separately. (See Table 4.9.) The third hypothesis was supported, therefore, by this result.

Table 4.9
Two-way Analysis of Variance Means and Cell N of Identification by
Stigmatization and Level of Attribution

Stigmatization	Individual	Structural
Yes	1.92 (n = 51)	2.44 (n = 72)
No	2.73 (n = 57)	2.68 (n = 92)

Total n = 272

Results—Coded Responses

On the basis of the results presented above regarding the quantitative measures of identification, one would expect that those people who expressed a higher level of identification with the individual portrayed, would also emphasize structural factors in their impressions of homeless people, garnered from media portrayals. In other words, people's impressions would be generalized to outcomes of class, status or other social, political or economic forces rather than framed in terms of individual and group characteristics.

The question arises, to what extent does the strength of the research participants identification with homeless people in a specific segment constitute a condition under which the individual-as-central sensibility will translate into or be generalized to structural attributions of homelessness in general. The data employed to address this issue are the responses to the question, "If your only exposure to homeless people had been the news segment you just saw, what would be your impression of homeless people?"

Responses were coded according to whether respondent's impressions included causal attributions to (1) individual or group factors, (2) structural factors, or (3) a combination of individual and structural factors. Some responses were not codeable under any of these categories and usually made reference to personal feelings, not causal attributions.

The results of the coding of open ended responses indicate that with the exception of one segment, the largest percentage of impressions referred to individual or group factors rather than structural factors. The segment for which the highest level of identification was reported did not elicit any impressions which included structural attributions for homelessness. On the other hand, the segment for which the lowest level of identification was reported had the second lowest percentage of responses mentioning structural factors.

However, at the other end of the scale, the two segments which elicited the highest percentage of impressions referring to structural factors engendered very different levels of identification. One of these segments which elicited the second highest level of identification, the percentage of impressions which were limited to individual/group attributions (60.4%) is about two and a half times the percentage of impressions incorporating structural attributions (23.25%).

The findings of the coding of the open-ended responses regarding people's impressions of homeless people as a result of viewing the segment, indicates that structural attributions were mentioned, primarily by those individuals who were exposed to the segment where life circumstances were attributed to social factors and in the highest cases where the individuals were nonstigmatized.

One might conclude, therefore, that when mechanisms that communicate otherness are not employed by the media system, viewer identification is most likely to occur, and that generalizations are more likely to be made from specific instances (homelessness) to a structural explanation of the causes of homelessness, in general. A textual analysis of the responses to those segments, which are non-stigmatized, including those where life circumstances are attributed to the individual (high identification) and to structural factors (high generalizability) reveal a much more complex pattern of responses. In particular, I note the range of interpretations, some contradictory and conflicting, about the news segment in particular and about homelessness in general.

Results—Open-ended Responses

In this section, I examine more closely the open-ended responses of viewers to two of the news segments in order to get a more richly textured sense of the relationship between content and interpretation. These statements are responses to the question, "If your only exposure to homeless people had been the news segment you just saw, what would be your impression of homeless people?" The first segment was non-stigmatized and the life circumstances of the individual were attributed to the individual himself rather than to other factors. This segment also generated the highest level of viewer identification. Impressions voiced by respondents who viewed this segment were, first, an acknowledgment that homeless people are a heterogeneous group:

"Like any other segment of society, there are good and bad homeless people."
"Even some 'good apples' can be homeless."
"This TV tape gives me a different view of some homeless people."
"Some people are homeless by choice. Some are homeless due to economic conditions beyond their control."

Second, the responses also reflect a lower tolerance for homeless people and the problem of homelessness, in general:

"Self-pitying wimps."
"A great percentage of them are just not trying harder to help out their situation. I believe that if there is a will, there is a way."
"My impression is that it is not all that devastating." "If homeless people can get a job, should keep it and gradually get off the line of homelessness."
"Unwilling to improve education/knowledge. Unwilling to retrain or improve. A lack of a commitment to survive. No instinct to really make it."

Responses to this story reflect an identification expressed in terms of individual characteristics, that is, control over one's destiny and pride. This segment also engendered responses which questioned why individuals who seemed so competent would be in such a situation. This suggests that by virtue of acknowledging similarities with the individual, a homeless person who appeared much like you and me, respondents viewed the person as having less credibility.

The second segment was non-stigmatized and the life circumstances of the homeless people portrayed were attributed to social factors. This segment generated the second highest level of identification. A number of common themes also arose in the responses people provided to the question: "If your only exposure to homeless people had been the news segment you just saw, what would be your impression of homeless people?" An interesting contrast arose in how people attributed the causes of the problem and the solution, which is consistent with Lewis' (1978) culture of inequality framework. Some responses reflected the impression that somehow this was an anomaly caused by bad luck or not getting the right breaks:

"They are people with bad luck."
"Just sometimes people get a bad break."
"One round of bad luck could put anyone in the same position."
"They are just like us without the breaks."
Other responses viewed the individual as central to the problem:
"They don't do enough to help themselves."
"They aren't attempting to solve their problem."
"They could be doing more."
A third set of responses view the solution to the problem as lying with the abstraction, that is "society":
"Would see the need for society to provide some form of temporary assistance."
"It is a difficult problem for our society because of the high cost of living."
"That they are innocent victims of our society through no fault of their own."
"The system needs to be adjusted so that those who truly have a need can receive help."

This segment engendered relatively high levels of identification and the highest number of responses which incorporated a structural level component. However, this incorporation of a structural level component was abstracted in the body of "society" and no response questioned existing political and economic arrangements. The evidence presented in this research suggests a number of points. First, the extent to which viewers identify with non-fictional characters can vary according to whether the portrayal attributes the life circumstances of the characters to individual or to social factors and whether the individual is stigmatized or non-stigmatized. Second, identification does not necessarily translate into viewers ability to go beyond individual explanations of the problem. This is particularly problematic since the practice of personalizing news stories which became particularly popular in the news media during the eighties (Bennett, 1988) may not be the most constructive means of communicating the multilayered nature of social problems. Finally, open-ended responses highlight the generation of a variety of conflicting understandings and interpretation of homelessness and homeless people in this culture. The viewers responses remind us the cultural themes which media images are vying to connect with. On the one hand, there is the culture of pluralism, the one that advocates an understanding of groups as possessing minor differences both within the group and with other groups. On the other hand, there is the culture of fortune and misfortune, that somehow when things go wrong, it is a result of "bad luck" and nothing more. The only references in the viewer's responses to non-individual type action are in terms of the nonspecific abstraction, society.

CONCLUSION

This chapter was introduced by reference to a face to face encounter with a homeless man. Most people do not have these encounters or at least try to avoid them at all cost. Knowledge and insight on the lives of homeless people and poor people, in general, is derived from mediated experience, what we read in newspapers, what we hear on radio, what we see on television. We know from previous research that the understandings based on this experience can be extremely distorted (Lang and Engel-Lang, 1953; Hartman and Husband, 1974). Nevertheless, we are willing to express our attitudes and beliefs regarding a variety of topics and issues about which we have no direct experience, yet feel knowledgeable about because of media exposure.

The research findings reported in this paper address the relationship between television news portrayals of homeless people and viewers identification with them. The results in this research are threefold. First, people tend to identify more with portrayals of homeless people where their life circumstances are attributed to social factors as opposed to individual factors. In addition, people tend to identify with homeless people who are not stigmatized. Second, when these two dimensions are combined there is an interaction effect where the highest level of identification is engendered by those portrayals which are characterized by individual attribution and non-stigmatization. Third, high levels of identification do not necessarily translate into interpretations of the plight of homeless as being the fault of current political or economic relations. Rather, interpretations of homeless people and the phenomenon of homelessness remain on the individual level.

Coding of the respondent's impressions of homeless people of the segments most likely to promote identification reveals that the "media effects process" is not at all divorced from the culture within which it operates. Although the media can address such issues of homelessness, even in attributing blame to the government, that the "common sense" manner in which the issues are addressed invites few alternative interpretations beyond a focus on presence or absence of individual effort. The media system and its portrayals cannot be examined in isolation from a culture where the individual is central, even in cases where other factors are deemed to be involved. In social psychological terms, this tendency to overestimate dispositional factors while underestimating situational factors is termed the fundamental attribution error (Ross, 1977).

The findings in this research punctuate how a particular worldview can be and is privileged over another. Using Lewis' (1978) culture of inequality framework, the individual as central consistently colored respondents interpretations of the situation, even where other agents including the government were specifically accused of causing the problem, even where others were praised for tackling the problem, the final judgement and interpretation lay with the individual. Where the situation was attributed to the individual, identification was higher even when the situation was fairly bad and/or not improved. The influence of culture is consistently evident in the responses to these segments.

Most importantly, this research demonstrates the relevance of incorporating television into discussions of culture since it constitutes a major source of meanings and understandings in the society. Furthermore, these meanings and understandings may serve to reinforce rather than challenge cultural assumptions, in this case, about the causes of homelessness. As a major source of information on issues not directly experienced by many, television contributes to the legitimacy of current economic and political arrangements. In this way, it plays a major role in connecting the various components of the "archaeology of culture," a culture where the experience of seeing and not questioning the existence of a homeless person has become normal, a culture where the gap between the "other" America and the rest of us is widened rather than narrowed.

REFERENCES

Aydin, C. E. (1987*). Use of the Mass Media for Social Comparison by Breast Cancer Patients.* Unpublished Paper. Annenberg School for Communication, University of Southern California.

Ball-Rokeach, S. J. and Reardon, M. (1988). *Media System Dependency Theory.* Unpublished Manuscript. Annenberg School for Communication, University of Southern California.

Bandura, A. (1982). "Self-Efficacy Mechanism in Human Agency." *American Psychologist.* 37 (February): 122–147.

Bandura, A. (1986). *Social Foundations of Thought and Action: Social Cognitive Theory.* Englewood Cliffs, NJ.: Prentice Hall.

Bennett, W. L. (1988) *News: The Politics of Illusion.* (2nd Ed.) New York: Longman.

Campbell, R. and Reeves, J. L. (1989). Covering the Homeless: the Joyce Brown Story. *Critical Studies in Mass Communication.* 6, 21–42.

Cohen, S. (1980). *Folk Devils and Moral Panics.* London: Martin Robertson.

Cohen, S. and Young, J. (1973). *The Manufacture of News. Deviance, Social Problems and the Mass Media.* London: Cons'.

Collins, R. (1975). *Conflict Sociology: Toward an Explanatory Science.* New York: Academic Press.

Festinger, L. (1954). A Theory of Social Comparison Processes. *Human Relations.* 7, 117–140.

Fiske, S. and Taylor, S. (1984). *Social Cognition.* New York: Random House.

Galtung, J. and Ruge, M. (1973). Structuring and Selecting News. In Stanley Cohen and Jock Young. *The Manufacture of News: Social Problems, Deviance and the Mass Media.* London: Cons', 62–72.

Gans, H. J. (1979). *Deciding What's News: A Study of CBS Evening News, NBC Nightly News, Newsweek and Time.* New York: Pantheon Books.

Gecas, V. (1982). Self-Concept. *Annual Review of Sociology,* 8, 1–33.

Goffman, E. (1963). *Stigma: Notes on the Management of Spoiled Identity.* Glencoe, New York: Free Press.

Gramsci, A. (1971). *Selections from the Prison Notebooks.* New York: International Publishers.

Gray, H. (1986). Social Constraints and the Production of an Alternative Medium. In Sandra J. Ball-Rokeach and Muriel G. Cantor, *Media, Audience and Social Structure.* Beverly Hills: Sage, 129–142.

Gray, H. (1989). Television, Black Americans, and the American Dream. *Critical Studies in Mass Communication.* 6, 376–386.

Hall, S. (1982). The Rediscovery of ideology: return of the repressed in media studies. In M. Gurevitch, T. Bennett, J. Curran and J. Woollacott (Eds.). *Culture, Society and the Media.* London: Methuen. 56–90.

Hall, S. (1986a). Cultural Studies: two paradigms. In Richard Collins, James Curran, Nicholas Garnham, Paddy Scannell, Philip Schlesinger, and Colin Sparks (eds.) *Media, Culture and Society: A Critical Reader.* London: Sage, 33–48

Hall, S. (1986b). Gramscils Relevance for the Study of Race and Ethnicity. *Journal of Communication Incruiry.* 10 (2), 5–27.

Hall, S. and Jefferson, T. (1975). *Resistance through Rituals: Youth Subcultures in Post-war Britain.* London: Unwin-Hyman.

Hardt, H. (1986). British Cultural Studies and the Return of the "Critical" in American Mass Communication Research: Accommodation or Radical Change? *Journal of Communication Inquiry.* Vol. 10. No. 6. 117–124.

Harrington, M. (1988). *The Other America: Poverty in the United States.* New York: Penguin Books.

Hartley, J. (1982). *Understanding News.* London: Methuen.

Hartman, P. and Husband, C. (1974). *Racism and the Mass Media.* Totowa, NJ: Rowman and Littlefield.

Hebdidge, D. (1979). *Subculture: The Meaning of Style.* London: Methuen.

Horton, D. and Wohl, R.R. (1956). Mass Communication and Parasocial Interaction. *Psychiatry.* Vol. 19, 215–29.

Iyengar, S. and Kinder, D. R. (1987). *News that Matters.* Chicago: The University of Chicago Press.

Iyengar, S. (1989). How Citizens Think About National Issues: A Matter of Responsibility. *American Journal of Political Science.* 33 (3), 878–900.

Iyengar, S. (1990). Framing Responsibility For Political Issues: The Case of Poverty. *Political Behavior.* Vol. 12 No. 1. pp. 19–40.

Iyengar, S. (Forthcoming). *Framing Effects in Politics: Television and Political Responsibiliy.* Unpublished Manuscript, University of California, Los Angeles.

Iyengar, S. and Lenart, S. (1989). Beyond "Minimal Consequences": A Survey of Media Political Effects. In Samuel Long (Ed.) *Political Behavior Annual.* Vol. 2. Boulder: Westview Press, 21–38.

Jhally, S. and Lewis, J. (1992). *Enlightened Racism: The Cosby Show, Audiences, and the Myth of the American Dream.* Boulder: Westview Press.

Kelley, H. H. (February, 1973). The Process of Causal Attribution. *American Psychologist.* 107–128.

Kelman, H. C. (1961). Processes of Opinion Change. *Public Opinion Quarterly.* Vol. 25, 57–78.

Kluegel, J. R. and Smith, E. R. (1981). Beliefs about Stratification. *Annual Review of Sociology.* 7, 29–56.

Lang, K. and Engel-Lang, G. (1953). The Unique Perspective of Television and Its Effect: A Pilot Study. *American Sociological Review.* 18, 3–12.

Lembo, R. and Tucker, K. H. (1990). Culture, Television, and Opposition: Rethinking Cultural Studies. *Critical Studies in Mass Communication.* 7 (2), 97–116.

Lewis M. (1978). *Culture of Inequality.* Amherst: University of Massachusetts Press.

Liebes, T. and Katz, E. (1990). *The Export of Meaning: CrossCultural Readings of Dallas.* Oxford: Oxford University Press.

Lippman, W. (1922). *Public Opinion.* New York: Free Press.

Livingston, J. (1991). *Paris Is Burning.* Prestige Films

Livingstone, S. M. (1990). *Making Sense of Television: The Psychology of Audience Interpretation.* Oxford: Pergamon Press.

McLeod, J. Brown, J. D. Becker, L. P. and Zieke, D. A. (1977). Decline and Fall: A Longitudinal Analysis of Communication Effects. *Communication Research.* 4 (January).

Mead, G. H. (1934). *Mind, Self, and Society.* Chicago: University of Chicago Press.

Meyrowitz, J. (1985). *No Sense of Place.* New York: Oxford University Press.

Norusis, M. J. (1986). *SPSSPC+.* Chicago, Ill: SPSS Inc.

Patterson, O. (1989). Toward A Study of Black America: Notes on the Culture of Racism. *Dissent.* Fall, 476–486.

Pettigrew, T. F. (1979). The Ultimate Attribution Error: Extending Allport's Cognitive Analysis of Prejudice. *Personality and Social Psychology Bulletin.* 5: 461–76.

Pettigrew, T. F. (1985). New Black-White Patterns: How Best to Conceptualize Them? *Annual Review of Sociology.* 11, 329–46.

Petty, R. E. and Cacioppo, J. T. (1981). *Attitudes and Persuasion:Classic and Contemporary Approaches.* Dubuque, Iowa: Wm. C. Brown Company Publishers.

Piven, F. F. and Cloward, R. A. (1971). *Regulating the Poor.* New York: Pantheon.

Press, A. (1989). Class and Gender in the hegemonic process: class differences in women's perceptions of television realism and identification with television characters. *Media, Culture and Society.* 11, 229–251.

Price, V. (1989). Social Identification and Public Opinion: Effects of Communicating Group Conflict. *Public Opinion Quarterly.* 53: 197–224.

Raven, B. H. and Rubin, J. Z. (1976). *Social Psychology: People in Groups.* New York: John Wiley and Sons, Inc.

Rosengren, K. (1986). Linking Culture and Other Societal Systems. In Sandra J. Ball-Rokeach and Muriel G. Cantor, Media, *Audience and Social Structure.* Newbury Park: Sage Publications.

Rosengren, K. E. and Windahl, S. (1979). Mass Media Consumption as a Functional Alternative. In Denis McQuail (Ed.) *Sociology of Mass Communications.* Middlesex: Penguin. 166–194.

Ross, L. (1977). The intuitive psychologist and his shortcomings. In L. Berkowitz (Ed.), *Advances in Experimental Social Psychology* (vol. 10, pp. 173–220). New York: Academic Press.

Shaver, K. G. (1985) *The Attribution of Blame: Causality, Responsibility and Blameworthiness.* New York: Springer-Verlag.

Sherif, M. and Sherif, C. W. (1956). *An Outline of Social Psychology.* New York: Harper and Row Publishers.

Stafford, M. C. and Scott, R. R. (1986). Stigma, Deviance and Social Control: Some Conceptual Issues. In Ainlay, S.C., Becker, G. and Coleman, L. M. (Eds.) *The Dilemma of Difference: A Multidisciplinary View of Stigma.* New York: Plenum Press.

Thompson, K. (1986). *Beliefs and Ideology.* New York: Tavistock Publications.

Tuchman, G. (1978). *Making News: A Study in the Construction of Reality.* New York: Free Press.

Turner, V. (1985). *On the Edge of the Bush: Anthropology as Experience.* Tucson, AZ: University of Arizona Press.

Waring, R. (1990). *Social Identity and Media System Dependency Theory.* Paper presented at the annual meetings of the American Sociological Association. Washington. August.

Williams, R. (1976). *Keywords.* London: Fontana.

Williams, R. (1980). *Problems in Materialism and Culture: Selected Essays.* New York: Verso.

Wilson, W. J. (1978). *The Declining Significance of Race.* Chicago: The University of Chicago Press.

Wilson, W. J. (1987). *The Truly Disadvantaged: The Inner City, the Underclass, and Public Policy.* Chicago: The University of Chicago Press.

Wilson, W. J. (1989).The Ghetto Underclass: Social Science Perspectives. (Ed.) *The Annals of the American Academy of Political and Social Science.* Vol. 501. Newbury Park: Sage Publications. (January).

Wilson, W. J. (1991). Studying Inner-City Social Dislocations: The Challenge of Public Agenda Research. *American Sociological Review.* Vol. 56, 1–14.

Wright, C. (1986). *Mass Communication: A Sociological Perspective.* New York: Random House.

Chapter 5

Informing and Educating the Media–A Hopeful Perspective on the Media and the Homeless

Jeremy Reynalds

The stereotyping of homeless people as crazy or drunk comes from the usual point of contact between media people and the homeless—the street. "Those you find on the street ARE crazy and drunk. You want to fix it? Get media people interested in the work of the homeless and rehabilitation programs" (Henderson, 1997).

As founder and director of Joy Junction, New Mexico's largest emergency homeless shelter, I have dealt with the local media for over a decade. They have always responded positively to my requests for stories about both Joy Junction and its clientele. I contend that some of the reasons for the Albuquerque media's positive treatment of the homeless has been due to my long-term attempt to inform and educate the media about the true nature of homelessness.

I have made a personal commitment to provide the local media with the best and the most current information I have about the homeless. That commitment entails a tremendous amount of work. I deal with the media as follows. I begin with an assumption that the people working in the media want to be knowledgeable, and that when they cover the homeless, they are coming to the subject with no predetermined biases. I go out of my way to let the media know about everything happening at the mission that has any news value and in which I think they might be interested. Often, however, this involves shaping the discussion in a fashion that helps media people recognize the interest this information might have for them.

I initially contact the media by sending a press release. However, I don't just write the first thing that enters my head. First, I identify what I hope to achieve from the release. I decide what message I want to communicate or what image I want to convey. The following is an example.

Joy Junction, like many other homeless providers, goes through a summer giving slump. Donors seems to take a hiatus from giving, and the press isn't really interested in the homeless during the hot summer months. However, the needs of the shelter remain relatively constant. So what do we do? In this particular situation, my job is two-fold. First, I must provide a compelling reason for the media to cover the summer slump story, and secondarily to write my release to I tell the entire story quickly, clearly and accurately. To make my point I need to say that the shelter doors are still open during the summer months, that we are experiencing a heavy workload with few resources and that I am appealing for additional community help. If I keep this concept before me as I write the release, it will stop me from rambling.

It is hard work, but very rewarding, to deal with the media. It is important to remember that there has to be a double motivational factor here. I have to motivate a television assignments editor. If the story is to get on the air, I have to provide the station with sufficient information to allow the reporter or writer to successfully inform and motivate their audience.

An assignments editor for television news, or a city or metro desk editor for the print media, is the person who makes the initial decision about whether to cover an event. This individual could be called the gatekeeper to the newsroom. In a television newsroom, an area where I have the greatest experience, the assignments editor has the most thankless job in the newsroom. He or she sits for long hours to decipher police scanners, answering the newsroom phones, collecting all the news releases spit out by the fax machine, checking on facts for reporters in the field, and getting yelled at should there happen to be a story in a competing medium that he or she hasn't picked up on. In order to understand life in the media, I have worked for months at a time in the newsrooms of two television stations, two radio stations and a daily newspaper. Among other tasks, my assignments included long hours on the assignments desk as well as writing news stories.

The assignments editor in a television newsroom is the person who gets to first read the news releases from homeless providers. Because of the many demands made on these individuals, I usually fax to the newsroom and only follow up with a phone call if it's an event that I consider to be of great importance. While the assignments editor doesn't have the final say in putting a story on the air, he or she can stop it from even being considered. Consequently, it is very important to be familiar about the constraints and demands of the job.

After motivating the assignments editor, I next have to motivate the audience: that includes knowing what exactly to send to the media. Something that has produced many responses for me is telling the media that due to an ever-increasing number of people requiring services, the mission is experiencing a food shortage. Releases concerning this issue have resulted in a number of stories about Joy Junction over the years. Coverage has ranged from mini stories (or briefs) in the metro section of the local paper to a live broadcast where I talked back to the anchor, and opened a refrigerator door live on a newscast to show all the viewers our minimal supplies of food.

Releases concerning the plight of the homeless in cold weather have also produced good coverage for the shelter, and have succeeded in keeping the plight of the homeless before the community. But as I have explained, this takes hard work, and an absolute willingness to drop any prearranged plans and be available for the media. For example, during a prolonged spell of cold weather we recently had in Albuquerque. I sent at least one release—and sometimes two—a day (on weekends as well) to the media detailing our transportation service for the homeless as well as providing a count of how many people we sheltered the previous night. These releases resulted in quite a bit of publicity for the shelter and the homeless.

The local ABC affiliate called me recently late one afternoon and asked if its crew could ride along with our van as we picked up people that night. I agreed. I canceled my plans for the evening and rode along with the van driver, accompanied by the cameraman. The assignments editor also asked me if I would be willing to do a live shot from the shelter for the late news, and answer a few questions from the anchor in the studio. I quickly agreed. To help show the viewers how cold it was that night, I was also willing to stand outside the shelter in the snow on that freezing cold evening. I had very little warning for the entire experience and it didn't take place during my normal working hours.

Was it worth it? Absolutely! The entire segment lasted more than a minute, which translates into thousands of dollars worth of free time on the city's most watched newscast. But in order to make it a reality, I had to let the media know what was going on that night and tell them what we were doing to relieve the dangerous conditions for the homeless. I then had to cooperate in the making of the story. Removing any of these factors can negate a successful story, since the media won't chase down an uncooperative shelter provider more than once, and maybe not at all.

I also attempt to determine who influences my intended audience. I don't discount individuals whose views don't agree with my political or theological preferences. We have a local "shock jock" in Albuquerque whose on-air personality runs counter to everything I stand for and believe in. However, I have done numerous on-air appearances with this individual, and over the years he has been a tremendous asset to the shelter. His most recent activity for Joy Junction was to raffle a "Tickle Me Elmo" doll, which raised over $2,000 dollars for the shelter.

Providers must also educate themselves about the needs of the various media. Providers involved in a very complex story with intricate details should consider staying away from television. The nature of television makes it less than useful for a complex, involved situation. A newspaper or radio talk show is better suited to deal with a detailed story. It's important to remember that because television news is essentially a headline news service, long and involved stories will suffer.

However, if there is a visually friendly story, I automatically inform television news. For example, if a business calls and wants to take some of the children staying at the mission on a ride in a hot-air balloon. That is the sort of story with which a television producer may choose to end a newscast with this type of story. It's called a "kicker," and producers are always looking for nice, happy story that stays in people's minds.

Radio news is styled in the same way as television news, but without the visuals. It can be very effective in announcing details of a food shortage, as well as other situations such as "A cold snap in XYZ city filled the city's homeless shelters last night. ABC Mission's Joe Blow says."

Due to the cold weather, I was recently a guest for a few minutes on KKOB AM, Albuquerque's 50,000 watt news talk station. Prior to my segment, the host had been talking about the treacherous road conditions and how they were affecting driving. He then segued to me, asking how the cold was affecting the homeless. I told him a few stories, and he asked how listeners could help. I offered suggestions and the interview ended. A portion of the interview was then played back on the next newscast from the station. Again, this interview was contingent on my being available after hours. The media need news when they need news, not just when it happens to be convenient to homeless providers.

As part of my attempt to inform and educate the media, I also try reinforce positive images about both the shelter and the homeless, and overcome negative image. Many cities nationwide have to cope with people. Homeless—or supposedly homeless—people who stand on street corners holding signs proclaiming their willingness to work for food and money. Concerned citizens attempting to help these individuals have quickly discovered that many of these "sign people" don't want to work. They just want a handout. More and more average, middle-class Americans are working harder than ever for their paycheck, so their sympathy for the homeless quickly dries up when they see signers who really don't want to work.

Constant reinforcement of a positive truth can help overcome some of that negativity. In much of our promotional material, I write over and over again, "Joy Junction, a hand up, and not a hand out!" I also write phrases such as, "We don't take in the chronic derelict who has no desire to get back on his feet again. We care for the temporarily economically disadvantaged who want to get reintegrated back into mainstream community life as quickly as possible."

These statements effectively communicate our operational philosophy, it and makes our donors feel much better about entrusting us with some of their hard-earned funds. I also want to reinforce that we are the biggest shelter in the state, and operate without any government funding or United Way membership. Consequently, the phrases, "New Mexico's largest emergency homeless shelter," and "Joy Junction operates without any government funding" appear on all of our promotional material. These phrases have started showing up in many of the reports done on the shelter by the media.

I am always aware of the different deadlines faced by the various media. Every shelter provider who wants the benefits of repeated media exposure must made a determined effort to study local media, learn how they work and be aware of their schedule. While there is obviously no deadline as such for "hard news," which is journalistic terminology for shootings, car crashes, rapes, fires and so on, with the exception of weather related stories, much of what occurs at a mission is "soft news"—news that deals with, for example, a homeless person getting back on his feet again, or somebody who has struggled against great odds to raise funds to build a new mission building.

Television news generally has early morning and early afternoon meetings both to firm up tentatively scheduled events and to decide what will be covered for the day. The assignments editor will bring a list of stories to the meeting that he or she thinks should be covered that day. Many of these suggestions will end up being stories. Some won't. It all boils down to a sort of consensus, with the news director having the final say.

Our city's morning paper has a deadline of 9 P.M. the night before. However, providers need to bear in mind that's when the reporter has to have copy on the editor's desk, it's not appropriate to fax a release at 8:55 P.M. and expect it to be turned into a story for the following day's paper.

Our city's afternoon paper publishes two different editions and therefore has two deadlines. However, usually the only things that will change throughout the day are updates on—or the addition of—any breaking news. As you can see, there are a lot of things to think about when dealing with the media. It all adds up to a lot of hard work that pays off with good press.

My successful dealings with the media have not necessarily been duplicated nationwide. In a recent interview, Mary Brosnahan, the executive director of the National Coalition for the Homeless, told me the media don't stereotype the homeless; they just ignore them. "In the past two-and-a-half to three years, I think we have seen the whole issue of homelessness upstaged through welfare reform," she said (Brosnahan, 1997).

Brosnahan said there are a couple of ways to help return the issue back on the front burner. First, that it's very effective to get homeless people to speak out on their own behalf. "There's nothing that explodes myths more than having an articulate homeless—or formerly homeless—person speak out on an issue."

Just as important, Brosnahan said, is investing the time to inform and educate reporters Second, it takes a great deal of time and energy to successfully handle all the press received by the coalition, however, time and energy is what it takes to get positive media coverage on a regular basis.

Paul Henderson agreed with Brosnahan's comments. He said that homeless people who do get into the system often become invisible to the media. "This is the point at which intervention with media people should take place in order to demonstrate that there are all shades of homeless people," he said (Henderson, 1997).

The *Albuquerque Journal* is New Mexico's largest newspaper; it has provided comprehensive and positive coverage of both Albuquerque's homeless in general and Joy Junction, in particular. I recently spoke with the *Journal's* managing editor, Rod Deckert, and the metro editor, Judy Giannettino, about the charge that the media negatively stereotype the homeless. Giannettino said the charge isn't fair. While stating that it is important not to generalize, she said, "Some homeless people ARE drunk, schizophrenics. That's who they are."

Giannettino and Deckert said they cannot recall the newspaper's reporters showing any slant or bias against the homeless and that the Journal works very hard to keep biases out of stories. Giannettino said overall she feels the Journal has done a good job covering the homeless, and has tried to be reflective of the community. While she thinks homelessness is a problem in Albuquerque, Giannettino said she doesn't feel it's an issue that residents worry about. She said it is important to remember that if it weren't for the media covering the homeless, the average citizen wouldn't be aware that there is a homeless problem.

Reed Upton is a news anchor and reporter for Albuquerque's 50,000 watt KKOB AM, which has the only serious radio news operation in Albuquerque. Upton doesn't think the media have stereotyped the homeless either nationally or locally. To a large degree, he believes, the media have been very sympathetic to the plight of the homeless. "Most of the media are very susceptible to what homelessness is all about," he said (Upton, 1997). How does KKOB portray the homeless in Albuquerque? Upton said there's a pretty neutral presentation. "I don't think we portray them as any class," he said. While some of the station's talk show hosts may at one time have portrayed an unsympathetic picture of the homeless, that's changed. "I don't see that view in any of the Albuquerque media," he said. While the issue of homelessness has perhaps begun to drop on the "important issues scale," that can be combated by homeless providers being more pro active in their telling of the homeless story, and sending more press releases to their respective media outlets.

Both nationally and regionally, the homeless have been portrayed very favorably, according to Upton, if a stereotype has been applied it has been a very sympathetic one, he said. Upton recalled the media outcry in San Francisco a few years ago when the mayor decided he was going to take shopping carts away from homeless people. In general, Upton believes, the national media have tended to portray the homeless as a middle-class couple who has lost everything, which tends to engender public sympathy. "I can't think of a single incidence of a media outlet portraying the homeless as psychotic," he said (1997).

Eric Sherman, a freelance journalist who writes for a number of national magazines including *Home Office Computing, Datamation* and the *Boston Globe*, agreed with Upton. "My impression is not that the press presents things in this manner," he said (Sherman, 1997).

Albuquerque Journal reporter Rick Nathanson believes his paper has done an excellent job of covering the homeless, "because the *Journal* recognizes this is not a seasonal issue," he said (1996). Nathanson said he doesn't believe there is any attempt by the media to portray the homeless as mental hospital patients who were deinstitutionalized.

The *Journal* even went one step further in an attempt to find out who the homeless really were. While doing a series of reports on the homeless for the *Albuquerque Journal* in late 1987, Nathanson lived on the Albuquerque streets for two days and two nights. He said he found a number of types of homeless people, including the mentally ill, and reported that there are a variety of reasons people are homeless. He did encounter some panhandlers who were homeless by choice. During his interview with me, Nathanson called this group "the fringes of society—tired of answering to anyone. That's their job" (Nathanson, 1996).

Another group Nathanson encountered was the homeless mentally ill. The people, Nathanson said, who were "having grand conversations with themselves." Nathanson recalled one individual who believed the government was looking for him because he had encoded information in his brain.

Nathanson also met people who had been traumatized by their experiences in Vietnam.

According to Nathanson, one group of the homeless he met was even shunned by other homeless people: the paint sniffers. Nathanson said most of the members of this group were illegal immigrants from Mexico, who tended to get very combative with each other. Nathanson recalled one such incident triggered by misplaced money. "That triggered the insults. They were beating each other with contruction debris," he said (1996).

Mark Horner is a reporter with the local CBS affiliate in Albuquerque, KRQE-TV. He said he has never thought of the homeless as being former mental hospital patients deinstutionalized in the 1970s. Horner said that while homeless individuals who are lazy, crazy, psychotic and coped attract a lot of attention, he doesn't think people like that are typical of the homeless. Horner said that although there are homeless people on the streets who intentionally attempt to deceive the average person, he doesn't resent them. "But I'm not going to give them money. I still have compassion for them. I think we're all subject to the same sort of temptations and demons," he said (Horner, 1996).

Dr. Ed Eyring, a mission director in Washington, D.C., has had numerous successful dealings with the media. His experience confirmed what the members of the media I talked to had told me. As a rule, the media do not negatively stereotype the homeless. While he has only been at his present position in Washington for about eight months, he told me that his shelter has received good coverage, "something like 20 major TV spots in that time," he said (Eyring, 1997).

Eyring has found the Washington press to be pretty fair to the homeless. "They don't talk about them in derogatory tones," he said (1997). Eyring said he has found members of the media to be very friendly to him—so much so that on a number of occasions he has been called by reporters and asked which aspect of the shelter's operation he would like them to concentrate on for their next story.

How does the *Albuquerque Journal* cover the Albuquerque homeless from its point of view? What exactly is the *Journal* looking for? Rod Deckert explained that the paper's primary mission is to report the news and not to write advocacy stories to help eliminate the problem. But, "if we write stories and educate the public and they respond, that's good. We're not advocates as an entity," he said (Deckert and Giannettino, 1996).

But what is news? Having worked on the assignment desk for a local television station and observed the news gathering process in full swing over a number of years, defining "news" seems sometimes to be a somewhat arbitrary decision. Does the accessability of a shelter provider to the media play any part in helping determine whether a story gets coverage?

Giannettino said the newspaper appreciates the easy accessability of some of its contacts, but that those who aren't so easy to reach aren't just ignored. "We'll keep calling," she said. However, she added, "Does accessability and being available work for Marty? (Albuquerque Mayor Martin Chavez?) You bet it does!"

KKOB's Reed Upton said that when a shelter operator doesn't respond, it changes his attitude toward the person. "I'm not going to waste my time dealing with them," Upton said (1997). And quite frankly, the response from some Albuquerque area shelter operators has been "very poor." Upton said it almost seems as if there's a fear of the media.

What would Upton like to see happen? More cooperation by the homeless agencies with the media; cooperation that would include sending out more press releases to make sure the media are adequately informed about situations and upcoming events. "I don't believe you can send out too many press releases. If it's a story, it's a story," Upton said (1997).

According to Upton, additional information would result in benefits for everyone. It would increase public awareness of the homeless problem in a city, as well as giving homeless agencies a leg up in fundraising. Just as important, Upton added, it would increase community awareness of the options available in a community for addressing the homeless problem.

Rod Deckert agreed; he said the media need adequate information to write a good story. "I think we're like a lot of other cities. Our initial impression is a windshield survey. People with shabby clothes pushing a cart full of junk," he said (Deckert and Giannettino, 1996).

In addition to making sure the various media in a town are well informed, Upton would like to see homeless agency personnel educate themselves about the needs of the media with whom they deal. He gave KKOB with 48 deadlines daily as an example. When news staff make a call to an agency executive, it's very important that the call is responded to in a timely fashion. "With a newscast every half hour, time and deadlines are a heavy part of day-to-day existence," Upton said (1997).

Mark Horner said any attempt to educate the media should be done tactfully. He gave an example of how to approach the press: "We think we have something here that is going to shed some light on whom the homeless are in this country" (Horner, 1996). Homeless providers approaching the media should carry out their task in a "non-confrontational manner," Horner said (1996). If the media sense they're being manipulated, their reaction will be to turn their backs.

Horner said one way for homeless providers to help ensure fair coverage is to get to know the reporters and the news directors. That can have very positive advantages, Horner said. "They will get a feel for you. You'll get an innate sense of whether you can trust people, and whether or not your words will be manipulated," Horner said (1996).

What suggestions did Deckert have for improved coverage? He said he would like to see more situations where reporters and photographers are "in direct contact with the homeless on their turf." He said Nathanson's series of articles was an example of this. After having lived on the streets—even though it was only for two days—and having covered the homeless, what would Nathanson like to see? Just like Upton, Nathanson said homeless providers need to educate themsleves about the nuances of the media. Homeless providers need to understand that different media have different constraints.

Nathanson said if homeless providers are serious about getting the issue of homelessness out in the public eye, they need to be know that different aspects of homelessness are best suited to different media. Television is best suited to a more visual situation, talk radio tends to focus around more controversial issues, and newspapers provide a more "balanced treatment. You'll never see a serious discussion of the issues on a local newscast" (Nathanson, 1996).

According to Nathanson, agency personnel who deal with the media have to guide journalists in their coverage. He suggests service providers be prepared to (1) tell the reporter about the issue under consideration, (2) provide a balanced picture, and (3) provide the names of some people who don't agree with your perspective. It is essential to be absolutely truthful with the media, even when doing so might result in negative publicity. "They will never question you when you're pitching something that makes you look good," he said. Reporters have long memories, Nathanson warned. But when you're honest with them, "they'll always be there for you," he said (1996).

KRQE's Horner called the media a valuable resource for homeless providers, and had several suggestions on how providers could spark interest by the media in their agency. We've all seen that stereotypical homeless person. To dispel that negative image, Horner suggested making a video titled "Destroying the Myth." On the video should portray a number of hard-working formerly homeless individuals who had turned their lives around. "Show me three or four who are willing to work their butt off. Show me the rule rather than the stereotypical," Horner said (1996).

Horner agreed with Nathanson that providers need to educate themselves about the needs of the various media. Despite being a television reporter, Horner didn't deny that more in-depth coverage is going to come out of the newspaper. "For TV it has to be sexy and exciting," he said.

Horner emphasized that when homeless advocates work successfully with the media, it is a winning situation for everyone. But what about when that co-operation doesn't happen? "The electronic media stay in the shallow end of the pool. There is no joining of the resources to reach the potential depth of who the homeless really are," he said (Horner, 1996).

Eyring doesn't know why some providers are antagonistic to the media. His philosophy is summed up well in one sentence: "I just take the view that they have a pretty good hearts and they're out to help us," he said.

Eyring has a very proactive stance in dealing with the media. He claims he takes an educator's rather than an advocate's position in dealing with the media and likes to make the media feel at home when they visit the mission. According to Eyring, such a philosophy makes the media "stay and stay and stay." He gave an example. "We had a fellow from National Public Radio who came back at least six times to record the sounds of people eating in the dining room. We have nothing to hide," he said (1997).

In the end, the job of dealing with the media puts the shelter director in the same role that Mark Twain and the author of John's Gospel occupied—they were storytellers and so are we. But we tell the stories of the homeless to the news media and they echo our stories into thousands and even millions of homes.

Our stories need to be well told. They need a human-interest focus. They must suggest that the homeless need help and that they have the potential to benefit from that help. The stories must always be truthful; if we seek to deceive, the media will find out the truth sooner or later. But a story—even a true one—can be told with emotion, drama, and a lot of heart. And that is the kind of story that gets a response from journalists and their audiences alike.

REFERENCES

Brosnahan, Mary (January 1997). Telephone interview with Author.

Deckert, Rod and Judy Giannettino (December 1996). Personal interview with the Author.

Eyring Ed. Telephone interview with the Author (January 1997).

Henderson, Paul. E-mail to Author (January 1997).

Horner Mark. Personal interview with the Author (December 1996).

Nathanson Rick. Personal interview with the Author (December 1996).

Sherman, Eric. E-mail to Author (January 1997).

Upton, Reed. Personal interview with the Author (January 1997).

Chapter 6

Discourse Analysis of Television News on Public Antagonism Against the Homeless

Insung Whang and Eungjun Min

Endless research and media reports in the 1980s taught us to view the issue of homelessness as a national "emergency" (Hopper and Baumohl, 1994). Now the emergency is often perceived as a serious "threat" to our well-being. An old woman living in a suburban area outside of Seattle complains that since her church provides a shelter for the homeless, the property value of her house has decreased significantly ("ABC World News," December 21, 1993). One resident in Portland called 911 after learning that a homeless man had dug through his trash can in the middle of night. There have been major crackdowns on the homeless in several big cities ("ABC World News," December 21, 1993). Certainly, public hostility toward the homeless is one of the most important societal issues today as antagonism against the homeless has been increasing since the beginning of the 1990s. This trend is probably due to what the media call "compassion fatigue" or "intolerance" among the mainstream public. Stereotypical portraits of homeless people as skid-row alcoholics and happy wanderers (Snow, et al., 1994) seem to be replaced with a threat to the society.

This chapter examines the way in which homelessness is represented in television news narrative and its relationship to reality construction. This study assumes that news communication creates and maintains our reality. In other words, the study will explicate the process of the signifying rules and practices of television news narrative communication by which particular meanings of homelessness are constructed. Hence, the research question is How does television news narrative treat the issue of hostility toward homelessness, that is, "Are the homeless portrayed as the victims of social problems or problem makers?" First, we will identify underlying paradigmatic symbolic patterns by adapting Levi-Strauss's theory of binary opposition. Second, we will examine how the paradigmatic principles work in the syntagmatic development of the story as a whole by making use of Propp's and Todorov's insights about syntagmatic narrative process to see how it ideologically deals with the social issue of homelessness. Finally, we will explain the discourse dimension of television news narrative by examining how semiotic modes of expression in television narrative such as camera work, sound, editing, lighting, among other are related to the whole paradigmatic/syntagmatic patterns of narrative by using basic concepts of visual semiotics by Kozloff (1987), Eco (1976), Seiter (1987), Silverman (1983) and Metz (1974).

The purpose of this study, in a broad sense, is to provide some knowledge about the formal logic of television news narrative by showing that the world in which we live is rendered meaningful and thus understandable to us. The systematic study of syntagmatic structural rules of television news narrative in particular is more contributive than the paradigmatic one. In fact, few studies (Fiske, 1987, p. 139; Hartley, 1982) have dealt with this aspect of television news narrative. The most commonly used theories in the structuralist approach to television communication tend to be Propp's theory on narrative schema (his theory of "spheres of action" in particular) and Levi-Strauss's theory of binary opposition. In applying these theories to television studies, however, the research tends to examine only the deep structural paradigmatic rules of television narrative and thus ignores the other half of the story dimension of narrative, the syntagmatic aspect of narrative. Many studies (Ekdom, 1981; Campbell, 1986; Campbell and Reeves, 1989; Penner and Penner, 1994) tend to focus on typological aspects of narrative by classifying the types of narratives or narrators. Campbell's (1986) study, for example, analyzes a news magazine program, "60 Minutes" and comes up with four types of narrative formulas including detective, analyst, tourist and referee. His study tends to mainly focus on categorizing the style of reporters in terms of his four types of formulas. In short, such research has not fully explored the syntagmatic aspect of television narrative which eventually serves as another determining structural principle in orienting the story as a whole on the macro level as it controls the horizontal development of the narrative, leading toward a certain narrative closure and rendering the episode meaningful and understandable.

NARRATIVE ANALYSIS OF TELEVISION NEWS

Story Dimension

The study of television narrative can be approached from two dimensions of signification: story and discourse. The story dimension consists of two aspects as it deals with the deep and surface structures: a paradigmatic and a syntagmatic analysis respectively. For this study, Levi-Strauss's concept of "binary oppositions" provides a useful tool for analysis. Like myths, television news stories are constructed in terms of paradigmatic binary oppositions. The social types of characters, for example, can be represented in such conceptually opposite terms as We : They, Good : Evil, Hero : Villain, Helper : Victim, Normal : Abnormal, Honesty : Deception. The settings are identified in terms of Nature : Culture, Home : Street, Home : Foreign, among others. In television narrative, pairs of binary oppositions are metaphorically transformed into other pairs, usually moving from the abstract level to the concrete. An abstract pair of Good : Evil, for example, then may be transformed into a concrete pair of Rich : Poor, or of Homeowner : Homeless. Most of the time, the anchor or reporter as "framing narrator" mediates between two "polar" states by retaining the "duality" character which is "ambiguous and equivocal" (Levi-Strauss, 1964/1969, p. 226).

Two homologic oppositions, Us : Them :: The Ordinary : The Homeless and Absence : Presence :: Issue : Events were identified for the analysis. According to Hartley (1982), one of the things we should do in analyzing the news story is to look for what is *not* there, what is absent, not selected, discursively repressed (pp. 117–119). Therefore, the underlying meaning of news narrative is not to be found in the explicit manifestation of the events, but instead in its significant absence (Brunsdon and Morley, 1981, p. 137). Also Hartley (1982, p. 116) suggests that the news proceeds on the basic Us : Them opposition in which the former includes the culture, nation, public, viewer, family, newsreader and news institution, and the latter, striker, foreign dictator, foreign power, the weather, fate, bureaucracy and accessed voice. In addition, he argues that once an individual or topic has been stereotyped it will always be presented in terms of the stereotype, and further, it will never be selected as newsworthy unless it does or says something that fits the stereotype (p. 116). The search for these binary oppositions helps us understand how the social types (class, values, status, among others) of participants (actors) are constructed through their manifested representations by the sign systems.

The next step concerns the syntagmatic analysis of news stories by means of Propp (1968) and Todorov's (1977) theoretical schemes. Their partial conclusions indicate that any narrative has its own plot that allows the story as a whole to move on from a certain state of equilibrium (beginning) to another state of equilibrium (closing) if the latter is to confirm the former or is to arrive at a state of equilibrium which is different from the former. Between these two equilibriums are always contradictions (conflicts or disruptions), which are then usually resolved by certain mediator(s) or helper(s). As many (Fiske, 1987; Tuchman, 1978; Hall, 1981; Gitlin, 1986) indicate in their research, one of the techniques commonly used for this practice is so called "personalization" of the serious and hard issues. In this respect, this study compares the states of the opening and closing equilibriums for every news story in the sample to see if there is any consistent form of news narrative in the process of syntagmatization. The study also attempts to identify what kinds of syntagmatic rules are practiced most often, and how are these rules associated with the society's cultural values or ideologies.

Discourse Dimension

The study of discourse dimension examines the relationship between the visual/aural expression and the "orientation" or "point of view" of the narrative as a whole; that is, how camera work, editing, lighting, music, sound, and so on are related with the overall point of view. The visual presentation which mostly consists of news-camera work in particular seems to function as a determining role in embodying a point of view in the television news narration. Although television's "institutional" relations require the news events to be narrated without adopting the point of view of any party or person, as Hartley and Montgomery (1985) argue, the news narration cannot escape the self-embedded effect of the visual codes of television narrative. Due to these unavoidable restrictions resulting from its "formal" relations, "*All* shots have a point of view, whether it is *internally* motivated by the placing of a character, or *externally* motivated by the positioning of the imaginary observer (viewer)" (p. 246). The proper understanding of the visual then requires studying how various signs as a total signifying system work in the narrative.

Narrative Moments

In an attempt to identify a consistent organizing principle on the horizontal dimension, this study analyzes a structural pattern of four significant narrative moments for the present sample. We have labeled these four narrative "moments" as those of *framing* ("Here's our story"), *differentiating* ("Are 'they' really different from 'us'?" If so, how?), *reversing* ("Who's to blame?") and *closing* ("Here's our solution"). This syntagmatic categorizing was based on each moment's narrative "function" that was abstracted for the most part from the verbal development of the narrative.

ANTAGONISM AGAINST THE HOMELESS

Sample

Since NBC first reported the antagonism against the homeless in 1990, a total of nine stories related to the issue of hostility toward the homeless from three traditional network's evening news (ABC/CBS/NBC) were identified between 1990 and 1995 in the *Television News Index and Abstracts*. Five of them, however, had to be excluded since their connection to the issue, is too minimal to be considered for this chapter. A story on funding the homeless program in Boston (November 23, 1994), for example, examined the possible threat to programs for the homeless when the Republican leadership takes over the Congress. The story was rather indirect to be considered for the sample. Only four stories (two special reports and two regular reports) were exclusively on the issue of hostility: (1) NBC's "Focus" (07/07/90, 5:20 mins); (2) CBS's "Eye On America" (12/23/91, 4:27 mins); (3) ABC (12/21/93, 2:40 mins); and (4) NBC (10/05/94, 2:00 mins).

For the purpose of this chapter, CBS's "Eye on America" was selected for the analysis. This particular report was more inclusive and described the public's growing antagonism against the homeless people than the rest of the sample. The excluded reports were mostly on various ordinances and crackdowns against the homeless in major cities. For example, Peter Jennings (ABC, 1993) was reporting from the U. S. conference of Mayors on the state of the homeless in this country. For the most part, the report was not about the public's antagonism against the homeless, but about law and order against the homeless. The selected CBS special report is, however, a story about the conflict between the middle class community and the homeless.

Framing (Sequence 1)

In the first sequence, the anchor does not set up a basic Us:Them opposition explicitly. The anchor, however, introduces two emotion-related terms (compassion fatigue and intolerance) in relation to the topic for setting the opposition:

some people with "compassion fatigue" and "intolerance," and a different group of "everyday" people. Here the issue of homelessness is framed as a matter of emotional conflict between two groups of people in this sequence. This means that the structural cause of the problem at the macro level is readily absent from the scene. Therefore, it can be assumed that the narrative has already begun with the following homologic oppositions: Absence (Structure/Institution) and Presence (Individual).

Differentiating (Sequence 2)

The reporter's voiceover on actual tape focuses the viewer's attention on the middle class's rally against the homeless. The rally signifies the middle class's antagonism against the homeless. This oppositional pair (middle class versus homeless) is then metaphorically and/or metonymically, and verbally and/or visually transformed into more abstract concepts, that is, Us : Them. There is a significant visual connection between Sequence 1 and Sequence 2 that eventually contributes to locating the news team and the middle class's rally on the same camp. In the beginning of Sequence 1, as the anchor begins with his studio report through the mode of "direct address" to the camera, the title of the program segment, "Eye On America" is seen over his left shoulder in the frame as a part of the background visual. As the studio report proceeds, the anchor, who has been initially placed slightly left from the center of frame, is being slowly moved into the center. At the same time, the title of the segment disappears out of frame gradually as the camera pans slowly to the left. In this shot, the relationship between the segment title, "Eye On America" itself and the anchor's mode of address is semiotically significant. The anchor's mode of direct address to the camera creates an imaginary space, which is to be mutually shared by the viewer and the narrator. This imaginary space binds the viewer and the narrator together temporally and spatially as the narrator's address makes the viewer feel that the temporal and the spatial gaps between he/she and the narrator collapse, creating a common ground of "here and now." When the anchor uses the term "we" or "us" during the report, "Tonight, we will examine" or "Most of us think" for example, the anchor deftly locates the viewer's orientation in the same line as his. Therefore, the existing gap between the anchor's and the viewer's "points of view" disappears. This merging then eventually creates the collapse of the difference between the narrator and "you" (the viewer), and thus combines two parties into a single unit, "we."

There is another semiotic collapse between the "Eye" (the actual presentation of which is not a word but a symbol shaped like an eye) in the logo and the "eyes" of the viewer and the anchor. That is, the "Eye" in the logo looks at "us" (the viewer) just the same way the anchor's "eyes" do; the actual gap between the "eyes" of the anchor and that of the logo symbolically collapses. Consequently, there is also a collapse of the viewer's eyes and the "Eye" in the logo. This means that the news' "Eye" on America is semiotically identified as "our" (the viewer's) eyes on America.

At the ending part of sequence 1, the computer generated flying particles gradually form a shape (with the title, "Eye On America" on it) which resembles the "stripes" part of the American Flag. As the visual of Sequence 2 opens, the previous computer generated graphic is being wiped out to reveal the close-up shot of the real American Flag hanging on the ceiling of the huge homeless shelter. The camera tilts down then to hold a medium-shot of the reporter with an extreme long-shot at an extremely high angle of the scene inside the shelter which becomes the reporter's background scenery. The scene is then cut to a series of shots that reveal a group of the homeless lying down or sitting up on their beds. Their faces are not yet discernible since the shots are taken still at long distances and in high angles.

What should be noted in this series of shots is the transition of the scene from the computer generated graphic "stripes" to the stripes of the real flag, and the optimum camera framing of the reporter with the background of inside shelter and a series of following shots of the homeless taken from a high position. All of these symbolically may signify the superior (higher) position of the reporter and the viewer as the representative of "normal" America, in contrast to the inferior (lower) position of the homeless people. The reporter who is making a direct address to the viewer is seen at the medium-distance and in normal-angle. His voiceover narration here at the scene of the homeless taken at an (extremely) long distance and in (extremely) high angle endows the reporter with a higher status of authority, credibility and neutrality.

In the meantime, the scene of the homeless in the shelter is then cut to a street scene in which a homeless person is seen at a distance strolling along the by street with a grocery cart filled with his miscellaneous articles. While this homeless person is moving off screen to the left side of the frame, a woman's voice (from the anti-homeless rally) is fading in as if it were a voiceover narration on the scene. This voiceover like quality functions symbolically to "dominate" the visual, thus creating a Dominance : Subordination opposition. The street scene, with the woman's voiceover effect, is then bridged with a series of shots, which show, what they call, the "middle class" citizen's anti-homeless rally scenes from different places. This scene is comprised of 9 shots that show three rally speakers and the applauding audiences alternatively. It begins with a medium-shot of a middle-aged female speaker whose voice sounds furious, and proceeds with three shots of the audience applauding the speaker. It is then followed by a series of five shots that also show hostile rally scenes including two shots of speakers, 1 of outdoor picketing and 2 of the audience applauding. During the outdoor picketing scene, a placard is seen reading "Bums" with a line drawn diagonally across it and "Make Santa Monica Safe!" To identify the homeless as "Bums" is again verbally supported in the following shots where the speaker uses the same term, "the Bowery bums." As the rally speakers keep addressing themselves as the "middle class" "citizen" or "community" and the homeless as "bums," one may come up with another oppositional homology of "Citizen" : "Bum." In addition, the reporter's verbal quotation in the beginning of Sequence 2, "Don't put the homeless in middle class America's *back* yard," sets up a metaphoric interpretation of the oppositional pairs, The Middle Class versus The Homeless and Front versus Back.

In addition, the matter of "nominated/not nominated" and "accessed voices/silenced voices" is semiotically significant in this sequence. The reporter (Bob Faw), the news program producer (Jon Meyersohn) and two rally speakers' names (Dorothy Fitzpatrick and Robert Stranieri as "Resident") are verbally or visually "nominated" on the one hand, while the homeless are not. The former had "access" to voice, while the latter did not. All of these verbal and visual modes of presentation may be then formulated as follows:

US	THEM
Normal America	Abnormal America
Superiority/High	Inferiority/Low
The Anchor/Reporter/Viewer	The Homeless
The Middle Class: "Citizen"	The Homeless: "Bums"
Front	Back
Voicing-over	Voiced-over
Accessed Voices	Silenced Voices
Names Nominated	Names not nominated
Optimum Framing	Unfavorable Framing
(MS/SA)	(ELS/LS/HA/LA)

*MS (medium shot); ELS (extreme long-shot); LS (long shot); LA (low angle); SA (standard angle); HA (high angle)

Furthermore, the issue of homelessness has been translated into a matter of conflict between the middle class and the homeless. The Institution : Individual opposition, has been transformed into a practical, The Middle class : The Homeless opposition. This transformation has been made possible simply by the absence or disappearance of structural explanation of the issue from the story. The narrative's tendency of appealing to our common sense sentiment also helps make the transformation easier. The uncomfortable part of the issue disappears when the narration turns the viewer's attention toward its immediate effects in our everyday life. Eventually, the focus of the narrative is shifted to the concrete and pragmatic experiences which are practiced mostly at the emotional level. This change of focus has already been started by the reporter's verbal in Sequence 2 when he repressed alternative viewpoints and selectively quoted the middle class's complaint, "One reason homelessness in America is such a big problem is because so many people are shouting, 'Don't put the homeless in middle-class America's back yard.'"

Reversing I (Sequence 3)

In this sequence, the furious reaction by the New Yorkers to the City's plan to locate twenty-four new shelters in middle class residential areas throughout the city is described. The visual and verbal aspects of the narrative again reinforce the opposition already established in the previous sequences, but this time with more concrete and extreme sentiment indicated in the metaphorical use of such terms as "shunting them (the homeless)," "warehousing them," "down-and-outs," "digging in garbage cans" and "cancer" to refer to the inhumane quality of the homeless people.

The opening of the sequence begins with a series of shots of the homeless at a medium or long distance. The primary actions of the characters include hanging around, standing in a fixed position with shabby and dirty clothes and rags on, going nowhere, literally floating on the streets and sometimes sleeping inside make-shift cardboard shelters on the sidewalk. These shots are now very typical and thus serve as metonymic symbols for telling how "they" are different from the rest of us in terms of clothing, behaviors and attitudes. Compared with the previous shots of the middle class people in decent clothing and acceptable attitudes, the juxtapositions of these shots give us the sense of difference that exists between "us" and "them." This constructed sense of difference is once more verbally confirmed by the narrator's voiceover which dominates the silent visuals. The use of slang and everyday language mediates between two worlds and thus makes the unfamiliar familiar. Due to its ideological and magical power, on the other hand, it confirms our sense of difference and makes it more concrete and firm while eliciting our sense of sympathy for "them."

These shots are followed by a professional's comment on the failure of the past housing policies (the government policy makers are "exnominated") in an actual interview shot, and functions only as an "inoculation" effect that eventually strengthens (Barthes, 1957/1972, p. 150) the claims made by the middle class community. This "inoculation" effect is supported by the following actual rally footages and interviews of the middle class residents, of which the visuals and accessed verbals appear dominant compared to the other side where no accessed voice is allowed for the sake of its own interest. This is one of those major tactics commonly used throughout the whole sample that, in Barthes' words, "immunizes the contents of the collective imagination by means of a small inoculation of acknowledged" fact (p. 150). The voices that back up the homeless' side in most cases turn out to be "controlled doses" (Fiske, 1987, p. 39) that allow the dominant ideology to set the limits on the positioning of the homeless characters in the news stories. The negative construction of the homeless is then again reinforced by the metaphorical use of the term "cancer" by Lorraine Sorge (a middle class interviewee) for the homeless, as she asserts, "It's like a cancer. They're spreading a cancer into a healthy community." As Sontag (1978) suggests, the metaphor of illness is often used to speak of the various kinds of dark sides in a society, for example, slums and pornography shops. "Cancer" in particular is one of those which is commonly used and thus popular to us just as in J. Edgar Hoover's favorite metaphoric use of the term referring to communism or the same use for Nixon's administration (Conrad and Schneider, 1980, p. 252). "When we have a sense of evil but no longer the religious or philosophical language to talk intelligently about evil," Sontag (1978) argues, "we search for adequate metaphors" in order to comprehend it; "And the cancer metaphor is particularly crass. It is invariably an encouragement to simplify what is complex and an invitation to self-righteousness, if not to fanaticism" (pp. 82–83). By appealing to our "common sense stock of knowledge," the "cancer" metaphor for the homeless simplifies the complex nature of the homelessness problem and thus masks the structural causation of the issue.

Besides this, the voiceover-like narration by an interviewee, Harold Donnelly displays the middle class's dominance over the homeless in the scene in which a homeless woman positioned with her back to the camera is seen digging in a garbage can on the street. On the contrary, the homeless themselves have never had a chance for their voices to be heard to defend themselves. The following oppositions may be formulated for this particular sequence:

US	THEM
The Middle Class	The Homeless
Superiority	Inferiority

Being Dominant	Subordinated
"Healthy" Society	Social Disease ("cancer")
Victim ("done to")	Cause ("doer")
Accessed Voices	Silenced Voices
Optimum Framing	Unfavorable Framing
(MS/SA)	(ELS/LS/HA/LA)

Reversing II (Sequence 4)

On the whole, this sequence is devoted to confirm the reversed direction of the cause-and-effect relation between society (us) and individual (the homeless). The advocates for the homeless finally allowed to speak for themselves, however, the passive defending style turns out to be an inoculation that ironically strengthens the reversed causal relation. This inoculation effect is achieved by the newsmaker's deft selection of the shots and their timely arrangement in its relation to the overall flow of narrative.

The sequence now focuses the viewer's attention on the side of homeless advocates, who are mostly seen busy defending themselves against the middle class worry about what the homeless might be able to do. After more than half of the narrative has passed, the homeless advocates begin to have their voices accessed. Yet, this only reaffirms the primary binary oppositions, Us : Them and Absence : Presence. Ultimately, the accessed voices on the part of the homeless are not seen successfully claiming their interests, but only having the Cause : Victim, The Homeless : The Middle class oppositions hardened.

As the sequence opens, Willie Washington, a homeless advocate, in response to the middle class's complaints from the previous sequence, begins to defend the homeless by arguing that he applies very tough rules to the homeless people who participate in his program so as to have them under control and thus not to allow the things the middle class ("we") worry about to happen. His claim is defended in the series of following shots, which seem to demonstrate how tough rules work in controlling the homeless. One interesting point is that the voices of the actual homeless are yet to be heard even though the sequence is especially arranged for defending the homeless. The guide's tough leadership indicated in his verbal command, "We're all going to Rockefeller Center. I expect that everybody behave like *real adults*." The brief question and answer scene between the reporter and Willie Washington once more makes the viewer become fully convinced of the toughness and effectiveness of the rules:

> *Willie Washington*: Each client is occupied daily, full day, from the time they wake up until the time they go to bed.
> *The reporter*: And if he violates the rules, he's out?
> *Willie Washington*: He's out.

The reporter's question seems trivial since it does not get down to the nature of the issue, nor to the context of the problem, but only confirms that the homeless are always the part that initiates the social problem, not vice versa. It is also true in the case of the following interview scene where Raymond Diaz from New York City Human Resources Administration is asked a similar trivial question:

Raymond Diaz: Good programs historically have helped people take control of and change their lives.
The reporter: Would you want people like that living next to you?
Raymond Diaz: (disgusted) Yes.

Above all, the reporter's wording of the question here, being out of context, tends to arouse antagonism between the homeless and the rest of us. At the same time, this trivial question, along with the former one with Willie Washington, only proves the journalist's routine of personalizing the issue, which eventually makes the narrative more melodramatic. Raymond Diaz's disgusted "Yes" to the reporter's question is then covered up by the following shot in which the opponent, Lorraine Sorge, a middle class resident, shows her full confidence in reacting to Diaz by "That dreaming. Let's get down to reality." The juxtaposing of these two contrasting scenes is not coincidental again, since the narrative flow of the whole story is always under control of a well organized framework. Therefore, what the viewers see on the screen is only a group of fragmentary events which do not have real relationships to each other but produce meanings only after being knitted together and reintegrated by a higher level of authority.

In brief, the examination of the structural causation, the hidden state of affairs, is absent from the scene again, while the focus of narrative has been put on the realization of the immediate effects of the problem both on the middle class and on the homeless. What is unique in this particular sequence is that the narrative now has achieved the reversed version of the cause and effect relation, and thus translated the homeless, a victim of social problems, as the cause of the problem itself (the "doer") and the society as the victim (who is "done to").

Closing (Sequence 5)

The narrative closure here basically reaffirms the binary oppositions which have been initiated as early as the beginning of the narrative. While the reporter closes the narrative with a concluding remark that "Ultimately, it is a question about power and priorities," it merely sounds like it is hanging in the air since power and priorities have already been sold out to the middle class to which "most of us" belong. The structural discussion of the "issue" has already disappeared, once again leaving behind only the fragmentary "events" on the front stage. The homeless have come to be blamed as the cause of the social problem. Hence the final interpretation of the story as follows:

US	THEM
The Middle Class	The Homeless
Superiority	Inferiority
Healthy Society	Disease
The Victim	The Cause
("done by")	("doer")

ABSENCE	PRESENCE
The Structural Causation	The Events
The Cause	The Effects
(Structural/Institutional)	(Individual Experiences)

The visual discourse reinforces these oppositional relations in the closing sequence. On the one hand, a series of normal angle shots of the middle class people have been taken at the optimum range of medium shots without any ambient sounds except for the audience's cheering applaud. On the contrary, the shots of the homeless including David Taylor, the only homeless person who has been given an accessed voice throughout the whole story, were taken at high angle views and at long distances. Finally, the mayor, David Dinkins' voice as well as David Taylor's has only functioned as a lead-in for the dramatic effect induced by a concluding metaphorical comment for the rally by the middle class resident, Dorothy Fitzpatrick, that "Forget the melting pot. You've got a boiling pot, and you better turn down the flame." The location of this last shot just before the reporter's final comment signifies her importance in terms of narrative flow. She is the person who has actually set off the narrative flame in the beginning and put it out at the end. Again, the juxtaposing of these two shots apart like this seems not accidental, but rather well-planned. Therefore, it can be argued that her narrative function has helped in establishing a particular orientation of the narrative in general. Yet, within the given framework, she has also been playing a function that confirms the underlying dominant point of view.

CONCLUSION

Through a close textual reading of four news stories, this analysis has provided a detailed approach which illustrates how the syntagmatic organizing pattern in collaboration with the deep structural binary oppositions works in the narrativistic construction of a particular version of homeless reality. In other words, it purports to study how a particular version of reality in a reality of the homeless in particular is constructed in television network news. A few points regarding this study should be noted here. While this study has attempted to render the whole structural patterns both at the visual and aural levels, it has relied more on the characters' verbal narrations than on the visual presentations. Second, it should be mentioned that the narrative structures, four narrative moments on the syntagmatic dimension in particular, are not necessarily able to be applied to other news programs, this formulation needs to be tested against other regular news segments if they are to be claimed as such at a more general level. Third, this study has not dealt much with the sociological aspects of the issue of homelessness, since the main purpose of this study has been to understand the television news medium's social practice in the construction of a particular reality of the homeless.

Finally, this study takes a subjective, interpretive approach to the reading of television news narrative in an attempt to understand the structural encoding principles which have been consciously or unconsciously practiced in the television journalist's news making process. Besides the above limitations, this study has not investigated the inter-textual relationship of television news programs with other popular cultural news forms such as news magazines and newspapers. It would be necessary to compare the would-be different narrative structures embedded in various mass mediated cultural products, if one attempts to understand homelessness as a minority culture in mainstream society in its full mass mediated social context.

REFERENCES

Altheide, D. L. (1976). *Creating reality: How TV news distorts events.* Beverly Hills: Sage.

Barthes, R. (1972). Myth today. In R. Barthes, *Mythologies* (A. Lavers, Trans.). New York: Hill and Wang. (Original work published 1957)

Barthes, R. (1977). Introduction to the structural analysis of narratives. In R. Barthes, *Image-music-text* (S. Heath, Trans.). New York: The Noonday Press. (Original work published 1977)

Bentele, G. (1985). Audio-visual analysis and a grammar of presentation forms in news programs: Some mediasemiotic considerations. In T. A. van Dijk (Ed.), *Discourse and communication: New approaches to the analysis of mass media discourse and communication* (159–184). Berlin: Walter de Gruyter.

Brunsdon, C., and Morley, D. (1981). Everyday television: Nationwide. In T. Bennett, S. Boyd-Bowman, C. Mercer and J. Woollacott, *Popular television and film* (118–141). London: BFI.

Campbell, R. (1986). Narrative, myth and metaphor in 60 Minutes: An interpretive approach to the study of television news (Doctoral dissertation, Northwestern University, 1986). *Dissertation Abstracts International, 47,* 2783A.

Campbell, R. (1987). Securing the middle ground: Reporting formulas in 60 Minutes. *Critical Studies in Mass Communication, 4*(4), 325–350.

Campbell, R. (1991). *60 Minutes and the news: A mythology for middle America.* Urbana, IL: University of Illinois Press.

Campbell, R., and Reeves, J. L. (1989). Covering the homeless: The Joyce Brown story. *Critical Studies in Mass Communication, 6*(1), 21–42.

Collins, C. A., and Clark, J. E. (1992). A structural narrative analysis of Nightline's "This Week in the Holy Land" *Critical Studies in Mass Communication, 9*(1): 25–43.

Conrad, P. and Schneider, J. W. (1980). *Deviance and medicalization: From badness to sickness.* Columbus, OH: Merrill.

Eco, U. (1976). *A theory of semiotics.* Bloomington, IN: Indiana University Press.

Ekdom, L. R. (1981). An interpretive study of the news: An analysis of news forms (Doctoral dissertation, The University of Iowa, 1981). *Dissertation Abstracts International, 42,* 4634A.

Fiske, J. (1987). *Television culture.* London: Methuen.

Fiske, J. (1991). For cultural interpretation: A study of the culture of homelessness. *Critical Studies in Mass Communication, 8*(4), 455–474.

Foucault, M. (1979). *Discipline and punish: The birth of the prison* (A. Sheridan, Trans.). New York: Vintage Books. (Original work published 1975)

Gitlin, T. (1980). *The whole world is watching: Mass media in the making and unmaking of the new left.* Berkeley: University of California Press.

Gitlin, T. (1986). Introduction: Looking through the screen. In T. Gitlin (Ed.), *Watching television: A Pantheon guide to popular culture* (3–41). New York: Pantheon Books.

Hall, S. (1981). The determinations of news photographs. In S. and J. Young (Eds.), *The manufacture of news: Social problems, deviance and the mass media* (rev. ed., 226–243). London: Constable.

Hartley, J. (1982). *Understanding news.* London: Methuen.

Hartley, J., and Montgomery, M. (1985). Representations and relations: Ideology and power in press and TV news. In T. A. van Dijk (Ed.), *Discourse and communication: New approaches to the analysis of mass media discourse and communication* (233–269). Berlin: Walter de Gruyter.

Hopper, D. and Baumohl, M. (1994). Rethinking advocacy. *American Behavioral Scientist, 37*(4), 522–534.

Kozloff, S. R. (1987). Narrative theory and television. In R. C. Allen (Ed.), *Channels of discourse: Television and contemporary criticism* (42–73). Chapel Hill: The University of North Carolina Press.

Levi-Strauss, C. (1963). *Structural anthropology* (C. Jakobson, and B. G. Schoepf, Trans.). New York: Basic Books. (Original work published 1958)

Levi-Strauss, C. (1969, 1983). *The raw and the cooked: Introduction to a science of mythology*, Vol. 1 (J. and D. Weightman, Trans.). Chicago: The University of Chicago Press. (Original work published 1964)

Metz, C. (1974). *Film language: A semiotics of the cinema* (chap. 2). New York: Oxford University Press.

Morse, M. (1986). The television news personality and credibility: Reflections on the news in transition. In T. Modleski (Ed.), *Studies in entertainment: Critical approaches to mass culture* (55–79). Bloomington, IN: Indiana University Press.

Penner, M. and Penner, S. (1994). Publicizing, politicizing, and neutralizing homelessness. *Communication Research*, 21(6), 766–781.

Pietila, V. (1992). Beyond the news story: News as discursive composition. *European Journal of Communication*, 7(1), 37–67.

Propp, V. (1968). *Morphology of the folktale* (2nd and rev. ed.; L. Scott, Trans.). Austin: University of Texas Press. (Original work published 1928)

Seiter, E. (1987). Semiotics and television. In R. C. Allen (Ed.), *Channels of discourse* (17–41). Chapel Hill: The University of North Carolina Press.

Silverman, K. (1983). *The subject of semiotics*. New York: Oxford University Press.

Snow, D., et al. (1994). Distorting tendencies in research on the homeless. *American Behavioral Scientist*, 37(4), 461–475.

Sontag, S. (1978). *Illness as metaphor*. New York: Vantage Books.

Todorov, T. (1977). *The poetics of prose* (R. Howard, Trans.). Ithaca: Cornell University Press. (Original work published 1971)

Tuchman, G. (1978). *Making news: A study in the construction of reality*. New York: Free Press.

Zettl, H. (1984). *Television production handbook* (4th ed.). Belmont, CA: Wadsworth Publishing.

Chapter 7

The Representation of the Homeless in U.S. Electronic Media: A Computational Linguistic Analysis

Rebecca Ann Lind and James A. Danowski

Investigating media representation of various social and cultural groups is valuable for several reasons. Of primary importance is the acknowledgment that the media do not merely report events—media reports are assumed by many observers to be representations of reality. Further, media reports themselves are tied to the reporter's perceptions (Kern, 1981; Mowlana, 1984; Said, 1981), and according to Trew (1979, p. 95), "all perception involves theory or ideology and there are no 'raw,' uninterpreted, theory-free facts." Indeed, before one's perceptions can be reported, they must be encoded, Roeh (1981, p. 78) argues that this is also inherently a value-laden process: "no author or speaker is free of the necessity to choose words, syntax, and order of presentation. It does make a difference if 'friction' and not 'dispute' is chosen." Thus values and attitudes are embedded within even the simplest descriptions.

Additionally, media representations of social or cultural groups which may reflect stereotypes are worthy of examination. It has been argued that stereotypes are not merely descriptive; they exist within a historical context and contain elements of both description and evaluation (Gorham, 1995; Seiter, 1986). Stereotypes are not entities in themselves; they exist only because people construct them, and myths and stereotypes about the homeless in America abound (see, for example, Mowbray, 1985; Grunberg, 1992). Many of these stereotypes stigmatize the homeless—Guzewicz and Takooshian (1992, p. 68) wrote that "portrayals of the homeless in American culture have long stressed laziness, immorality, drunkenness, and other character deficits"—and perpetuate the myth that individuals who are homeless have chosen that lifestyle. To what extent are these myths and stereotypes evident in the electronic media in the mid-1990s?

This chapter analyzes the representation of the homeless in U.S. electronic media by studying the transcripts of approximately 35,000 hours (about 130 million words) of television and radio content aired on ABC, CNN, PBS, and NPR from May 1993 to January 1996. This study improves upon previous research by analyzing a larger body of text than has any previous related research and by utilizing a more rigorous methodology than is typical of much content analysis. This research uses a form of computerized network analysis which, according to Danowski (1993), provides qualitative analysis by using quantitative procedures. Danowski's Wordlink program allows us to discover and map the relationships among words within messages; in this case, it allows us to interpret the underlying themes and structures present in mediated representations of the homeless. It allows us to discern the frequency with which certain words, terms, concepts, attitudes, and values are associated with the homeless.

An investigation such as this one becomes even more important when considering the extent to which the electronic media provide information to the American public—for example, Roper (1985) found that most Americans cite television as their most important source of news. Also, the cultivation research of Gerbner and others argues that by viewing television, people assimilate values and feel they understand what is going on in the world, and research has discovered similarities between the content of media portrayals of homelessness and public opinion of and knowledge about the homeless (Lee, Link, and Toro, 1991).

There is very little research investigating the representation of the homeless in the media. Although these few studies present conflicting findings as to whether the media primarily attribute the responsibility for being homeless to the individuals themselves or to external social factors, and the extent to which the homeless are presented as stigmatized, the bulk of the research has determined that most media portrayals blame homelessness on the homeless and often depict the homeless as deviant.

In a narrative analysis of 92 newsmagazine articles and 111 CBS news stories about the homeless appearing between 1980 and 1990, McNulty (1992) concluded that the news media perpetuated the notion that homeless people have brought this condition upon themselves. While some characterizations of homelessness are more sympathetic than others, "the overall tone of news coverage suggests that the homeless are ungrateful victims of individual weakness or personal choices who have come to depend too heavily on public charity and service" (McNulty, 1992, p. 183). Campbell and Reeves (1989) analyzed ABC, CBS, and NBC news coverage of one homeless woman (Joyce Brown) and found that "homelessness is primarily attributed to personal deficiencies, drunkenness, and mental illness" (p. 39). Penner and Penner (1994) investigated 213 comic strips and 126 editorial cartoons featuring homelessness that appeared in San Francisco newspapers between 1989 and 1992. They discovered that 57 percent of the comic strips and 30 percent of the editorial cartoons served to "neutralize" homelessness by "focusing blame on the homeless themselves for their condition, rather than on concern for their welfare or the need for government action" (p. 767).

However, Lee, Link, and Toro (1991) analyzed 205 *New York Times* articles about homelessness appearing between 1980 and 1990, and found that structural, not individual, explanations for homelessness dominated, although this dominance decreased over time. Still, nearly half the articles (45.6 percent) contained references to deviant behaviors among the homeless, and some forms of deviance (alcohol or drug abuse, begging, loitering, and crime) received increased coverage over time.

Power (1991) also found that the majority of news stories about homelessness aired on ABC, CBS, and NBC between 1982 and 1988 attributed responsibility for the situation to social factors, rather than to the homeless individuals themselves. In addition, Power found that, contrary to other research, the majority of news stories did not portray the homeless in a stigmatized fashion, although stigmatized portrayals increased noticeably over time. Power acknowledged that these findings may be due to shortcomings in his coding system, which focused on the specific individuals involved in the story rather than on "the homeless" in general, and that the coding procedures may not have been sensitive enough to capture and reflect the presence of stigmatization.

The Center for Media and Public Affairs' *Media Monitor* (1989) analyzed news coverage of the homeless on network news (ABC, CBS, NBC) and major newsmagazines (*Time, Newsweek, U.S. News and World Report*) from November 1986 through February 1989. This analysis revealed that "News of the homeless revolved around two questions: Who are they, and what is being done to help them?" (p. 2). The *Monitor* found that coverage of the homeless focused on discussions of the homeless individuals rather than on the causes of homelessness. Even though limited attention was paid to causes, they were indeed discussed. The most commonly-mentioned causes related to housing market forces; government inaction was also mentioned, as were labor market forces and the mainstreaming of the mentally ill. Only 4 percent of sources providing their opinions about the causes of homelessness "attributed the plight of the homeless to their own personal problems, such as mental illness, lack of motivation, or drug and alcohol abuse" (p. 3).

However, the *Monitor*'s exploration of the media's focus on the characteristics of homeless individuals notes that the media present a "human face of homelessness" (p. 6), which seems to contradict prior research that found a focus on individuals was associated more with blaming than with humanizing. Further, the study fails to provide any information about the extent to which media coverage overall made reference to deviant behaviors among the homeless. Analysis of 174 "personal anecdotes" contained within the stories revealed that only one homeless person was identified as a criminal, and only 7 percent were identified as drug or alcohol users. While useful, this analysis does not reflect media descriptions of the homeless which occur outside the parameters of the personal anecdote.

In this chapter, we use Power's concepts of "stigmatization" (discrediting the homeless based on appearance, character, among others) and "attribution" (identifying the cause of homelessness as relating to either individual or societal factors) to guide our investigation of the representation of the homeless in American electronic news and information media.

We also analyze media coverage of the homeless along several other dimensions. First, even though Guzewicz and Takooshian (1992, p. 68) argue that "many of us tend to lump all the homeless together into a single, faceless category," which would reinforce the notion of the "Otherness" of the homeless as described in Power (1991), the *Media Monitor* (1989) found that media coverage focused on the characteristics of individual homeless people and thus humanized the homeless. Other research has also claimed a similar focus on the individual, though with a differing result. Therefore, even though our analysis is not able to determine whether these references place blame, present deviance, or humanize, we investigate the extent to which the electronic news media focus on individuals and people, as opposed to portraying the homeless as an undifferentiated mass.

Second, prior research has found that "in addition to portraying the homeless themselves, the media provided images of public reaction to them" (*Media Monitor*, 1989, p. 5), finding two-thirds of public reaction to the homeless was compassionate or supportive. This mediated depiction of people's response to the homeless is not incompatible with the results of various surveys of public attitudes, which have found Americans to be generally supportive of and sympathetic toward the homeless (Benedict, Shaw and Rivlin, 1988; Lee, Link and Toro, 1991; Link et al. 1995; Toro and McDonell, 1992). Although we cannot claim that mediated representations directly influence people's reactions to or identification with the homeless (see Lee, Link, and Toro, 1991; Power, 1991), it is still worthwhile to investigate the extent to which media coverage of the homeless is presented in a context of compassion.

Third, since prior research (Lee, Link and Toro, 1991; *Media Monitor*, 1989) has shown that media coverage of the homeless often refers to policies, programs and services (both existing and proposed) designed to help the homeless, we investigate the extent to which electronic media reflect consideration of potential solutions to the problems of homelessness.

Finally, since the homeless "constitute an obligatory part of the 'coping in bad weather' story, the Thanksgiving story [and] the Christmas story" (Power, 1991, p. 1), and since research has found seasonal variation in media coverage of the homeless (*Media Monitor*, 1989), we investigate the extent to which seasonal markers are part of the portrayal of the homeless in the media.

In this research, therefore, we investigate the extent to which six themes are evident in electronic media's representation of the homeless: (1) stigmatization; (2) attribution; (3) individualization; (4) context of compassion; (5) programs, policies, and solutions; and (6) seasonal markers.

METHOD

"You shall know the meaning of a word by the company it keeps." This concept is often presented by scholars of computational linguistics who study statistical patterns in large collections of texts. These scholars argue that people have varying meanings for words, and that some meanings are idiosyncratic, while others (macro-level meanings) are widely shared and may be linked with membership in particular social, ethnic, or language communities. Wittgenstein's work provides the theoretical rationale for using statistical text analysis to identify societal or macro level meanings for words.

One way to estimate the macro level meanings of words is to look at the frequency with which words appear in close proximity. In other words, we can infer words' meanings from the statistical distributions of their co-occurrences. We can be relatively confident that a language community (in this case, the audience of news and public affairs programs on ABC, CNN, PBS, and NPR) exhibits a great deal of agreement about the meanings of those words. We therefore can infer the meanings of particular words (in this case, "homeless") by investigating their surrounding word context.

A useful method for making such inferences is to take a large set of textual content, called a corpus, and perform statistical analysis of word co-occurrences. The basic unit of analysis is the word pair—two words that cooccur, or are used together. The method we used in this study was to filter two and a half years' worth of transcripts of news and public affairs programs, using computer programs that function like an information refinery. In this study, our software was set to slide a window through the text and find all words that appeared seven words before and seven words after the target word "homeless." The program recorded and counted the windowed word pairs.

RESULTS

The corpus we analyzed contained approximately 130 million words. We searched for word pairs that combined references to the homeless with references reflecting the main themes we identified in previous research. Specifically, we looked for the presence of word co-occurrences which would serve to link the homeless with stigmatization, attribution, individualization, compassion, programs/policies/solutions, and seasonal markers.

The first thing that became obvious as we searched the corpus is that the homeless receive relatively little attention in American news and public affairs programming. We found a grand total of 3,134 references to the homeless in the nearly 130 million words we analyzed—only 0.0024 percent of all words. This means that the word "homeless" appeared only about once every 41,500 words. It is evident, therefore, that the homeless are not at the top of the media agenda. Still, even though coverage of the homeless is relatively rare, there is value in determining the extent to which even limited coverage perpetuates or ameliorates popular myths.

Stigmatization

To investigate the depiction of the homeless as stigmatized, we searched the corpus for words related to deviance, unacceptable physical or social behaviors or appearances, and criminal activities (whether as victim or perpetrator). Examples of stigmatizing words include "drug," "panhandlers," "abusers," "addicted," "begging," "derelicts," "scruffy," "crazy," "alcohol," "rags," "soiled," "naked," "erratic," and so forth. We separated words which were stigmatizing in a general sense from those which were overtly related to crime and criminal activity, arguably a specific form of stigmatization. Examples of these words include "arrested," "crime," "homicide," "stole," "illegal," "prisons," "parole," and so on.

Our analysis revealed that general stigmatizing words were included in the same window as "homeless" 572 times. The most frequent word pair (at 45 occurrences) was "mental/ly-homeless," followed by "drug/s-homeless" (37 occurrences, excluding references to specific drugs, such as crack and cocaine). Stigmatizing words associated specifically with crime co-occurred with "homeless" 336 times, led by "police/man-homeless" (37 occurrences) and "kill/ed/ing/er-homeless" (35 occurrences).

Both of these forms of stigmatization would be considered what Power (1991) described as stigmas of individual character. A different sort of stigma is stigma of the body, which includes physical deformities. We argue that this conceptualization should be expanded to include illness, disease, and infection. To the extent that the homeless are portrayed as physically unwell and possibly contagious, they are indeed stigmatized. Thus, we searched the corpus for words such as "sick," "infected," "illness," "disease," "virus," among others. We found words associated with stigmas of the body co-occurred with "homeless" 487 times. The most common co-occurrences were "health-homeless" (67 occurrences), "AIDS/HIV-homeless" (53 occurrences), and "ill/ness/es-homeless" (35 occurrences). A wide variation on the theme of death and dying (words such as "death/s," "dead," "body," "bury," "casualties," "coffin," "dying," "fatalities," and so on) was quite evident, at 76 total co-occurrences with the word "homeless."

When these three forms of stigmatization are combined, we find that of the 3,134 total references to the homeless, 1395 present a stigmatizing image. The fact that nearly 45 percent of all homeless references contain an allusion to some form of stigma indicates the perpetuation of the image of the homeless as deviant.

Attribution

Power (1991, p. 75) defined attribution as "the process of locating or identifying the cause or responsibility for an outcome." Thus, the state of being homeless could be attributed either to the homeless individuals themselves (due to drug abuse, mental illness, alcoholism, among others or to societal or other factors beyond the homeless individuals' control (unemployment, shortage of low-income housing, deinstitutionalization, the economy, and so on). Media content which attributes the cause of homelessness to the individual is quite similar to content which reflects stigmas of individual character, and there is significant overlap between the two. However, in this case, we considered only those words depicting circumstances that traditionally may be assumed to lead to homelessness (drug abuse, release from prison, the desire to lead the homeless lifestyle, mental illness) and not those words reflecting circumstances that—while still stigmatizing—may be the result of homelessness ("beggars," "dirty," "prostitute," and so on), or may be stigmatizing without having any relationship to the causes or effects of homelessness ("harass," "gay," "lesbian," and so on).

Upon analyzing the corpus, words reflecting individual attribution for homelessness co-occurred with our target word 250 times. These emphasized drug abuse and mental illness. For example, when we combined all references to drugs and alcohol ("abusers," "crack," "users," "addicted," "dependency," "drunk," "alcoholism," among others), we found 132 co-occurrences with the word "homeless." When all references to mental health ("mental," "crazy," "disturbed," "psychiatric," "idiot," among others) were combined, there were 60 co-occurrences with our target word. Taken together, drug abuse and mental illness represent about 77 percent of the total number of individual attributions for homelessness.

In examining the extent to which the cause of homelessness is attributed to societal or other factors beyond the homeless individuals' control, we found the word "homeless" co-occurred with housing-related words ("housing," "building," "rent," "affordable," "dwelling," among others) 168 times, and with employment-related words ("work," "pay," "jobless," "hiring," "unemployed," and so on) 260 times. Natural disasters ("flooding," "earthquake," "hurricane," and so on) were paired with "homeless" 65 times, while "homeless" co-occurred with words such as "economy," "recession," "poverty," "Reaganomics," and so on 92 times. The word pair "deinstitutionalization-homeless" appeared only once in the entire corpus. All together, these various forms of external attribution occur in conjunction with "homeless" a total of 586 times. Therefore, while about one-third of all mentions of homelessness contain some reference to its possible causes, the attention paid to external causes is nearly three times greater than that paid to individual causes.

Interestingly, words which reflected overt attribution, such as "because," "why," "cause," "reasons," "blame," "responsible," and so on, co-occurred with "homeless" only 148 times of the 3,134 total times "homeless" appeared in the corpus. Thus the audience is usually left to infer causality based on the details contained within the report.

Individualization

The corpus was examined for the co-occurrences of the word "homeless" with nouns (excluding proper nouns) which would indicate that the homeless were being presented as "subjects," rather than as a mass. We searched for words such as "people," "man," "woman, "sister," "child," "family," "teenagers," and so on. There was a total of 1,751 such co-occurrences, led by "person/people-homeless" (848 occurrences), "man/men-homeless" (204 occurrences), "woman/women-homeless" (100 occurrences) and "family-homeless" (72 occurrences). It would thus seem as though many references to the homeless do speak of and consider the homeless as individuals. However, it seems that the terms "homeless people" and "homeless person" are qualitatively different from terms which describe the homeless as having some connection with and in some way being related to society—evidenced by the use of words such as "vets," "sisters," "students," "youth," "grandchildren," "fathers," "elderly," "parents," and so on If the more generic nouns "people" and "person" are excluded from the analysis, we are left with 903 word co-occurrences which present the homeless as individuals, fewer than one-third of all references to the homeless. Still, even when including "people" and "person," only about 56 percent of all references to the homeless are individualized.

Context of Compassion

To investigate the extent to which the homeless were portrayed within a context of sympathy, support, and compassion, we looked for the co-occurrence of our target word "homeless" with words which seemed evocative of compassion and support. These included "understanding," "compassion," "sympathy," "suffering," "shivering," "tragedy," "remind," "invisible," "neglected," "tolerance," "loneliness," and so on. We found 517 such co-occurrences, with the most common being "cares/s/ing-homeless" (99 occurrences) "see/ing-homeless" (78 occurrences), and "hard-homeless" (19 occurrences). The most prominent theme in this category of response presented the hard conditions of homelessness as "hell," "suffering," "overwhelming," "tragedy," "brutal," "harsh," "horrendous," and so on—these words co-occurred with "homeless" 139 times. Another obvious theme had to do with a broad awareness of homelessness; words such as "forgotten," "seeing," "hidden," "notice," "invisible," "ignored," and so on co-occurred with "homeless" 143 times. At 517 total references, a context of compassion is found in fewer than 17 percent of the 3,134 references to the homeless.

Programs, Policies, Solutions

Here we looked for words of varying types. First, we searched for words which reflected programs and solutions that dealt with the immediate needs of the homeless—words such as "shelter," "food," "charity," and so on, we found 997 such references in the window with the word "homeless." The most frequent were "shelter/s-homeless" (264 occurrences) "help/s/ed/er/ing-homeless" (157 occurrences), and "hunger/ry-homeless" (50 occurrences). The broad food/hunger theme, comprised of words such as "hungry," "kitchen," "feeding," "cooking," "meals, "pantry," "stew," "cake," "eggs," and so on, was one of the most obvious features in this category, co-occurring 278 times with our target word.

Second, we searched for words which reflected an emphasis on policy, on working on a larger scale and addressing the larger issues underlying homelessness. These words included "government," "president," "mayor," "taxes," "programs," "reforms," "system," "funds," "prevent," "eliminate," "stop," "solve," "end," and so on There were 657 such references, led by "homeless-program/s" (73 occurrences), "homeless-Clinton" (38 occurrences), and "homeless-end" (22 occurrences).

Third, we searched for words which reflected policy or solutions involving some form of activism or empowerment. While these can indeed be considered part of the larger solution theme, it is interesting to consider them separately. There were 170 such references; the most common were "advocate/s/acy-homeless" (79 occurrences), "voice-homeless" (54 occurrences), "coalition-homeless" (31 occurrences), and "activist/s/ism-homeless" (21 occurrences). The word pair "empower/ed-homeless" occurred 8 times.

Thus, when collapsing these last two policy/solution categories, we have found 827 co-occurrences with the word "homeless." Adding to these the 997 references to solving the more immediate needs or problems of the homeless, we find a total of 1824 word co-occurrences reflecting programs, policies, and solutions. This is indeed a large proportion (about 58 percent) of all references to the homeless, but the relative prominence of this category is inflated by virtue of the fact that we included references to solutions for immediate needs such as meals.

Seasonal Markers

Overall, seasonal markers were relatively rare in our corpus, occurring in conjunction with "homeless" only a total of 307 times, or fewer than 10 percent of the 3,134 references to our target word. The two main types of seasonal markers acknowledged in prior research reflect concerns due either to weather conditions or to the Christmas Holiday season. An investigation of the corpus indicated a third concern which can be related to a season of a different sort—tourism.

We found 109 weather-related co-occurrences with the word "homeless." Most of these dealt with inclement winter weather; for example, "cold/er-homeless" occurred 24 times, and "winter-homeless" occurred 12 times. The most obvious focus was on cold conditions, with words such as "cold," "freeze," "subfreezing," "frigid," and "arctic" appearing in conjunction with "homeless" 36 times. Our finding that when weather is mentioned, the weather is bad, is reinforced by the relative frequency with which the months of the year are mentioned. Excluding May and March (which we didn't count due to possible alternate meanings of those words), we found a total of 123 co-occurrences of various months with "homeless." The winter months (November, December, January) accounted for more than half of all mentions, at a total of 68 co-occurrences. July and August, which can also present harsh conditions for the homeless, accounted for 26 of the co-occurrences.

There were only 37 holiday-related seasonal markers co-occurring with "homeless." The word pair "Thanksgiving-homeless" occurred 15 times, and "holiday/s-homeless" occurred 13 times.

The final type of seasonal marker we found represented tourism issues. These were just about as common as traditional holiday references (at 38 occurrences), and seemed to be a function of the 1996 Olympic Games held in Atlanta, Georgia. The word pair "Olympic/s-homeless" occurred 14 times, "games-homeless" appeared 6 times, and "tourist/s/ism-homeless" appeared 6 times. Evidently someone was concerned about how the presence of the homeless during the Olympic Games would reflect on the host country.

Summary by Topic

Table 7.1 provides the summary counts for all word pair frequencies by topic area. The table also includes the percentage value, based on the 3,134 total appearances of the word "homeless" within the nearly 130 million words contained within the corpus. These topics are presented in the order in which they were discussed in this chapter.

Table 7.1
Summary of Homeless Representation by Topic

Topic	Frequency	Percent
Stigmatization	1,395	44.51%
Individual	250	7.98%
External	586	18.70%
Individualization	1,751	55.87%
Context of Compassion	517	16.50%
Immediate	997	31.81%
Long-Term	827	26.39%
Seasonal Markers	307	59.80%

* Percent of the 3,134 total references to "homeless" contained in the corpus.
** Total Attribution: 836; 26.68% Total Programs/Policies/Solutions: 1,824; 58.20%

CONCLUSION

Overall, this analysis has found very little coverage of the homeless in American electronic media. It stands to reason that when the media ignore a specific cultural group, most audience members will not be particularly well informed about that cultural group. Under these conditions, negative stereotypes may thrive, unencumbered by depictions which may serve to debunk popular myths.

But to what extend does media coverage reflect or combat these myths about the homeless? Certainly, this study found that the homeless continue to be extensively stigmatized in news and information programs. The presentation of the homeless as mentally ill and/or substance abusers, as involved in criminal activities, and as being in poor health (often with contagious diseases) is common.

This finding becomes even more powerful when interpreted in conjunction with our investigation of the context of compassion. There are relatively few associations between compassion and the homeless (unless one considers references to resolving the immediate needs of the homeless, which we have not). The stigmatized image of the homeless that the audience receives is not countered by an alternative image encouraging sympathy and support.

Furthermore, the great emphasis on the immediate needs of the homeless, when considered in concert with the stigmatization and the lack of compassion, seems to reinforce an image of the homeless as constantly needy though perhaps undeserving. The homeless therefore come across as strange, scary, filthy, demanding creatures who don't really seem to deserve our sympathy but who are always after us for something, whether it be spare change, a meal, a change of clothes, or a warm place to spend the night.

However, our analysis did find that, although the media pay relatively little attention to the causes of homelessness, the state of being homeless was significantly less frequently blamed on homeless individuals than it was on a combination of things such as unemployment, a lack of affordable housing, the economy, and natural disasters. This finding implies a fairly positive portrayal of the homeless, though we must reiterate that only about one quarter of all references to the homeless (836 of 3,134) contained any indications of attribution, and of these, about one third did attribute blame to the homeless themselves.

An additional finding of this research is that the homeless are more often than not depicted as individuals—as people, sisters, parents, teenagers, and so on While our methodology doesn't allow us to determine whether this individualization serves to humanize the homeless or to more easily blame them for their situation, it seems clear that, on the whole, the homeless are not depicted in the media as an amorphous mass. Still, there is room for progress in this area; nearly 45 percent of references to the homeless did not contain the type of personal individual reference we used in our analysis.

In sum, we conclude that the homeless have very little shelter in the electronic media. One may speculate that the media's adherence to internal and external norms of "objectivity" might encourage reporters to avoid more compassionate treatment of the homeless. The responsibility of reporters, some might argue, that is to relate the facts, and that encouraging support, sympathy, and compassion for the homeless falls within the domain of charitable, religious, or other social institutions—not the media.

Nevertheless, to the extent that people's contact with the homeless comes from the media, and society's fleeting images of homelessness are given cultural interpretation by the media, we argue it is important that mediated representations of the homeless continue to be critically analyzed. It is difficult to imagine successfully resolving the complex issues underlying homelessness while myths and stereotypes about the homeless continue to be perpetuated.

NOTES

All segments of the following programs aired between May 1993 and January 1996 were analyzed: ABC: "Breaking News," "Good Morning America," "News Special," "Nightline," "Prime Time Live," "This Week with David Brinkley," "Turning Point," "World News Saturday," "World News Sunday," "World News Tonight," "20/20." CNN: "Both Sides with Jesse Jackson," "Capital Gang," "Crossfire," "Diplomatic License," "Evans and Novak," "Future Watch," "Health Week," "Health Works," "Inside Business," "Inside Politics," "Larry King Live," "Moneyline," "Moneyweek," "News," "Newsmaker Saturday," "Pinnacle," "Reliable Sources," "Science and Technology Week," "Showbiz Today," "Special Assignment," "Talkback Live," "Your Money." NPR: "All Things Considered," "Morning Edition," "Weekend Edition." PBS: "American Experience," "Charlie Rose," "Frontline," "Nova," "Wall Street Journal Report," "Washington Week in Review."

REFERENCES

Benedict, A., Shaw, J. S., and Rivlin, L. G. (1988). Attitudes toward the homeless in two New York City metropolitan samples. *Journal of Voluntary Action Research, 17 (3–4)*, 90–98.

Campbell, R. and Reeves, J. L. (1989). Covering the homeless: The Joyce Brown story. *Critical Studies in Mass Communication 6(1)*. 21–42.

Center for Media and Public Affairs. (1989). The visible poor: Media coverage of the homeless 1986–1989. *Media Monitor, 3(3)*.

Danowski, J.A. (1993). Network analysis of message content. In W. D. Richards Jr., and G. A. Barnett (Eds.), *Progress in communication sciences, Vol XII* (pp 197–221). Norwood, NJ: Ablex.

Gorham, B. (1995, August). *Stereotypes in the media: So what?* Paper presented to the Association for Education in Journalism and Mass Communication, Washington, DC.

Grunberg, J. S. (1992). The social life of homelessness: Myths and social standing. *Journal of Social Distress and the Homeless 1(2)*. 131–144.

Guzewicz, T. D. and Takooshian, H. (1992). Development of a short-form scale of public attitudes toward homelessness. *Journal of Social Distress and the Homeless 1(1)*. 67–79.

Kern, M. (1981). The Invasion of Afghanistan: Domestic vs. foreign stories. In W. C. Adams (Ed.), *Television coverage of the Middle East* (pp. 106–127). Norwood NJ: Ablex.

Lee, B. A., Link, B. G., and Toro, P. A. (1991). Images of the homeless: Public views and media messages. *Housing Policy Debate 2(3)*. 649–682.

Link, B. G., Schwartz, S., Moore, R., Phelan, J., Streuning, E., Stueve, A., and Colten, M. E. (1995). Public knowledge, attitudes, and beliefs about homeless people: Evidence for compassion fatigue? *American Journal of Community Psychology, 23(4)*, 533–555.

McNulty, B. R. (1992). *Homeless and hopeless: Resignation in news media constructions of homelessness as a social problem.* Unpublished Doctoral Dissertation, University of Pennsylvania.

Mowbray, C. T. (1985). Homelessness in America: Myths and realities. *American Journal of Orthopsychiatry, 55(1).* 4–8.

Mowlana, H. (1984). The role of the media in the US-Iranian conflict. In A. Arno and W. Dissanayake (Eds.), *The news media in national and international conflict* (pp. 71–99). Boulder, Co: Westview Press.

Penner, M. and Penner, S. (1994). Publicizing, politicizing, and neutralizing homelessness: Comic strips. *Communication Research, 21(6).* 766–781.

Power, J. G. (1991). *Mass communication of otherness and identification: An examination of the portrayal of homeless people in network television news.* Unpublished Doctoral Dissertation, University of Southern California.

Roeh, I. (1981). Israel in Lebanon: Language and images of storytelling. In W. C. Adams (Ed.), *Television coverage of the Middle East* (pp. 76–88). Norwood NJ: Ablex.

Roper, B. (1985). *Public attitudes toward television and other media in a time of change.* NY: Television Information Office.

Said, E.W. (1981). *Covering Islam: How the media and the experts determine how we see the rest of the world.* NY: Pantheon Books.

Seiter, E. (1986). Stereotypes and the media: A re-evaluation. *Journal of Communication, 36(2).* 14–26.

Toro, P. A. and McDonell, D. M. (1992). Beliefs, attitudes, and knowledge about homelessness: A survey of the general public. *American Journal of Community Psychology, 20(1),* 53–80.

Trew, T. (1979). Theory and ideology at work. In R. Fowler, B. Hodge, G. Kress, and T. Trew (Eds.), *Language and control* (pp. 117–156). London: Routledge and Keegan Paul.

Chapter 8

Blaming the Homeless: The Populist Aspect of Network TV News

Insung Whang and Eungjun Min

Tom Brokaw once said, "homelessness is not a seasonal phenomenon. This is a fixed pattern now" ("NBC Nightly News," December 5, 1986). It is, however, a media event of the winter season and a fashionable cause for the media. While the flood of reports and commentaries try to make people concerned about the issue, they fail to make any meaningful assault on the fundamental causes of the problem. One of the typical ways of portraying the issue is that the image of an individual with a unique circumstance is carefully chosen to illustrate the problem. News reports, then, become dramatic documentaries about unfortunate individuals.The real issue is lost in the midst of humanism. As Tom Brokaw said, the phenomenon is not a seasonal, but fixed pattern. It is also true that the television news tells of the homeless stories is a seasonal phenomenon with a fixed pattern.

"BLAMING THE VICTIM"

What are these people really, then? How are these people conceived of in society? What do others think is the origin of these people? According to a common belief among many journalists and politicians, the homeless of America are generally considered to consist of former mental hospital patients who were deinstitutionalized in the 1970s. Hence, the popular myth is that the homeless people are mentally disordered and thus psychotic, lazy, crazy, drunk, doped, among others (Snow, et al., 1994, p. 462; Hopper and Baumohl, 1994). This is the essence of the so-called "victim blaming" perspective.

Generally speaking, victim blaming is an attitude of ascribing social problems to psychological/psychiatric conditions rather than seeing them from sociological, political and economic perspectives. Between two contrasting perspectives of social deviants, that is, whether they are the problem itself or only victim's of it, the victim blaming attitude exclusively identifies the homeless as the problem itself (Ropers, 1988, p. 29; Ryan, 1976, pp. 3–23). Carefully listening to the victim-blamers, Ryan (1976) criticizes their attitude as an ideological process in the following:

Victim-blaming is cloaked in kindness and concern, and bears all the trappings and statistical furbelows of scientism; it is obscured by a perfumed haze of humanitarianism. Blaming the Victim is an ideological process, which is to say that it is a set of ideas and concepts deriving from systematically motivated, but *unintended*, distortions of reality. In the sense (of Karl Mannheim), an ideology develops from the "collective unconscious" of a group or class and is rooted in a class-based interest in maintaining the *status quo*. (pp. 6–11)

What is implied in the victim blaming theory is then, in short, an inverted logic of cause and effect so that cause becomes effect and vice versa. Ryan (1976) describes the process of this inversion of cause and effect as follows:

All of this happens so smoothly that it seems downright rational. First, identify a social problem. Second, study those affected by the problem and discover in what ways they are different from the rest of us as a consequence of deprivation and injustice. Third, define the differences as the cause of the social problem itself. Finally, of course, assign a government bureaucrat to invent a humanitarian action program to correct the differences. (pp. 8–9)

Contrary to the psychological victim blaming attitude toward the social problem of homelessness, the critical scholars approach the problem from a macro perspective, arguing that the answer for the origin of homelessness should be sought primarily from the context of economics (Rossi, 1994; Penner and Penner, 1994; Fiske, 1991; Ropers, 1988; Kozol, 1988; Ryan, 1976). They argue that the current problem of homelessness is rooted in three areas of the economy: the recession of the early 1980s that caused millions of job and home losses; the lack of affordable homes and federal cutbacks for low-income housing subsidies; and "the gentrification of the cities" that took away cheap flophouses and skid row districts where the poor used to live (Campbell and Reeves 1989, p. 22; Rossi, 1994).

SEMIOTICS AND SYSTEMATIC DISCOURSE THEORY

The primary concern of this chapter is to examine the populist aspect of television narration, that is, for example, how socially and politically important issues end up being transformed into trivial stories about personal events. This populistic trend of the news has been pointed out by Gitlin (1986) as he argues, "television" often "loves nothing more than a story about a 'little guy' who stands up to the 'powers that be'" in "anti-establishment" themes (p. 15). Both NBC and ABC, for example, featured a heroic act of a homeless couple (Tom and Pauline Nichter) who found a wallet containing "thousands of dollars" and returned it to the owner ("ABC World News," March 3, 1993; "NBC Nightly News," March 6, 1993). The underlying assumption was that the homeless are not descent enough to return that amount of money, therefore it was newsworthy.

Specifically, this chapter attempts to identify the narrative structures of television news in their relation to story (what happens to whom under what conditions) and discourse (how the story is told by using what codes and conventions) by using semiotic theories (Leach, 1976; Chatman, 1978; Hartley, 1982; Hartley and Montgomery, 1985) and Fiske's (1991) systematic discourse theory. In other words, it tries to combine an interpretive analysis with the conditions under which viewers will identify with homeless people presented in news stories. Television narrative, as Hartley and Montgomery (1985) argue, "renders the world of objects, persons, events and processes on the one hand, and the way in which that same utterance (narrative) sets itself into relation with a recipient (reader, viewer or hearer) on the other" (p. 233). Put in a broad way, "wider cultural processes are not merely invoked within textual features," but rather "textual features play an active, political role in cultural relations of power" (p. 260).

According to Leach (1976), both story and discourse dimensions are closely related to the terms, "metaphor" and "metonymy." The metaphor exists "when A stands for B" and "there is *no* intrinsic prior relationship between A and B, that is to say A and B belong to different cultural contexts" (p. 14). In the metaphorical connection between New York and The Big Apple, for example, two terms do not belong to the same cultural sphere, but have an arbitrary relationship. The relation between two elements is one which is not natural, but asserted and conventionalized. On the other hand, a relationship of metonymy is where A stands for B, that is, "a part stands for a whole" when "there is an intrinsic prior relationship" between two elements, A and B (p. 14). In this case, the relationship is contiguous, rather than asserted. The substitution of crown for the monarchy or sovereignty in the European cultural context, for example, demonstrates a metonymic relationship, as long as the former is a significant attribute of the latter. These modes of representation contribute to the construction of reality in television.

To avoid representative and conclusive nature of sample and analysis, as evidenced in the tradition of positivism, the study also uses John Fiske's (1991) systematic discourse theory. The sample does not have to be representative but systematic:

By this I mean that they are instances of a system in practice. The homeless men in Midtown are not representative of the homeless in general—they are white, male, Midwestern, single, and so on—but insofar as their experiences are systemic we can generalize from them, not to other homeless, but to the workings of the system (Reagannomic capitalism) within which these specific conditions of homelessness have developed. (1991, p. 469)

Fiske suggests the linguistic system should be inserted into the context of living social relations to "understand both the system that structures the whole way of life and the ways of living that people devise within it" (p. 469). This study attempts to identify various problematic structural elements between them.

SAMPLE

The sample for this analysis was selected from "mini news-magazine" segments in the evening network news programs between 1985 to 1994 (*Television News Index and Abstracts*). Among these mini news-magazine segments are NBC's "Special Segment," "America Close Up," "Assignment America," "Focus" and "What Works"; ABC's "Special Assignment" and "American Agenda"; and CBS's "Inside Sunday," "The Best of US" and "Eye On America." They report on a single topic in more depth, lasting between three and eight minutes, longer than other customary stories on the evening news which last about half a minute to three minutes. The authors found that not only is the number of homeless stories decreasing (1985–1991: average fifty stories per year; 1992–1994: average twenty-two stories per year), but the contents and ways of portraying the issue are typical (winter weather, Thanksgiving meals, etc.) and trivialized. For the newsmakers, the homeless are becoming just a part of downtown scenes in big cities.

The sample size ended up with fifty-four stories that relate to the issue of homelessness in one way or another. Twenty-nine stories had to be excluded, however, since their relation to the issue, "homelessness," is too minimal to be considered as samples for the present study. For example, NBC, in its "Assignment America" segment of May 19, 1989 evening news, covered a story on "Outward Bound" of New York City, a social program which allows inner-city children and corporation executives to face survival challenges and thus build confidence. Even though this segment described, as a part of the story, how the program participants lived like homeless people, it was not considered worthy enough to be selected for the sample. In other words, if any story was not directly related, or not dealing with the issue of homelessness as the primary topic of the segment, it was excluded. From the rest of the twenty-five stories, for the purpose of the study, twelve segments were selected: (1) four "general description of the homeless," (2) three "mental illness and the homeless," (3) one "homeless teens and social disorder," (4) two "the homeless and housing," and (5) two "the homeless and rehabilitation."

ANALYSIS

Unfamiliar "Regular" Scenes

As exemplified in most of the sample narratives for the present study, "sitting on the street bench" is one of those regulars very often used by the news teams to signify "homelessness." Other regulars may include scenes in which the homeless in dirty clothing are seen aimlessly standing here and there, waiting in soup lines, walking along the streets, pulling grocery carts along the streets, sleeping on the sidewalks, digging in trash cans and so on. These scenes are so typical that the viewers can not miss their signification once exposed to them.

On the verbal level, the reporters' typical description of being homeless as "lonely," "isolated" and "alienated" is supported by its visual counterpart in terms of ordering and timing: for "lonely," a close-up shot of washed-out looking woman with matted hair and deep-set eyes staring in vain; for "isolated," an extreme long-shot in high-angle of a man with shabby clothing and hat on, sitting and dozing by the escalator; for "alienated," a long-shot of one person (his or her sex cannot be discerned due to the face being covered by dirty blanket) sleeping on a street bench. The effectiveness of this acute way of juxtaposing shots along with the reporter's voiceover contributes to confirming that what is being said is "real." Their realities are meaningful only within the overall flow of the narrative which has already been tightly organized and thus controlled both by the anchor and the reporter.

To be meaningful within a given framework, each semiotic element is selected by the newsmakers not on a random basis, but on the basis of careful paradigmatic considerations to maximize their dramatic effects. They are webbed together in such a complex way that their strategical use in metaphoric and metonymic significations is not to be easily identified. This effect is achieved by the use of a complex combination of three semiotic, visual and aural elements including: "camera-work" such as fast-zoom, dissolve and fast tilt-up in a row; "lighting" techniques such as counterlight picturings and dark room shots; "sound effect" including the siren of an ambulance and the "howling wind."

At first sight, the siren has a metonymic signification for something urgent which usually turns out to be unfortunate according to "our" "common sense:" "accident," "death," "fire," "crime," and so on. The siren also serves as a metaphoric signifier for referring to something more abstract which seems "undesirable" such as "abnormality." This metaphoric use of the siren, along with the visuals, is then metonymically connected to the "howling wind." The howling wind as an ambience also connotes, in its relation to a scene's context, something undesirable, which may occur in the dark side of life. In sum, as analyzed so far, the eventual effects induced in the visual and aural semiotics of these two scenes are very productive, and this is due to their complex web of semiotic devices including paradigmatic selections, syntagmatic arrangements, and symbolic devices of metaphor and metonymy.

One of the regulars often seen in the homeless stories is street pigeons. Four of the sample stories contain shots of the homeless with street pigeons. For example, in a typical shot of the homeless sitting on the street bench in one of CBS's "Eye On America" episodes (December 23, 1991), a pigeon is seen flying down on the ground just in front of a crippled homeless person on the street. Similarly, one of ABC's "American Agenda" episodes (December 6, 1988) also features a pigeon staggering in front of a homeless person sitting on a street bench. The signification of the "pigeon" here is that the bird has more than a neutral status. It is a metonymic signifier for "the homeless," which now works inter-episodically across the visual narratives about the homeless. The viewers exposed to this kind of "reiteration," have become accustomed to the unfamiliar scenes that have metonymically been transformed into the familiar. In addition, this "pigeon" also has a metaphoric meaning for the homeless while holding metonymic significance. That is, as the homeless are juxtaposed with the bird within the same frame, their status is semiotically relegated to the world of birds. This is, of course, different from a typical movie shot where an ordinary person is feeding the birds around him or her in such places as public squares or riversides.

They're Not Us: Us versus The Homeless

These unfamiliar scenes confirm this: "they are not us." In addition to these images, our basic opposition, Us : Them is also clear in the beginning of most stories. Hartley (1982, p. 116) suggests that the news proceeds on the basic Us : Them opposition in which the former includes the "culture," "nation," "public," "viewer," "family," "newsreader" and "news institution," and the latter, "striker," "foreign dictator," "foreign power," "the weather," "fate," "bureaucracy," and "accessed voice." In addition, he argues that once an individual or topic has been stereotyped it will always be presented in terms of the stereotype (Hartley 1982; Penner and Penner, 1994).

Stories typically begin with questions like "how they ended up on the street" and "how we can treat them now." Above all, as explicitly expressed in anchors' addresses, "During winter storms like that one, we worry most about people who." And what is featured in the above quotation is an initial narrativistic shift of the viewer's attention from the serious aspect of the issue to our common sense (individual vs. issue). The anchors draw our attention to the fact that some people have no place to go in such a cold and stormy winter, which touches our sense of humanity. The mentally ill homeless, for example, should be taken off the streets on the grounds of "our" humanitarian morality, since "leaving them alone (on the streets)" is morally wrong because it "condemns many to a lifetime of unheeded voices and endlessly walking the streets."

The strategy of appealing to our basic sense of humanism is semiotically productive in constructing imagined reality due to the anchor's or reporter's direct mode of address. The form of direct eye-contact address by the anchor/reporter marks the heart of television news narrative's textual strategy. This strategy helps create an imagined, but realistic space of here and now (Berger and Luckmann, 1967, p. 29) in which the temporal and spatial distinction collapses on the part of the viewer. This happens so naturally and unobtrusively that the constructedness of narrative is difficult for the viewer to realize.

On the visual level, the message in the "hanging" box located over the right or the left shoulder of the anchor often contributes to the establishment of Us : Them opposition. This "hanging" box is a common device used in television newsmaking, which provides the viewer with supplementary information by means of symbolic representation which is directly or indirectly connected with the story topic (Morse, 1986, p. 70). In some stories, the anchors stress the fact that homeless people are "without families" before they die or disappear. The oppositions in this way look very transparent to reality, and thus, at the same time, the viewer has a feeling that what will follow "looks like" and "sounds like" (Hartley, 1982, pp. 72–73) a story about some people without families. Therefore typical homeless stories induce the viewer to see how "they" are different from "us."

In the process of Us : Them opposition, however, the verbal (the reporters' voiceover in particular) seems to dominate the visual. The visual presentation appears to have an enslaved life unless its isolated shots are semiotically connected to each other within the overall narrative scheme. The verbal elaboration of differences are often deftly exploited and translated as the cause of the problem itself. The characterization of the homeless' difference, for example, marked by alienation, loneliness and isolation are sometimes displaced with what is commonly implied in more radical terms including "alcohol," "crime," "drugs" and "mental illness." Obviously, sleeping outdoors or standing on the street does not necessarily mean that the homeless are alcoholics or drug addicts.

While the camera captures the graffiti on the wall saying, "God Bless This Home," and the homeless are inside a tunnel below the street, the reporter's voiceover reads, "For the 30 to 40 percent who have some kind of mental illness, many of their families want to help " ("ABC World News," Dec. 8, 1988; "CBS News," Nov. 23, 1994). The verbal presentation here tends to force the arbitrary meaning of the visual to be understood as evidence of what is being said. Through these types of verbal characterizations, the homeless' differences are portrayed as the main cause of the problem. Moreover, even the homeless' personal problems such as "lack of money" or "apathy" are converted into a cause of the problem. In short, the viewers may see symbolically oriented objects as metonymically reminding us of pre-established concepts of their differences. As the viewers have become familiar with their abnormal features shown many times, their clothing, weird behaviors and gestures as well as their dark side are now a metonymic signifier as a whole for their difference. Again, the homeless issue is transformed into an individual family problem and the society becomes the victim.

The Homeless: Voiceless Community

The image of the "problem-maker" is reinforced by the marginalized voices of the homeless. First, the visual appearances of the homeless, even when their voices are accessed, function as a lubricating role for the smooth flow of the narrative. Their voices are oftentimes semiotically stolen, appropriated by the reporter and are devoted to a certain purpose of the narrative. When an unidentified homeless man shown in an extreme close-up shot at a high angle or a close-up of hands receiving pills is uttering something, it is not heard and only functions as an ambient sound. In other words, the chief function of their voices, semiotically lacking in autonomy and thus embedded in the narrative is to grant a credible quality to the textual reality constructed by the reporter's direct address. Even images of aggressive moves to secure and renovate abandoned buildings for their housing ("ABC World News," Feb. 23, 1993) are suppressed and marginalized in the name of "illegal occupation." Second, the "Them" side is always represented by carefully selected individuals who are semiotically exploited only to tell the immediate effects of the issue, that is, "how they feel about being homeless or mentally ill." Third, just as their detailed appearances are hard to discern visually, most of the subjects' faces cannot be distinguished due to superimposed black blobs on them or because of the use of long-distance shots. The implication of this is that they are again not to be identified as autonomous individuals, but only as a collective function that serves as a human lubricant for the slick flow of the narrative as a whole.

The image of professional characters is no exception, as it is also meaningful only within the overall context of the narrative. The professionals' (homeless advocates, government officials, medical doctors, psychiatrists) accessed voices often serve the predictable narrative. Their verbal presentations are readily exnominated as a collective abstract authority. By referring to the federal government, a private foundation, eight cities or authorities as information/action sources, the anchor/reporter appears to be telling the truth about objective and reliable facts. While he or she is given a comparatively favorable semiotic framing , the expert interview scene usually functions as a lead-in role for the opening of the following sequence. It seems that once both the homeless and professional's voices are semiotically deprived of their genuine quality and expression, and their reaction to the issue is restricted, it only tends to corroborate the reporter's control of the narrative.

In addition, no homeless people, even those who are allowed to speak, have been nominated either visually or verbally, whereas the reporter has been visually nominated during the actuality report. There is another practice that is commonly used during the reporter's direct address in actuality sequences. In actuality report scenes, the reporters, at first glance, may seem to participate as character narrators due to their plausible involvement in the scenes with other homeless characters. However, the reporters, by keeping moderate distance between them and other characters featured behind them, in Genette's (1980) words, "Never yield the privilege of the narrative function" (p. 247) to any other and thus "play only a secondary role, which almost always turns out to be a role as observer and witness" (p. 245).

Within the same shot, the optimum framing of the reporter facing the camera at a mid-shot range sharply contrasts to the background scene (behind the reporter) which provides a long-shot of the homeless people with their backs to the camera in low-angle. The optimum framing of the reporter with a slow zoom-in from the medium-distance to medium close-up with good lighting endows his/her status with a natural-looking, rational, neutral and realistic quality. All of these discourse routines of "nomination" (the reporter), "nonnomination" (the homeless) and considerable camera work give the textual reality more of a quality of neutrality, factuality and authority. Finally, the anchor's position always relieves the viewer from the tension accumulated thus far and gives us the impression that he really cares for us, as he is seen sitting and pondering in his chair like Rodin's famous sculptor, "The Thinker" at his studio desk.

Absence of the Real Homeless

In some stories, the narrative's humanistic translation of the issue is also backed up by the reporter's direct address to the camera (seemingly to us) in most of the endings of the stories, where the reporters attribute the major cause of homelessness to personal problems such as the breakdown of the family. Some stories begin with "a recent study" on the issue, which confirms the thesis that the family breakdown is the cause of being homeless. This notion is usually then supported by a follow-up interview with a professional psychiatrist, who stresses the necessity of rebuilding supports for homeless families. To present this thesis, the following sequence introduces to us a real case, a transitional house in Boston, Massachusetts, where a group of homeless families live as a surrogate family and can stay there as long as a year (ABC, December 6, 1988, "American Agenda").

	Video	Audio
1.	ES, LA show a transitional house; decent-looking two-story house.	*REBECCA CHASE* A transitional house in Brockton, Massachusetts,
2.	LS, SA babies and mothers in the room; looks comfortable, cozy and warm.	*REBECCA CHASE* where homeless families can stay as long as a year.

3.	MS, SA woman feeding her baby by window; light coming through window.	Off screen Kathy Maguire (Transitional House Director): We try to strengthen the family wherever that's possible.
4.	MCU, SA Maguire; white woman; white shirt, glasses; TC name.	On screen Kathy Maguire: If that's not possible, then we just try to help people to get a surrogate family.
5.	MLS, SA young women Listening; camera zoom/pan left to reveal another women, a consultant at desk; office setting.	*REBECCA CHASE* Here, people find the kind of that families used to give, whether it's looking for a job,
6.	MS, SA woman looking after baby in walker.	*REBECCA CHASE* taking care of the children,
7.	MCU, SA woman cooking, in profile; camera tilts down to CU hands and eggs being fried; in kitchen.	*REBECCA CHASE* or just someone to talk to.
8.	CU, SA woman in from previous shot.	On screen woman: me crazy if I thought of myself as homeless right now. I like to think of this as my home, and it is.
9.	Dissolve to LS, SA elderly man sitting on street bench; shabby clothing; in street, in front of him, trash-can and pigeon faltering.	*REBECCA CHASE* So, for those who are living on the street, in...
10.	LS, SA man sitting on subway stairs; beside his feet, vinyl bags.	*REBECCA CHASE* subways or in emergency shelters,
11.	Dissolve to LS, HA women baby-sitting in transitional house; light coming through window.	*REBECCA CHASE* the cure is not simply a roof...
12.	MCU, HA woman in back caressing her baby in front leaning against her; good sun-lighting through window.	*REBECCA CHASE* over their heads, but creating substitutes for broken families.
13.	Dissolve to ELS, SA women baby-sitting.	*REBECCA CHASE* That may be more difficult than building houses, but,

14.   Dissolve to MS, SA woman   *REBECCA CHASE*
       in profile holding baby.   just as essential.
       in front in arms while   Rebecca Chase, ABC News,
       standing by window;   Brockton, Massachusetts.
       camera slowly zoom to MCU;
       good-lighting through
       window; warm and cozy.

*ECU(extreme close-up); CU(close-up); MCU(medium close-up); MS(medium shot); MLS(medium long-shot); LS(long shot); ELS(extreme long-shot). HA(high-angle shot); SA(standard angle shot or eye-level); LA(low-angle shot).

This sequence is visually comprised of some routine shots of the inside of the house. These shots reveal babies and kids playing together with their mothers in mostly normal angle and mid-range shots, and two actuality interview scenes in normal angle and (mid) close-ups, which emphasize commonsense family values. No extreme camera work such as extreme close-up, extreme long and high/low-angle shots has been taken in the house. This is a sharp contrast to other typical shots where the homeless are often viewed from weird angles or distances. That is to say, the orientation of the discourse has reached a certain point of resolution that confirms "family values" as its major thesis. Finally, as the reporter is wrapping up the sequence with her voiceover narration that once again stresses the value of family unity as the "cure" to the problem, the visual part presents typical homeless images of those who are on the streets (Shots 9–10). The visual image of these two shots suggests that the voiceless homeless on the street, are not autonomous individuals but a collective, and symbolize the breakdown of the family. In addition, the last shot (Shot 14) just before the anchor's studio report in particular, demonstrates a dramatic effect as it features a woman holding a baby in her arms and looking out the window from inside the transitional house. The initial medium-shot of that woman in normal angle with warm and soft lighting is slowly zoomed in on and becomes an optimum medium close-up. This scene is semiotically very productive in supporting the narrative's temporal but ideological resolution suggested in this sequence. Meanwhile, the structurally oriented issue has been translated into a matter of individual family events rather than a societal issue.

According to Hartley (1982), "Meaning in news-discourse is not only determined by what is there, but also what is absent, not selected, discursively repressed" (p. 117). Therefore, what has to be looked for is not the manifested part of the story, but what is semiotically repressed and silenced. The anchors usually suppress stories when they define the topics by narrowing down the focus. To define the topics in such a way leaves behind the fundamental point of the issue which has to do with the structural causation of the problem. This happens partially because the narrative makes an appeal to the viewer's (supposedly "our") commonsense knowledge and humanitarian sentiment. By turning our attention away from the complex aspect of the issue to its immediate effects in our everyday lives, the narrative gets away with the burden of proof.

In addition, what has not been told is the structural causation of the issue, that is, the socioeconomic and political—cultural problems which are considered a fundamental origin of the problem of homelessness. This absence of structural interrogation is not simply a result of professional negligence, but a matter of ideological practice, which has already been so deeply embedded in our culture that it can also be found in many other forms of social practice.

CONCLUSION

In general, it can be argued that the issue of the homeless has not been viewed in a serious way. Put another way, the structural, difficult nature of the issue has been altered into a soft matter of humanism. During this process, the issue itself, as is often the case, seems to have disappeared, since the narrative has dealt with the issue in such a way that only provides us with some isolated examples to show the problem's immediate effects on the personal level. The major purpose of the visual presentations in particular, seems to be to dramatically portray the homeless as different from us. The visual presentations of the homeless are not allowed to hold any autonomous meanings that could have their repressed and silenced voices be heard in society. Consequently, their individualities as human beings have disappeared while leaving behind only their impersonal collective functions which then serve as a lubricating role for the realistic flow of the narrative. In this way, the narrative has been as successful in mediating the viewer and them as it has been in translating an unfamiliar world into a comprehensible one for the viewer. This achievement has been possible partly due to semiotic exploitations both on the level of the visual and the verbal by means of metaphoric/metonymic transformations of the abstract into the concrete and the concrete into the abstract.

Back to the beginning, the anchor turns his eyes from the monitor and addresses the camera (us) his/her final words. As is always the case, both the first and the final shots are the only ones that are taken in the studio, and since they are the most neutral and objective looking shots in the whole discourse, they warrant the anchor's higher status as a real heterodiegetic camera narrator, compared to other characters including the reporter. Thus, the anchor's gaze functions as an ultimate window through which, in Morse's (1986) words, all other 'views' of the world must be relayed, including the public's view of itself (p. 67). Due to this authoritative, omnipotent and reliable quality of the anchor's position, he is able to comfort the viewer and relieve the tensions accumulated throughout the narrative. His concluding remarks sound as if he were saying to us, "We have some problems out there. But don't worry. I'll take care of them. Everything will be fine. You have a good night."

REFERENCES

Altheide, David L. (1976). *Creating Reality: How TV news distorts events.* Beverly Hills: Sage.

Barthes, Roland (1977). Introduction to the structural analysis of narratives. In R. Barthes, *Image-music-text* (S. Heath, Trans.). New York: The Noonday Press.

Berger, Peter L. and Luckmann, Thomas (1967). *The social construction of reality: A treatise in the sociology of knowledge.* New York: Anchor Books.

Brunsdon, Charlotte and Morley, David (1981). Everyday television: Nationwide. In Tony Bennett, Susan Boyd-Bowman, Colin Mercer and Janet Woollacott, *Popular television and film* (118–141). London: BFI.

Campbell, Richard (1986). *Narrative, myth and metaphor in 60 Minutes: An interpretive approach to the study of television news* (Doctoral dissertation, Northwestern University, 1986). Dissertation Abstracts International, 47, 2783A.

Campbell, Richard (1987). Securing the middle ground: Reporting formulas in 60 Minutes. *Critical Studies in Mass Communication*, 4(4), 325–350.

Campbell, Richard and Reeves, Jimmie L. (1989). Covering the homeless: The Joyce Brown story. *Critical Studies in Mass Communication*, 6(1), 21–42.

Chatman, Benjamin S. (1978). *Story and discourse: Narrative structure in fiction and film.* Ithaca: Cornell University Press.

Eco, Umberto (1976). *A theory of semiotics. Bloomington*, IN: Indiana University Press.

Eitzen, Stanley D. (1989). *Society's Problems: Sources and Consquences* (4th. ed.). Boston: Allyn and Bacon.

Fiske, John (1991). For cultural interpretation: A study of the culture of homelessness. *Critical Studies in Mass Communication*, 8(4), 455–474.

Foucault, Michel (1979). *Discipline and punish: The birth of the prison* (A. Sheridan, Trans.). New York: Vintage Books. (Original work published 1975)

Genette, Gerard (1980). *Narrative discourse: An essay in method* (J. E. Lewin, Trans.). Ithaca: Cornell University Press. (Original work published 1972).

Gitlin, Todd (1980). *The whole world is watching: Mass media in the making and unmaking of the new left.* Berkeley: University of California Press.

Gitlin, Todd (1986). Introduction: Looking through the screen. In Todd Gitlin (Ed.), *Watching television: A Pantheon guide to popular culture* (3–41). New York: Pantheon Books.

Hall, Stuart (1981). The determinations of news photographs. In Susan and Jonathan Young (Eds.), *The manufacture of news: Social problems, devianceand the mass media* (rev.ed., 226–243). London: Constable.

Hartley, John (1982). *Understanding News*. London: Methuen.

Hartley, John and Montgomery, Mark (1985). Representations and relations: Ideology and power in press and TV news. In Dijk Teun Adrianus van (Ed.), *Discourse and communication: New approaches to the analysis of mass media discourse and communication* (233–269). Berlin: Walter de Gruyter.

Hopper, Karl and Baumohl, Michael (1994). Rethinking Advocacy. *American Behavioral Scientist*, 37(4), 522–534.

Kozloff, Sara R. (1987). Narrative theory and television. In Robert C. Allen (Ed.), *Channels of discourse: Television and contemporary criticism* (42–73). Chapel Hill: The University of North Carolina Press.

Kozol, Jonathan (1988). Distancing the homeless. *The Yale Review*, 77(2), 153–167.

Leach, Ronald E. (1976). *Culture and communication: The logic by which symbols are connected.* Cambridge: Cambridge University Press.

Metz, Christian (1974). *Film language: A semiotics of the cinema.* New York: Oxford University Press.

Morse, Margaret (1986). The television news personality and credibility: Reflections on the news in transition. In T. Modleski (Ed.), *Studies in Entertainment: Critical approaches to mass culture* (55–79). Bloomington, IN: Indiana University Press.

Penner, M. and Penner, S. (1994). Publicizing, Politicizing, and Neutralizing Homelessness. *Communication Research*, 21(6), 766–781.

Pietila, Victor (1992). Beyond the news story: News as discursive composition. *European Journal of Communication*, 7(1), 37–67.

Ropers, Richard H. (1988). *The invisible homeless: A new urban ecology.* New York: Insight Books.

Rossi, Peter H. (1994). Troubling Families. *American Behavioral Scientist*, 37(3), 342–395.

Ryan, William (1976). *Blaming the victim* (rev. ed.). New York: Vintage Books.

Seiter, Ellen (1987). Semiotics and television. In R. C. Allen (Ed.), *Channels of discourse* (17–41). Chapel Hill: The University of North Carolina Press.

Silverman, Kaja (1983). *The subject of semiotics*. New York: Oxford University Press.

Snow, David; Anderson, Leon and Koegel, Paul (1994). Distorting Tendencies in Research on the Homeless. *American Behavioral Scientist*, 37(4), 461–475.

Television News Index and Abstracts (1985–1994) published by Vanderbilt University.

Zettl, Herbert (1992). *Television production handbook* (5th ed.). Belmont, CA: Wadsworth Publishing.

Chapter 9

Homelessness:
The Other as Object

Eric Mark Kramer and Soobum Lee

BIRTH OF THE STRANGER

The human animal is a very sociable creature. Indeed, it has become generally accepted (Lorenz, 1983; Geertz, 1973; Pribram, 1971; Kramer, 1992a) that the development of the human nervous system demands sociocultural interaction (communicative stimulation). The nurturing of natural abilities is precisely why no two clones would be identical. As Clifford Geertz (1973) put it, "a cultureless human being would probably turn out to be not an intrinsically talented though unfulfilled ape, but a wholly mindless and consequently unworkable monstrosity" (p. 68). Geertz, along with DeVore (1965), argues that *Homo Sapiens* literally have a social brain.

But what is the nature of social for this creature? In his classic works *The Naked Ape* (1967) and *The Human Zoo* (1969), Desmond Morris argues that, more than 10,000 years ago our Ice Age ancestors' brains were already as big and highly developed as ours are today (Morris, 1969, p. 13). In fact recent evidence from northern Germany and Siberia indicates that the social brain extends much further back in time to at least half a million years. Over nearly all of that time, the species lived in groupings of no more than 150 individuals. Their territory was vast. When a group became too big a splinter group would go off to establish its own home range.

It was not until after the last great Ice Age that larger settlements of a more permanent nature began to appear. After millennia of learning to be cooperative, probably through the "long hunting apprenticeship" of the species, the cultivation of two plants, barley and wheat (and a little later rice and maze), led to a surplus of food. The invention of irrigation and the storage of surplus demanded settlement which led to a new age of urban population density and specialization.

Permanent settlement is closely related to a perspectival attitude which is characterized by an emergent sense of self and a new sense of not only space but more importantly time; depth space and depth time (Gebser, 1949/1985; Kramer, 1992a). To be a farmer, the human animal had to "stretch his far-seeingness beyond anything he had previously experienced," certainly beyond the time frame of planning a hunt (Morris, 1969, p. 17). Not only did this new, temporally expanded horizon emerge, but another barrier to full fledged urban life was breached, the loss of tribal ("local") identity. As the social environment expanded, the self shrank and solidified into more of a self-contained individual than is evinced by un- and preperspectival tribal humans. The urban world gave birth to the stranger. Perspectival consciousness is characterized by functional fragmentation, merit, and instrumental value.

BELONGING

The point in this chapter is to ask what the phenomenon of the homeless has to say to us about the larger society that created it. The existence of the "home-less" tells us very much about the society that gave birth to such a designation. From the beginning, in-grouping and out-grouping are shown to be an essential process for social animals including humans. Stories of outcasting, that is of individuals being singled out and forced to leave the group womb are primor-dial. Three Biblical examples may suffice. The Archangel Lucifer (the Enlight-ened One) was cast out of heaven. The source of his great suffering (the greatest of all possible sufferings) was precisely his separation from his beloved divine companion. Campbell and Mayers (1988) put it this way, "The worst of the pains of hell, insofar as hell has been described, is the absence of the Beloved. So how does Satan sustain the situation in hell? By the memory of the echo of God's voice, when God said, 'Go to hell.' That is a great sign of love" (p. 204). The pain of love is in separation. Similarly, Adam and Eve were driven out of paradise into time (mortality) and space, and later Cain was driven out into the larger world where he would be marked as a wandering stranger. These stories indicate that for such a social creature as human, banishment is the worst of all possible sanctions. It also indicates the perspectival nature of the Judeo-Christian culture which is characterized by a correlation between dissociation and the consolidation of all divinity into a single "royal" god ("king of kings") (Gebser, 1949/1985; Innis, 1950; Ong, 1982). Perspectivism is characterized by a new sense of distance (not only spatial but also social and semantic) which isolates and thereby gives birth to monadology (individualism).

In the past official banishment was to the "outside." Now it is to the "inner" sanctum of prison (Foucault, 1975/1977). But in both cases, official banishment, by definition, reinforces the claim of ownership the group (the state for instance) has over the individual. Under official group sanction one is seen as part of a larger polis, to be a "charge of the state." To be marginal presumes an associa-tion with centralized power. But the peripheral condition of the homeless is not even recognized by the group. The group is not responsible for meeting their basic needs as it is with a prisoner. The modern homeless is literally no body because they do not appear in the collective memory of the group as a bureau-cratic entity. They are "invisible" in the sense that Ralph Ellison (1952) uses the term. No one cares, or takes responsibility for them.

Outcasting presupposes the rule of social norms and mores. To be a member means to follow the ways of the clan. To be social means to identify with a group. An identifiable group exists as such because its parameters are limited by the Other; by space, or another group(s). Being outcast or homeless among the insiders must be rationalized by the insiders. The insiders see themselves as rational and caring individuals who, through willing participation maintain a system that is also believed to be rational and caring. So, when confronted with such a wretched situation, the insiders must attribute the situation to the behavior and attitudes of the victim and not themselves or the system which affords them their insider identity. This way the insiders can feel good about their community and themselves. Thus, homelessness must be the effect of sinful behavior on the part of the homeless person. It may be the sin of gluttony (insatiable addiction to drugs), sloth, arrogance or pride (a refusal to conform), wrath (the homeless are that way because they are dangerous), and so forth. A necessary condition for group membership is a group, and a necessary condition for a group to exist is the existence of the Other, be it nature, other animal tribes, or other human groups. A necessary condition for identity to exist is difference. The inside requires the outside and vice versa. Seeing the outcast makes one feel good to be secure within the normative system of interaction. While the parasite is disposed, it is the parasite that enables the host's identity to exist and to enjoy its regal status. The host owes its very existence to the parasite, who by the very of act of taking aims from the host makes him or her a moral being. The parasite is the host's savior. To be a hostage is to be held against one's will by one's own morality. The homeless face is personal and painful to the mighty host because the homeless face demonstrates morality and is an inescapable moral face—the savior is also a judge.

Belonging is perhaps the most important sense for any social creature. It is so strong that Socrates chose suicide over living beyond the walls of Athens amidst the barbarians. To be outcast is in many ways worse than death for in death, one may still be part of the extended group, a martyr or even an ancestor worthy of worship. One will be missed because one belonged. But the very nature of groupness has at least three variants based on the three different consciousness structures or worlds elucidated by Jean Gebser (1949/1985).

THREE KINDS OF SOCIAL WORLDS

It is important at this point to elucidate the three primary consciousness structures evident throughout history and across cultures. Consciousness structure is manifested by differing valences of spatial and temporal awaring. The three structures are identifiable by the number of dimensions they manifest. After years of rigorous research into all manners of civilizational expressions including art, architecture, dance, music, philosophies, sciences, mythologies, religions, and so forth, Gebser (1949/1985) delineated three essentially different consciousness structures/worlds.

A quick note is necessary here to indicate Gebser's bracketing of Cartesian dualism. Gebser does not assume, in hypothetical fashion, a world and then awareness of it as a dualistic realism. There is no difference between perception and what is perceived and if there were to be such a difference it would be impossible to know. At least two decades before the deconstructive critique of this dualism, Gebser argued that to be logically consistent, all that is what we are aware of. To claim that there is some hidden reality behind or underneath mere perception is tantamount to hypothetical thinking. Since he was not attempting to replicate or experimentally test any culture, he chose to use a method later called descriptive-analytic by Michel Foucault (1969/1972). History in this sense is not gone but embedded. The now has a sedimentary quality. Gebser, like others, attempted to analyze the nonoriginary origin of sense. This method was independently devised by three different German thinkers. Friedrich Nietzsche (1887/1967) called it genealogy, Edmund Husserl (1952/1970) called it archeological phenomenology, (the investigation into the *Selbstverstandlichkeiten* or what is handed down as tradition, obvious or taken for granted by the intersubjective community—historically conditioned consciousness or always already world horizon) and Wilhelm Dilthey (1988) called it critical hermeneutics.

The key is to take context (including the "past") into account and to presume that artifacts can be "read." Artifacts hide nothing. They manifest the capacities, motives, wishes, beliefs, and wills of those who made them. In short, what Peter says about Paul may or may not be true, but what Peter says is directly available and it tells me much about Peter such as his skill at articulation, his interests, his feelings about Paul, and so forth.

Using Eric Kramer's (1997) theory of Dimensional Accrual/Dissociation, which he developed by expanding Gebser's work on comparative civilizations, one can begin to understand the phenomenon of homelessness as a uniquely perspectival expression.

Magic World

The magic world is univalent, one dimensional (Gebser, 1949/1985). According to Kramer (1997) this is manifested in a world where there is no difference, no separation between the signifier and the signified—no consciousness of space or time be they semantic or physical. Magic communication is idolic (Kramer, 1997). Incantation is magical speech. If writing exists at all, it is as magic "spell." Writing, which is a form of dissociation from bodily limitations and action, is a sign of an emergent mythic world. But in the magic world, words and deeds are identical. When writing does exist it is in the form of highly motivated pictographic images which are purely emotional, not analytical. A picture "of a thing," and the thing "depicted." There is no such thing as magical representation. In the magic world there is no "figural" ambivalence. Bivalent two dimensionality is characteristic of the mythic structure, which is discussed below, not the magic world.

The homeless face is inescapable. Ethics are not analytical but primordially incarnate. The smell of urine, the glassy eyes, the grimy fingers exhibit manifest morality—the bodily imperative that cannot be denied. The magic aspect insists that I and He are both human and that human quality cannot be escaped. Even in the act of turning away, ignoring, or rationalizing in all such efforts the homeless Other is the presumed source of the need to ignore, turn away from, or rationalize about. The homeless Other demands identify—for me to identify "with." When we are face to face the communication of identify and morality is instantaneous. It is always already. The message is "too fast" to dodge responsibility. Magic is spaceless and timeless. The imperative is prereflective.

For magic humans, if one steals a magic amulet (a crystal, sacred object, lucky rabbit's foot, *ad infinitum*) one has literally stolen the power. There is no "difference." If I steal an idol, I have stolen "god" and must suffer the most severe punishment. The magic world is not analytical in mood but rather emotional through and through. Care (will/intent) is a powerful force that underlies all efforts at communication so that in all cultures a magic dimension is present. An idol is more than "merely" a statue, or "merely" a work of art. The magic world is not spatial. Gods and spirits are not somewhere else such as on a mountain top or an even more dissociated heavenly realm. Therefore, reductionism, which is a spatial concept, is senseless. By contrast, reductionism is the very source of knowledge and sense in the perspectival world (Kramer, 1997).

The magic clan moves like a flock of birds or school of fish. There is no "personal choice." It is a tight unit of intertwined "members." Members is in quotation marks because there is no separation that would afford the spatial notion of "in." There is no "membership" "in" the magical group. For magic people, belonging is not contingent upon joining. "In-stitutionalization" does not exist. Officialdom emerges later with hierarchical, perspectival life. Belonging is eternal; before and after birth. The group and the member are identical. One does not "identify" with one's group in the sense the word "identify" is often used by perspectival people. Instead, the group and individual are the same. The blood of each is the same as all. Separation is practically unthinkable. Of the many scholars (Jung, Eliade, Bataille, Freud, among others) who have tried to describe magical awaring, Gebser's effort is presented here.

The concept *pars pro toto* (the part for the whole) is at the same time always a *totum pro parte* (the whole for the part)—where, curiously and without any probable etymological connection, totum suggests by chance totem. This interchageability goes even further: the rule may be changed into *pars pro parte* (a part for a part), and in this sense even into *totum pro toto* (all for all), without losing its validity. The effectiveness of such interchangeability is perhaps most strikingly demonstrated in the vicarious sufferings experienced in the course of ritual sacrifice. Exchange (*Tausch*)—in the realm of magic—is by no means deception (*Tauschaung*); it is rather the expression of the genuine validity of "equals" (Gebser, 1949/1985, p. 50).

Banishment appears only in mythic two dimensional cultures, and even then it is the most severe of all sanctions. An example of mythic banishment is "official" excommunication.

Mythic World

The mythic unperspectival world is bivalent, two dimensional. A nascent sense of separation begins to appear. This separation is a necessary condition for reflective thought, critique, and taking a discursive position as in ideological distinction. A reflective awareness of culture and nature begins to emerge so that both become available as independent realms for investigation (Kramer, 1992a). A rudimentary self emerges which is disruptive of the magic unitary clan. Myths are of heroic deeds, and the egoistic heroes of such stories are often problematic for the group as was Achilles in the *Iliad*, Odysseus in the *Odyssey*, Gilgamesh in the *Epic of Gilgamesh*, Jesus, and Buddha. They all present a nonconformist mind of their own.

Mythic communication is ambivalent, symbolic (Kramer, 1997). Figures of speech emerge as such. A separation appears between the literal and the figural. Various polarities such as message/intent, body/mind, primary/secondary qualities begin to emerge. Myths are written with metaphors. Language and speech begin to exist as a second order metaphor estranged from native. The identity of the signifier and the signified begins to weaken. If I steal a crucifix there may still be a strong emotional association with the object but the owner is not likely to say that I have stolen his or her god. Despite the emotional attachment, the owner knows that the object is just a symbol of faith. Symbolic communication presupposes a nascent separation which enables one phenomenon to stand in for another. But this substitution is not totally arbitrary, not totally dissociated. Metaphors can seem inappropriate. Drama emerges in the mythic world as the unifying ritual splits into the play and the audience. Theatrical distance emerges. Yet, if the audience cannot emotionally identify with the characters, then the magic of the theater fails. Complete objectifying dissociation requires a third dimension.

Perspectival World

Modernity is essentially perspectival. However, the magical and mythical modes of being are not extinct but coexist. The perspectival world is predominantly trivalent, three dimensional. It's mode of communication is signalic-codal. Perspectival consciousness presents depth space which is empty and in between things. Here emerges empiricism as thingism and alienation. The signifier and signified become accidentally associated (or more properly, dissociated). Language becomes completely arbitrary as does social identity. Dissociated analysis displaces emotional attachment. Communication is enhanced by codal processing as in the computer language of 0,1. The arbitrary perspectival world is characterized by a kind of freedom from community commitments and traditional parameters. Caste systems disappear and individual civil rights take on central importance. A pauper may become president. Identity is set adrift. Also what is made possible in the perspectival world is the exploration, mapping, codification (as in Newtonian physics), and colonization of space.

Ego hypertrophy is evident as the group disintegrates. Instead of a community, aggregation (of individuals) becomes the norm. The sphere of caring is truncated to the personal agenda of the modern perspectival individual. The individual tends to be on their own. Responsibility that was shared by the magic group now falls onto the slim shoulders of the individual. Rational meritocracy and democratic institutions displace tradition and irrational favoritism (unconditional clan loyalty). Analytics displaces an irrational commitment to superstitious ways. To care becomes inefficient. Mobility of all sorts (including progress) and measurement (the spatialization of all of life) mark the modern perspectival world. Relationships become instrumental and short lived. They last only until their mission is accomplished. All of life takes on a linear process of goal attainment. Efficiency becomes the super-value and speed is of the essence. Personal relationships become ever-smaller in scope. The magic tribe shrinks to the extended family which shrinks to the nuclear family which in turn is split.

THE MODERN STRANGER

The rise of ever larger and more permanent settlements led to sectoralization and specialization. The oldest known town arose at Jericho over 8,000 years ago but it was not the first fully urban settlement. The first empirical inter-city coordination, enabled by writing and specialized administrators emerged in Sumer, between five and six thousand years ago. Here, was born the first citizen or "super-tribesman" who "no longer knew personally each member of his community" (Morris, 1969, p. 18). According to Morris (1969):

It was this change, the shift from the personal to the impersonal society, that was going to cause the human animal its greatest agonies in the millennia ahead. As a species we were not biologically equipped to cope with a mass of strangers masquerading as members of our tribe. As a result of the artificiality of the inflation of human social life to the super-tribal level, it became necessary to introduce more elaborate forms of controls to hold the bulging communities together. The enormous material benefits of super-tribal life had to be paid for in discipline. (pp. 18–19)

Thus was born the need for law and complex ordination. Writing, the self, and text herald the emergence of a new world. All the major world religions emerge as transpersonal systems of law that are, to use Walter Ong's term "interiorized," by the development of sacred texts including the *Code of Hammurabi,* the *Torah,* the *Vedas,* the *Bible,* the *Analects of Confucius,* the *Koran,* and so forth (Ong, 1982, p. 178). The spiritual realm consolidates into a single Godhead, personality and judge. Writing replaced oral communication in ontic and power status.

Morris comes to the same conclusion as the great scholars of human interchange and communication Patrick Geddes (1915), Gebser (1985), and Lewis Mumford (1961). Mumford, Gebser, Geddes, and later Harold Innis (1950) and Ong (1982), concerned themselves with the dissociative aspect of increased population density and the rise of urban life. What Innis (1950) called "empire," Morris called the "super-tribe." Several major scholars agree that the shift from orality to writing created a "transpersonal," or virtual abstract "reality" (Gebser, 1949/1985; Sapir, 1921; Cassirer, 1946; Wallas, 1914; Innis, 1950; Becker, 1949; Ong, 1982). Ong (1982) has referred to this shift as the "technologizing of the word." It amounts to a completely new attitude (in Husserlian terms) or mood (Kramer, 1997). As Edwyn Bevan (1921) argued, the monarchical powers of Egypt, Persia, China, India and Rome were literally and essentially products of writing. In the urban world to be true and real is to be *literal* not figural. There are "figures of speech," which are ambivalent as compared with written law. Gebser (1949/1985) agreed with Edward Sapir (1949) that oral expression has a "latent luxuriance" and is an outlet for intense emotion more than intellectual discipline. The song became disciplined speaking, because it was too contingent, too ephemeral, became fixed in writing. Writing is not musical. According to Ong (1982), "Oral discourse has commonly been thought of even in oral milieus as weaving or stitching—*rhapsoidein,* to 'rhapsodiz,' basically means in Greek 'to stitch songs together'" (p. 13). According to Gebser (1949/1985), this is the essentially magical quality of speech (p. 52, 62, 106, 250–251, 348), and in fact Ong's phrase "oral discourse" is incongruent because the magic and mythic worlds of the muse and mouth are not discursive but incantatory. But the urban world is in Gebser's (1949/1985) terms "perspectival," individualistic, and mental-rational (p. 18, 61, 252, 255–259, 385, 429). The urban world gave rise to linear discourse, a form of speech which was competitive and temporally fragmented with dialectics splitting conversation into formalized debate. The three temporal aspects of debate were categorized by Aristotle as forensic, which is concerned with things of the past, epidectic, which is concerned with the present, and deliberative, which is concerned with future plans of action. This new mode of being stressed individual "positions" and confrontation.

The late modern world is marked by mass anonymity on one hand and hypertrophic egoism on the other (Gebser, 1949/1985, p. 22, 34, 153, 154, 158, 262, 357, 358, 531, 537). It is not adequate to discuss this difference in terms of individualism versus collectivism because the term collectivism means to collect individuals into an aggregate. This misses the fundamental sense of tribal "we" which is an "enmeshment" or "intertwining" (Gebser, 1949/1985, p. 48, 50, 52, 109, 348). The tribal human being is not only intertwined with the other "members" of the extended self (tribe) but with all of the "surrounding," so-called "external" environment ("nature"). What appears with the modern discipline of narrative logic is articulated by Erich Kahler (in *The Inward Turn of Narrative*, 1973) and Erich Neumann (in *The Origins and History of Consciousness*, 1954). The modern world is preoccupied with the self and text, which tends to be the articulation of inner, personal issues. Neumann argues that it is a move toward a self-conscious, highly personal, interiority (also see Gebser, 1949/1985, p. 11, 273, 350, 405, 468). This modern form of consciousness appears as individual intentionality. It is, as many so-called postmodern thinkers have argued, a consequence of writing. As populations grew, the self shrank. In the face of expanding space and populations of strangers oral cultures began to fade because orality could not cope with the distances involved the ordination of larger collectives. The impersonal letter gives birth to the bureaucracy and expanded power-organization. That is, power abstracted from the immediate here and now, power that requires communication beyond earshot.

This transpersonal world is the city. And it is here that anonymity and ego-hypertrophy (the "status seekers" to recall Vance Packard, 1961) come into being. The loss of direct personal contact, which marks the tribal milieu, was replaced by an essentially specialized and competitive world order. Here is born the impersonal "mob," the prototypical mass (Nietzsche, 1886/1967; Gebser, 1949/1985). For the first time in human history most of the people in one's social environment were strangers. The extended (tribal) self recoiled in the face of others that one could not identify with. Under such conditions, the social bond is greatly weakened. The competitive nature of in-group/out-group relations infects the city which is comprised of various sub-groups ("tribes") which spontaneously emerge due to the human need to belong to a group of meaningful size, where one belongs and has an identity.

The city is the place where most people are strangers to each other. It is not a village milieu. The most important difference between the city and the village is the sense of self as a member of an intimate group. In the village, personal knowledge is adequate and the personal nature of everyday intercourse generates an entirely different kind of interaction. As Morris (1969) has experimentally demonstrated, if a person feigns a collapse and lays in a thoroughfare of a village, the individual is immediately attended to by others. But if the same person pretends to be in need of aid by laying on a sidewalk in a major city, literally hundreds of persons will avoid that person as if they were invisible and go about their own personal agendas. The person laying on the sidewalk may only be attended to when specialized "officials" such as police arrive to investigate. In a village, such fragmentation as specialized "helpers/investigators" does not exist. Instead, anyone and everyone immediately stops to see what is wrong and to aid the individual. This is why Marshal McLuhan's notion that modern communications technologies will render a "global village" has been rejected by Daniel Bell (1973), Zbigniew Brzezinski (1970), Herman Kahn and Norbert Wiener (1967). In fact, Gebser's (1949) work, which laid the ground for much current communication and identity theory based on a spacio-temporal manifold, rejected McLuhan's "happy positivism" even before it was enunciated.

Rather than a global village, what is emerging is a global city. The difference is essential. The ideas of participation, involvement, trust, reciprocity, intimacy, and belonging, are central to the difference. In a village all others are, to use a phrase from Jean Paul Sartre "authentic."

THE MODERN WORLD AS A NECESSARY CONDITION FOR HOMELESSNESS

The modern perspectival attitude promotes the contradictory position that it values value-freedom. This ideological absurdity presents various adumbrations of delusion such as detachment, disinterest, and the principle of equivalencies applied to everything including human beings. But perhaps this absurdity is not delusional but rather a fairly clumsy rhetoric motivated by a desire to escape critique and "accountability." The claim to objectivity and value-freedom is, as Walter Benjamin (1928/1968) said over 50 years ago, either incredibly naive, incredibly cynical, or plainly incompetent (p. 95). Cynicism is the ultimate expression of uncaring. It is unique to the cosmopolitan mental-rational individual.

In the modern "value-free world," everyone and everything is equal, in fact identical clones. But this is not magical emotional identification. Rather, perspectivity analytically reduces everything, not to each other, but to some completely different (dead) stuff which is incapable of caring. Disintegration of the body via perspectival atomism is manifested as physicalism and behaviorism. In an absolutist proclamation reminiscent of the Pythagorean claim that "all is number," the modern metaphysics essentially argues that all is matter. Everything, including people are piles of essentially identical atoms. Whether one ascribe to causal or probabilistic epistemology, the logical result of physicalism is the same, the equation of everything with everything else. There can be no qualitative differences, only quantitative ones. Some piles have more atoms than others. Consciousness is defined out of existence as subjective nonsense even though only the synthetic activity of mind makes sense. Caring, belonging, trusting, and involvement are all ridiculed as ambiguous "feminine traits." They defy quantification and must therefore not really exist.

Since everything is dead atoms in a ninety-nine percent void, there can be no ethics. The necessary conditions for the existence of an ethical being are not recognized by physical behaviorism. Value judgments are defined *a priori* as subjective nonsense. Therefore, technological and other kinds of projects cannot be critically assessed in ethical terms. The value of the project cannot be discussed and debated. Only that which is quantifiable is real. Only falsifiable empirical statements have any meaning. This rhetorical trick of physicalism however, has not enabled it to out run reflection. It succeeds because of the political dimension it presents. Physicalism is violent and violating. It "takes command."

Physicalism and empiricism define a world wherein critique is no more than invalid opinion. This dominating metaphysics attempts to inoculate itself from consciousness (reflection). Without consciousness, the world functions as automata. Free will and responsibility are abolished. The universe runs on auto pilot; "god's will" in Cartesian terms or the "great chain of causation" according to Aquinas. Progress cannot be helped because of its manifest destiny. Value is reduced to instrumental utility. What is valuable is what achieves the desired goal. The fact that goals are desired, are emotional phenomena, is ignored. The fact that various hypocrisies and contradictions abound is overcome by shear will-to-power. The triumph of physicalism is not that the rhetoric it deploys protects it from any and all possible criticism. It does not debate. Rather, like all dominating philosophies it's rhetoric is but a veneer that covers the structure of power, a thin irrational rationalization. Physicalism (including cause-effect, stimulus-response behaviorism and empiricism) is an absurd metaphysical philosophy. It is absurd because it is a philosophy that claims that philosophy (thinking) does not exist accept as ink on paper. Empiricist literally have no ideas.

Ethics presupposes conscious reflection and choice, not material predetermination. Ethics presumes human being. In the modern physicalistic world, meaning is not real. Neither is quality or ideas or feelings. Interest in material production and concentration of power has promoted this antihumanistic ideology because it disables ethical reflection. Scientism serves the purpose of demanding the universe. As the highest authority, the logic of material science is used to justify disinterested social organization which reduces everything including people to resource base. According to scientism, only science can answer questions with any accuracy, validity, and/or consistency. Only the scientific method can resolve human questions. The philosophical corollary to the ideology of scientism is positivism with its verifiability principle. Moral and ethical questions are senseless. This is the basis of what several scholars including Max Weber (1905/1958) and Husserl (1952/1970) have called the crisis of modern Europe. Incidentally, this crisis is not limited to the insatiable demands and devaluating sentiments of the human sciences but also the physical sciences and their engineering derivatives because they too are human activities.

Because the modern sciences, in principle, ignore value judgments, the great (or even mundane) human questions cannot be seriously addressed. Questions of good and bad, right and wrong are deemed senseless. In such a world, only power is real. But, this is a false rhetoric because desires, values, passions, and wants remain at the core of the world. Because of this principle of devaluation, science becomes the most exploitable of all forms of knowledge, presumably beyond good and evil (to real Nietzsche). For instance, one can create a nuclear bomb but one cannot ask the question is it good to create a nuclear bomb? As a strict technician who flees from philosophical nonsense, who flees from consciousness and will, one becomes the most docile of all prostitutes whose tactile sense embraces all suitors equally. In Part Six (We Scholars) of *Beyond Good and Evil*, Nietzsche cautions against those positivists who scorn the personal and redeem us from our selves; those positivists who denounce as negative the passions and will. They reserve the highest honor of truth as salvific neutrality manifested as disinterested, detachment. The great leap forward amounts to the glorious *caput mortuum* of those primitive subjective fictions, virtue and caring.

The objective man who no longer scolds or curses as the pessimist does, the scholar in whom the scientific instinct, after thousand fold total and partial failure, for once comes to full bloom, is certainly one of the most precious instruments there are: but he belongs in the hand of one who is mightier. He is only an instrument—he is not an "end in himself". And the objective man is in fact a mirror: accustomed to submitting to whatever wants to be known, lacking any other pleasure than that provided by knowledge, by "mirroring"—he waits until something comes along and then gently spreads himself out, so that not even the lightest footsteps and the fluttering of ghostly beings shall be lost on his surface and skin. Whatever still remains to him of his "own person" seems to him accidental, often capricious, more often disturbing: so completely has he become a passage and reflection of forms and events not his own (Nietzsche, 1886/1972, sec. 207, p. 115).

Disinterested science, as Nietzsche pointed out, would be not merely a willess mirror but a masturbating mind, a self-polishing mirror that gained all its ecstasy from reflecting whatever happened to accidentally appear before it. Under such conditions, the hypertrophic ego displays itself as a pure self beyond good and evil, a god. This would be the triumph of W. Leibniz' windowless monad, the perfection of willess knowledge. The dream is to aspire to become the passive observer of mere mortal contortions, the ultimate voyeur whose transparency lets pass all information equally.

But of course this dream of being absolutely careless, is a ridiculously dystopia ideology. It is absurd because the egoism of being above valuation, of having no perspective (omniscience) betrays the most narcissistic of perspectives. Yet, one must ask how it is that it should come to pass that the highest virtue, the most noble of all aspirations is to become utterly careless and without will or directional consciousness (perspective). This grand transfiguration and redemption amounts to a denial of human awareness and the possibility that there might be any value to anything including human beings. This interpretation, this ideology Nietzsche (1887/1974) would elsewhere call the stupidest of all interpretations, because it would be one of the poorest in (Sec. 373, p. 335). The problem is not that the scientific interpretation of the world an inaccurate interpretation, one where the external world is not closely mimicked in perception, an unknowable anyway, but because the scientific interpretation is the least creative of all and like other dogmas, it demands a monopoly on truth. The drama of life, the great fears, daring and passions are reduced by the physicalist's watch phrase merely, or really. Love and hate are merely biochemistry and really neuronetworking.

But science and technology are tricksters. They are not so disinterested as they seem, but only very selective in their rhetoric. The method (tool) and the hand have been dissociated in the interest of creating what Roland Barthes (1957/1972) has called the alibi (p. 121). The objectifying tool and the intent are separated so that responsibility can be avoided. The arbitrariness, or unknowable intent, works to the advantage of the sign and ideology maker. He or she can always feign innocence and insist that that is not what I meant even though it is what they meant. Only those who care can be responsible. But the objective observer claims the ability, right, and even duty to merely reflect. Science and technology are the most powerful forces of socio-cultural change today. They constitute the most intense and effective expressions of desire. Desire to conquer the entire world, to predict and control all forces, domesticating them and bending them to the will of the controller, the one that is mightier. The industrial magician. Magic, make, mechanism machine, Germanic *Macht* (power), and *Moegen* (to want), and might all share the same root mag (h) (Gebser, 1949/1985, p. 46). Method serves the mighty. Because of their power to modify the world, desire seeks out technique to achieve its goals. Science proves most useful. The dissociation between the tool and the intending hand is the hallmark of modernity. The modern world values detachment in all epistemological projects from pure science to professional journalism. Objectifying the Other is the mark of the true truthsayer, the modern sophisticate who has raised him or herself above emotion and engagement. They are, like corporate entitles—totally systematic. Such is the ideal of the modern urban mind. Cool efficiency and blind balance and no to hold responsible. It's the system's fault. This is the perspectival version of the devil made me do.

VALUABLE PEOPLE AND THE INVISIBLE

Value itself is self-evident in the ways technology marks the face of the earth and modifies social organization. Those with technical skills are the most valuable to the passionate (entrepreneurs, dictators, saviors, movers and shakers, in a word magicians). By virtue of their ability to make things, technicians are assured a privileged place within the social structure. They are directed, coordinated, supported, in a word managed by transcending interests such as greed for power. This has always been the case from the time of magicians and wizards to prophets and engineers. Value is utility. In so far as a person is highly exploitable, they have value. Thus, students struggle to become educated at their own expense so that they will be valuable to employers. They make great and lengthy efforts to accumulate the various skills that they can then sell. Those who do well are big fish. The basis of this ideological prejudice is rooted in the instinctual drive to reproduce. The alpha males, the powerful bread winners are selected for by females who want assurances that their off spring will be secure. The logic of instinct manifested as the sex drive grounds the rationalizations for hierarchies. The interesting thing about the modern ideology is that it justifies the exercise of unequal power by promoting the idea that all is equal. Everything is equally available for domination and exploitation.

Under these conditions, the Cartesian dualism between skills and the person who "possesses them" is erased. The modern system of material production renders identities by equating people with their exploitable skills. Skills or talents that do not lend themselves to assimilation and exploitation are deemed worthless. Thus, the ability to think critically is not valued. In fact it is often regarded as an obstacle to the project of acquisition and concentration of power. By the criteria of the modern system, identity is manifest utility. What are you? I am a doctor, a welder, a mason, a computer programmer, and so on. People do not sell their skills or labor, but rather they sell themselves. The person and what is exploitable about them are identical. In the past, people were identified with their skills to the extent that their names indicated their craft. Thus we have Mr. Potter, Mr. Hammer, Mr. Porter, Mr. Goldsmith, Mr. Smith. But these skills where in the service of the craftsman. The dialectic of the enlightenment which separated the hand from the mind in the form of modern management did not yet exist (Horkheimer and Adorno, 1972). Today the system defines one. We no longer define ourselves. Identity is more dissociated and controlled from afar than ever before.

The Cartesian dualism which inoculated the ideology of exploitation for so long by making it appear that a person sold only their skills while the self was something different, has been exposed as a false rhetoric. If we take seriously the behavioral tenet that we are nothing but the some total of our bodily movements, then we are our skilled and unskilled actions (Braverman, 1974; Kramer, 1997). Therefore, if a person has no technical value they are "no body." Their body is of no value. Their movements are of no concern. No one cares about them. According to the logic of modern physicalism, care means that you are valuable to me. And since value has been reduced to utility and exploitable motion, I care about you only to the extent that I can exploit you. The unexploitable are not even afforded shelter or food.

In this modern metaphysics with its attendant value of overdetermined efficiency in material production, only behavior "counts." And the structural system takes moral president. Everyone must do their bit, pull their weight, which means to work to maintain the system or else the system will abandon them. The system determines the rewards and punishments on a reciprocal basis. If you maintain the system, it will maintain you.

New identities emerge. People can become "obsolete." As Geddes (1915) put it "technics takes command" so that people must be re-tooled for their own good. Benevolent management seeks to align the interests of the workers with those of the transcendental (which takes ontic priority) system so that everything will run more smoothly. But contradictions within the system prevent hegemony from becoming total. The world is open and so change is impossible to escape. The "criminal" time cannot be arrested. Mumford (1934) called the tendency toward totalitarian ordination the machine id, the externalization of will to power as machine might. Lackadaisical flux comes under control by the endlessly redundant motion of the clockworks which is the prototypical model for the machine world (Kramer and Ikeda, in press). But it must be understood that machine is not machine anymore than scientism is a science or computerization is a computer. In the latter case, what is at issue is not a metal box with wires in it, but a mode of being, a way of structuring interaction, valuation, morality, labor, et cetera. It is an ideology, an "ism." About the same time that machine precision was being brought to bear on all aspects of human behavior, both Max Weber (1905/1958), with his analysis of bureaucratic ordination, and Mumford recognized the danger of worshipping efficiency and the idea that each problem has one best solution so that thinking became synonymous not just with problem solving but with one (the best) way to think. Even Marx's claim to be "scientific" and that the revolution is inevitable was tainted by the romance of inescapable precision and "historical" logic. Though flux cannot be arrested, there is no guarantee which way things will go (Nietzsche, 1887/1974). Marx is a thoroughly modern thinker with great faith in historical logic. It is no mere coincidence that the most horrendous efforts at total social structuration and systematization, communism and Nazism, both claimed that transcendental "destiny" was on their side, and that they both planned to create the new improved material man. If one reads any of the propaganda generated by either the Soviet, Chinese, or Nazi systems it is practically identical in its utopian worship of logical control, centralization (in the service of efficiency), and techno-industrial prowess.

For the modernist, rationality comes to mean efficiency of material production. Rationality rejects value debate. One cannot ask whether or not bureaucratization is "good." Instead it is normalized and naturalized by the Hegelian notion (borrowed by Darwin) of linear progress and evolution.

The unproductive and unexploitable such as children, "dim wits," the "undependable," and the elderly must be segregated and warehoused. They must be isolated from the workers who are perpetually busy. The identity of humans is reduced to "functionalism." Dysfunctional individuals are worthless. They are "nobodies." They are invisible. They cannot secure a place, a "position" within the socioeconomic structure. They have no identity. They literally have no where to go. Since they are unproductive, they fail to pull their own weight, they are seen as a drag on the economy. They don't pay their own way. Hence, budgets are cut and a new type of human is invented, the homeless.

Never before the advent of industrial production have people been seen as "homeless" accept criminals ostracized and exiled from their group. Such a punishment was deemed so repulsive that Socrates, for instance, chose to commit suicide instead. Refugees from war, famine, and plague were "displaced" but not homeless. The homeless literally have no place where they "belong." They cannot be displaced because they have no place from which to be removed. The identity "refugee" always implies the dimension of home. I am a Cuban refugee, a Cambodian refugee, a Bosnian refugee, a displaced industrial worker. The "I am" and "place" are necessary conditions for refugee status. This is also the case with immigrants and migrants. This is a necessary condition for the double consciousness of diasporic pain which involves having two homes at once and confusion concerning motive, allegiance, and identity.

But the homeless do not even have the identity of being a nomad. They are not "at home" within a nomadic culture with all its complexities and traditions. A nomad has a place within the family lineage and they have a territory within which they move. Gypsies have a shared language and culture. But the homeless have no claims to place or time. They are isolated. They are disembodied and deminded. When they are gone, they are not missed because they "have" no friends, they "have" no "significant" others to mark their passage. They are not "had" by anyone. They do not "belong." They are meaningless. The others which constitute the system which presents functions and structures, places to enact to "belong" do not see them. The homeless are invisible. They have no bodies, they perform no function, they have no displacement, they are nobodies. They are passed on the street like ghosts. Only the "expendable" have value. The homeless are not even objects. And yet, the ever-present magical dimension of life gives them comportment, their hair and skin, their feathery clothes a force that is before words and certainly beyond good and evil.

In the modern world, to be ethical is to be disinterested and to objectify other humans. Hence the modern war on the subject and time. Time, the great criminals time and subjectivism, are to be "arrested" via the methodological process of automation, synchronicity, and generalizability. The subject, which is an expression of flux in the form of variance and multiple interpretations, is denied existence. Only static objects (structures) remain. The transcendental statistical mean is more real than lived-bodies. But this rhetoric cannot compete with the con-fronting of sentient soul to sentient soul.

Moderns pretend that subjects are contingent and expendable like the G.I. or general issue human being. While the individual is defined as irrelevant, the function within the reified structure endures. People come and go but the organization endures. In the modern world everything is fragmented so that production, for example, is broken down into simplified and redundant operations. This enables the interchangeability of workers without disrupting the overall production process. In the modern world people are redefined as structural functions and functions are simplified and standardized so that labor is devalued (it is not indispensable as is the case with highly skilled craftsmen). Quite the contrary, the modern perspectival world thrives on the dispensability of everyone and everything. People are temporary ("temps") within the permanent structure of the system. Mass production demands mass consumption, planned obsolescence and a throw away world.

In order to facilitate this worldview, a way to preserve power was invented. Capital, as pure power, can be "saved up," transferred, transformed, exchanged, converted, and grow. It is modern magic, pure, the potential to make things happen that never happened before. Capital has the proteus power of "liquidity." Capital is a modern expression of magical power. Capital can take many forms such as electronic signals, various monetary instruments, investments, and savings. Unlike magical and mythical attitudes (Kramer and Mickunas, 1992) wherein value was univalent, meaning inherent, in the modern world value is totally arbitrary, even quantified. Indeed, for many late modern nihilistic positivists and deconstructionists, value and meaning do not even merit existence. Modern value is often expressed as binary code or numerical accounting. But even though the ancient magic has simply been redefined through modern perspectival modes of articulation, it remains pure power. Like coal or oil, money exists as "deposited" and as a "reserve." Money is stored power, potential energy. But unlike coal or oil, money can reproduce itself.

In the modern world, if it is granted existence at all, value is totally arbitrary. Value is dissociated from any idea, art work, natural phenomenon like the Grand Canyon, or material artifact. Absurdly, however, money is not at all materialistic, rather it is the power to transform material relations. The modern world, despite its pretenses of being dedicated to direct (which means personal) empirical observation, is the most dissociated and abstract mode of being humans have yet articulated. Modern humans are suffering from extreme alienation/dissociation. The modern is dissociated from the natural variance of daylight/darkness through the season, from hot and cold via cybernetic "climate control," from the products of labor, from extended family relationships, and so on. The modern obsession with the metaphysics of quantification is pure abstraction. This modern metaphysical prejudice has been extended to human beings. As evinced by modern mechanized warfare, eugenics (including the technology of recombinate genetic engineering), and standardization in education, politics, sports, economics, linguistics, and so forth. In the twentieth century, humans are no longer believed to present any inherent value. The so-called "postmodernists" (the word "post" exposing the intense spatial prejudice which betrays the late modern hypertrophy), have declared the human "decentered," indeed, extinct. Reductionistic lingualism is their privileged truth. Everything is merely language which is further atomized into phonemes, semes, signifiers, etc... As objects available for various forms of exploitation, like cadavers to be dissected under the medical gaze, modern humans are confronting a crisis of nihilism unknown to "traditional" societies. One very important adumbration of nihilism is the sense of having no "place," no identity, to be invisible. The modern wasteland is populated by ghosts.

The essence of hopelessness, is to be "outside" the normative structures of a dominating social order.

THREE TYPES OF HOMELESSNESS

There are three forms of homeless people. One is the pseudo-Nietzschean (the Nazi version) hero variously portrayed as the drifter, wanderer that has no allegiance, no "ties" that bind. Hollywood has made millions producing seemingly endless variations of this version of the homeless, "footloose" "king of the road." Clint Eastwood characters, James Bond, Captain Kirk of the Starship Enterprise, Kane on Kung Fu (just to name a few) never have to worry about changing diapers, caring for aging parents, or going to the grocery store. They are homeless wanderers/vigilantes who articulate a militaristic version of the world, and who make no domestic commitments. They are modern individualists. They are often identified with weapons and war such as Remington Steele, Magnum P.I., Mike Hammer, Colt, Cannon, Barretta, The Rifleman, et cetera, ad nauseum. They stress the power of vision. They are spys, private eyes, detectors, observers, visionaries. They drift into town, hypnotize the herd-like population with charisma, power, and defiance of all norms and mores, in the higher value of ultimate good, law and order, and then drift on. Romanticism, with its intense dedication to personal preference, vision as the source of truth, is penultimately modern. Even modern empiricism in the form of "seeing is believing" is pure romantic individualism.

Another form of homeless person is the pathetic refugee. This is mythic homelessness. This person may be "displaced" by war or an economy that has forced them to exist outside the group including the labor market (chronically un- or underemployed). Unlike the romantic hero, such as the various incarnations of cowboy/gunfighter/spy/space traveler/explorer, this form of homeless person is powerless to alter his or her situation. They lack money. They do not wander because of a lust for independence, but are forced by circumstances beyond their control to do so.

The third form of mythic homeless is the social isolate/hermit/nomad that has rejected the habitat of "normal" social intercourse. This form is often dedicated to mythological exegesis and monastic discipline. Unlike the drifter who repeatedly encounters the civilized world of domesticated men, or the refugee who often lives among such men, the hermit shuns all contact. While the drifter is the enforcer of law and order, one who comes into the herd as a savior (shepherd) and "straightens things out," thus exhibiting his or her dominance, the hermit works on self-discipline.

All may be called marginal, but only if a center is presumed. For the magical nomad that spends his or her life traversing the vast oceans, deserts, or prairies of the world, there is no "edge" to life. And therefore, there is no center. To be homeless, presumes a home. Therefore, nomadic peoples are not homeless. Instead, everything, "inside" and "outside" constitutes "home." For the nomad, there is no edge to the camp. There is no fixed "outside" (or "inside"). There are no sides, just total identity. Modern materialists such as Caton (1990) often make the mistake that being "Homeless" means to have no fixed shelter or dwelling. But, "Home" is an empirical structure, but a sense of belonging. Homelessness is a function of urban civilization with its centralizing tendencies (that even extend to epistemology in statistical form). For a nomad, there is no "edge," indeed there are no sides or "outskirts" to reality/habitat. There is boundless sea or prairie, and sky. This constitutes a univalent mode of being prior to the separation (co constitutional genesis) of culture and nature. Instead of wild/domestic, and culture/nature, for the nomad there is only world. For nomadic peoples, humans have inherent value and identity. But for the modern, value is nonexistent and identity is totally arbitrary. Mobility for the modern is fundamentally different from nomadic movement. Social, economic, and geographic statuses, as well as other forms of mobility for the modern involve the contingency of identity. Thus, irregardless of one's family, age, sex, or other "inherent" characteristic, in the modern world, if one looses their money they can become homeless. Besides money, all other values are irrelevant. Status is achieved (contingent) not ascribed (inherent). "Displacement" presumes a modern trivalent mode of being we call perspectival/spatial.

THE VIEW FROM THE SOFA: WATCHING THE TELEVISED OTHER

The modern super tribe is marked by a dualism between intense individualism and mass anonymity. These two forces feed off of one another. Mass mediation is a late modern phenomenon. It exaggerates a single and very tiny perspective on reality to the status of Absolute Reality. Millions uncritically view the world through the single camera angle sharing a double consciousness—a disembodied consciousness like never before. The scope of a single camera is analogous to a single flashlight beam in the vast ocean. Through massive electronic networking this tiny and single conical segment is simultaneously consumed by a mass audience conferring the status of great value and importance onto it. Ironically, each viewer thinks that he or she saw "for themselves" with "their own eyes" a unique truth, but actually they have all seen exactly the same thing from the same angle, lighting, color, et cetera. This apparatus generates a very powerful false consciousness, a false independence of mind. The modern metaphysical prejudice of viseocentrism (not "phonocentrism") as Jacques Derrida (1976) claims, makes modern audiences more susceptible to manipulation than they believe (Kramer, 1992b). The more faith they put in what they see, the more completely they can be fooled (especially by digital technique). The modern audience tends to have the same memory, the same view, the same consciousness—mass consciousness. Because they all "share" a single view, reliability is assured. "Cameras don't lie." "A picture is worth a thousand words." Such sayings indicate the power of visual rhetoric. We all see the same thing, therefore it must be a fact. Viewer "counter arguing" and "resistance" is merely anecdotal, a false sense of independence. When "big news," like the Challenger disaster, or the Gulf War is happening, nearly all of the super tribe members rush to, and are fixated with " view" " story." In an effort to reduce uncertainty, they attend for hours to redundant information hoping for a shred of new news. Nothing else exists. Perspectival tunnel vision is shared on a massive scale, and everyone is looking down exactly the same tunnel.

Because of the intense metaphysical prejudice favoring material extension, spatial awareness (viseocentrism), if a story is not "good on camera" it is ignored. If the powers that be ignore it, the audience assumes that it must not be important. The homeless become even more invisible, especially since they do not sell products. Homelessness does not create what Vance Packard (1957) called a "buying mood." Hence, as many experts on the media have noted, cameras are "trained" to look at more visually interesting catastrophes and "personalities" that are created for the sake of selling (commercial entertainers). "Madonna has a baby" gets more global coverage than a thousand homeless who expire on the streets and whose bodies are never claimed. Does anyone wonder what happens to those objects? In every major U.S. city, every night a group of city employees makes the rounds to collect the dead and dispose of the "remains," the residue of the invisible. They leave without a trace. News cameras avoid this specter because it would be difficult for the couch potato to not feel guilty and change the channel.

And yet, news stories about homelessness in the United States have dramatically increased in recent years. The overall image of the homeless, however, has been biased. In other words, the news stories of the homeless typically emphasize deficiencies in individual members of the homeless group, but the news should take such an emphasis instead of arguing social inequalities. Despite this, the mass media has portrayed homeless people as alien representatives from another world.

Marcuse (1988) provided a theoretical background for understanding societal responses to homelessness, which he also categorized through the two methods of publicizing and neutralizing. These constructs are useful in explaining how the mass media depicts the topic of homelessness. On the one hand, the media employs the publicizing and politicizing method in portraying the plight of the homeless, as evidenced by being without shelter in bad weather and needing to beg for food. Alternatively, the media also employs the neutralizing method, which differs from the publicizing method by focusing blame on the homeless themselves for their condition, rather than on concern for either their welfare, or the need for government action (Penner and Penner, 1994). The individual, like Joyce Brown, becomes a "story."

Campbell and Reeves (1989) examine how network news makes sense of homelessness. More specifically, news covering the Joyce Brown stories placed the apparent deviancy of homelessness back into the consensus by translating the unfamiliar into the familiar world of the narrative. That is, network news transformed the troubling experiences of the homeless into familiar news packages. Such transformation is seen as imposing a distance between the audience and the objects of these stories. As an example, Campbell and Reeves observed the CBS account of the Joyce Brown story as follows: "Rather's narration also marks off the homeless as being outside his inner circle-the circle of common sense. Rather's language locates the homeless in the realm of difference, the other, the not us, them" (1989, p. 27).

Power (1991) explored the communication of "otherness" in network television news coverage of homelessness. According to his study, the communication of "otherness" is defined as "the employment of communication mechanisms that engender the perception of difference and inferiority" (p. 6). He interprets the texts of various news segments as evidence of a hegemonic process. On this point, Power regards this hegemonic process as a means by which people understand the media's portrayal of homeless people. Consequently, he claims that audiences merely demonstrate the capacity of understanding the phenomenon of homelessness in individual terms. The result of this study clearly indicates that the role that viewer identification plays in overcoming communication mechanisms engenders these vital perceptions of "otherness."

McNulty (1993) also examined news construction of homelessness as a social problem. Here, McNulty identified the precise methods by which news stories communicate the specific notion that certain types of people are homeless. According to this study, homeless people appear as "institution avoiders," "totally ill individuals," "families and children," "runaway and abandoned teens," and "threatening villains." Campbell and Reeves (1989) concluded that the conventional news narratives about homeless stories thus:

Television as an intimate medium sits in the comfort of our kitchens, living rooms, and bedrooms-our homes. At the same time television peeks at the plight of those without homes, it also imposes distance. The medium lets us see the homeless, identify briefly with their predicament, yet, in the end, it sustains the fragile boundaries that mark off the intruders (p. 40).

SEDUCTION OF TELEVISED IMAGES

Television provides an essential element for structuring contemporary existence. According to Baudrillard (1988), "In the image of television, the most beautiful prototypical object of this new era, the surrounding universe and our very bodies are becoming monitoring screens" (p. 12). As noted above, in our desire to be objective "good" observers, we are all spreading ourselves, our retinal surfaces out, so that, "not even the lightest footsteps and the fluttering of ghostly beings shall be lost" (Nietzsche, 1886/1972: Sec. 207, p. 115). In this sense, television constitutes an extended self upon which is reflected as real, simulated images and meanings. Increasingly, the self becomes simulation. Consequently, the implosion of the social subject in the masses becomes dependent on the seductive capacity of visual simulations. Generally speaking, in a world of simulation, appearances seem more real than the world of people and objects. As a result, the "real" has become the "hyperreal" product of media images. Moreover, Baudrillard's notion of "cold" seduction characterizes the media's performative function in what may best be described as a postmodern information society. This notion of seduction then informs us that third order simulacra do not represent the "original," "real world," but instead are often reproductions of reproductions (official models). For example, although the homeless story is based upon encounters depicting real-life events, those encounters are no less fictional than events in the ten o'clock news, or TV dramas for that matter. Consequently, the TV culture becomes the most important agent of collective, "cold" seduction in contemporary culture. Most recently, however, TV programs appear which directly simulate "real-life" situations, perhaps much in the same way TV evangelists appear to simulate religion. With such simulations appearing in the postmodern world, boundaries between "real-life" and "simulated life" continue to implode. For instance, TV news more is increasingly assumed to be the form of "required" entertainment, using both dramatic and melodramatic codes in which to frame their stories.

In other words, television is consumed by individuals in their own respective private psychic and physical understanding and space (Kramer, 1992b). Moreover, as McLuhan (1964) claims, each communication medium's message resides in its particular capacity to extend personal perception and, ultimately, to shape social organization. At this point, television thus extends the sense of vision, so that the viewer may gain the technological power of surveillance. This surveillance, however, is focused on particular subjects of interest, which means that a contingent ideology (or camera-angle view of reality) is thereby provided (Kramer, 1993). The problem (with respect to the Gebserian point of view) lies in the essential characteristic of perspectivism, which postulates the narrow sector, and subsequently inflates it to world status. Kramer (1993) suggests that the world-view (as propagated by television) may be represented by a camera angle controlled by commercial interests. In this sense, the seduction of televised images of the homeless as "otherness" (e.g., vagabond and/or refugee) is deeply associated with the commodification of pain and wanderlust.

CONCLUSION

In general terms, homelessness refers to persons who "have no fixed abode or nighttime shelter other than that provided by a private or public agency" (Caton, 1990, p. 20). Marcuse (1990) have extended the definition to include such categories as the "hidden" or "invisible" homeless. Basically, the term homeless brings into a set of meanings, drawing on pre-established ways of understanding precisely what homelessness represents. In essence, homeless communicates the absence of home, that which we take for granted and have come to understand as something that everyone should have. Homelessness, therefore, comprises a state which occupies a space outside the realm of common sense to the point that portrayals of homeless people takes place within the context of culturally established meanings, meanings derived from place within the system.

What has been set forth in this chapter is an explanation of the sedimented nature of the modern, mental-rational perspectival world and how it makes as all into strangers. In so far as we are all strangers, or estranged from each other, we are all made homeless. We lack the implicate mutuality that constitutes the sense of belonging and care. But the magic dimension, which is often ignored by the rational mentality, cannot be denied. The truth that is the embodied pain of homelessness defies reinterpretation (rationalization). In some sense, as Marcuse (1988) argued, television in its very act of publicizing the image of the homeless, neutralize the image. This is so because the image is highly dissociated. The object cannot look back and see us thus implicating us in his of her humanity (pain). We see the image and we satisfied (neutralized). But nothing has changed. Nothing has been done. The greatest threat to praxis is nihilism and dissociation. The homeless on television are reduced and equalized to the status of signs, like everything else. But face-to-face they are more than were arbitrary signs. Their humanity, value, humiliation, and pain is not accidental or arbitrary. We cannot remain totally detached "mirrors" as we may be while sitting on our sofas.

REFERENCES

Barthes, R. (1972). *Mythologies*. (A. Lavers, Trans.). New York: Hill and Wang. (Original work published 1957.)

Bataille, G. (1989). *The tears of eros* (P. Connor, Trans.). San Francisco, CA: City Light Books.

Baudrillard, J. (1988). *The ecstasy of communication*. New York: Semiotext.

Becker, C. L. (1949). *Progress and power*. New York: Knopf.

Bell, D. (1973). *The coming of post-industrial society*. New York: Harper and Row.

Benjamin, W. (1968). *Illuminations*. (H. Zohn, Trans.). New York: Harcourt, Brace and World. (Original work published 1928)

Bevan, E. (1921). *Hellenism and Christianity*. London: Metheun.

Braverman, H. (1974). *Labor and monopoly capital*. New York: Monthly Review Press.

Brzezinski, Z. (1970). *Between two ages*. New York: Viking Press.

Campbell, J., and Mayers, B. (1988). *The power of myth*. New York: Anchor Books.

Campbell, R. (1991). *60 Minutes and the news: A mythology for middle America*. Urbana, IL: University of Illinois Press.

Campbell, R., and Reeves, J. L. (1989). Covering the homeless: The Joyce Brown story. *Critical Studies in Mass Communication, 6*(1), 21–42.

Cassirer, E. (1946). *Language and myth*. New York: Harper and Brothers.

Caton, C. L. M. (1990). *Homeless in America*. New York: Oxford University Press.

Deleuze, G., and Guattari, F. (1984). *Anti-Oedipus: Capitalism and schizophrenia*. Minneapolis, MN: University of Minnesota Press.

Derrida, J. (1976). *Of Grammatology* (G. C. Spivak, Trans.). Baltimore, ML: The Johns Hopkins University Press. (Original work published 1967)

DeVore, I. (1965). *Primate behavior*. New York: Holt, Rinehart and Winton.

Dilthey, W. (1988). *Introduction to the human sciences: An attempt to lay a foundation for the study of society and history* (R. J. Betanzos, Trans.). Detroit, MI: Wayne State University Press. (Original work published 1923)

Eliade, M. (1963). *Myth and reality*. (W. Trask, Trans.). New York: Harper and Row. (Original work published 1961)

Elliott, M., and Kriva, L. (1991). Structural determinants of homelessness in the United States. *Social Problems, 38,* 113–131.

Ellison, R. (1952). *The invisible man*. New York: Random House.

Fiske, J. (1991). For cultural interpretation: A study of the culture of homelessness. *Critical Studies in Mass Communication, 8*(4), 455–474.

Foucault, M. (1972). *The archaeology of knowledge* (A. M. S. Smith, Trans.). New York: Pantheon. (Original work published 1969)

Foucault, M. (1977). *Discipline and punish*. (A. Sheridan, Trans.). New York: Vintage. (Original work published 1975)

Gebser, J. (1985). *The ever-present origin* (N. Barstad, and A. Mickunas, Trans.). Athens, OH: Ohio University Press. (Original work published 1949)

Geddes, P. (1915). *Cities in evolution*. London: Williams and Norgate.

Geertz, C. (1973). *The interpretation of cultures*. New York: Basic Books.

Horkheimer, M., and Adorno, T. (1972). *Dialectic of enlightenment*. New York: Seabury.

Husserl, E. (1970). *The crisis of European sciences and transcendental phenomenology* (D. Carr, Trans.). Evanston, IL: Northwestern University Press. (Original work published 1952)

Innis, H. A. (1950). *Empire and communication*. Oxford: Oxford University Press.

Innis, H. A. (1951). *The bias of communication*. Toronto: University of Toronto Press.

Jameson, F. (1991). *Postmodernism, or, the cultural logic of late capitalism*. Durham, NC: Duke University Press.

Kahler, E. (1973). *The inward turn of narrative*. Princeton, NJ: Princeton University Press.

Kahn, H., and Wiener, N. (1967). *The year 2000*. Croton-on-Hudson, NY: Hudson Institute.

Kramer, E. M. (1992a). Gebser and culture. In E. M. Kramer (Ed.), *Consciousness and culture: An introduction to the thought of Jean Gebser* (1–60). Westport, CT: Greenwood Press.

Kramer, E. M. (1992b). The origin of television as civilized expression. In J. Deely (Ed.), *Semiotics 1990* (27–36). Lanham, MD: University Press of America.

Kramer, E. M. (1993). Mass media and democracy. In J. W. Murphy and D. L. Peck (Eds.), *Open institutions: The hope for democracy* (77–98). Westport, CT: Praeger.

Kramer, E. M. (1997). *Modern/Postmodern: Off the beaten path of antimodernism*. Westport, CT: Praeger.

Kramer, E. M., and Ikeda, R. (in press). Japanese clocks: Semiotic evidence of perspectival mutation. *The American Journal of Semiotics*.

Kramer, E. M., and Mickunas, A. (1992). Introduction: Gebser's new understanding. In E. M. Kramer (Ed.), *Consciousness and culture: An introduction to the thought of Jean Gebser* (i–xxx). Westport, CT: Greenwood Press.

Levinas, E. (1994). *Outside the subject* (M. B. Smith, Trans.). Stanford, CA: Stanford University Press.

Lingis, A. (1983). *Excesses: Eros and culture*. Albany, NY: State University of New York Press.

Lorenz, K. (1983). *Die evolution des denkins*. Munich: Piper.

Lyotard, J. F. (1991). *The postmodern condition: A report on knowledge* (G. Bennington, and B. Massumi, Trans.). Minneapolis, MN: University of Minnesota Press. (Original work published 1979)

McLuhan, M. (1964). *Understanding media: The extensions of man*. New York: American Library.

McNulty, B. R. (1993). Homeless and hopeless: Resignation in news media constructions of homelessness as a social problem (Doctoral dissertation, University of Pennsylvania, 1992). *Dissertation Abstracts international*, 2146A.

Mickunas, A. (1973). Civilizations as structures of consciousness. *Main Current of Modern Thought*, (5), 179–185.

Morris, D. (1967). *The naked ape*. New York: McGraw-Hill.

Morris, D. (1969). *The human zoo*. New York: Delta.

Mumford, L. (1934). *Technics and civilization*. New York: Harcourt, Brace and World.

Mumford, L. (1961). *The city in history*. New York: Harcourt, Brace and World.

Neumann, E. (1954). *The origins and history of consciousness*. Princeton, NJ: Princeton University Press.

Nietzsche, F. (1967). *On the genealogy of morals*. New York: Random House. (Original work published 1887)

Nietzsche, F. (1972). *Beyond good and evil*. (R. J. Hollingdale, Trans.). New York: Penguin. (Original work published 1886)

Nietzsche, F. (1974). *The gay science* (W. Kaufmann, Trans.). New York: Vintage. (Original work published 1882)

Ong, W. (1982). *Orality and literacy: The technologizing of the word*. New York: Methuen.

Packard, V. (1957). *The hidden persuaders*. New York: Pocket Books.

Packard, V. (1961). *The status seekers*. New York: Pocket Books.

Penner, M., and Penner, S. (1994). Publicizing, politicizing, and neutralizing homelessness. *Communication Research*, (6), 766–781.

Power, J. C. (1991). Mass communication of otherness and identification: An examination of the portrayals of homeless people in network television news (Doctoral dissertation, University of Southern California, 1991). *Dissertation Abstracts international, 52*, 1557A.

Pribram, (1971). *Languages of the brain*. Englewood Cliffs, NJ: Prentice-Hall.

Sapir, E. (1921). *Language*. New York: Harcourt Brace.

Sapir, E. (1949). *Selected writings of Edward Sapir in language, culture and personality*. Berkeley, CA: University of California Press.

Snow, D., and Anderson, L. (1993). *Down on their luck: A study of homeless street people*. Berkeley, CA: University of California Press.

Wallas, G. (1914). *The great society*. New York: Macmillan.

Weber, M. (1958). *The Protestant ethic and the spirit of capitalism*. (T. Parsons, Trans.). New York: Scribner's. (Original work published 1905.)

Chapter 10

From Tramps to Truth-Seekers: Images of the Homeless in the Motion Pictures

Linda K. Fuller

> Believe me, Sara, the streets of this city are not kind to the homeless.
> —The mean Miss Minchin in the *Little Princess* (1939, 1995)

Hobo, vagrant, tramp, panhandler, bum, Sad Sack, vagabond, drifter, street urchin, down-and-out, the displaced, beggar, runaway, panhandle—rethink of all the epithets we have used over the years for the homeless. Review, also, places we were told where they might be found: Skid Row, soup kitchens, tenements, the Bowery, slums. The value of reviewing these changing linguistic and socioccritical descriptions over time is to help better understand messages that mainstream media has been feeding us, in a continuing effort to maintain the status quo.

Throughout its century of existence, the medium of the motion pictures has consistently dealt with the underclass of the homeless, albeit with differing perspectives. Beginning with the classic tramp character best exemplified by Charlie Chaplin (Haining, 1982), the movies have traditionally portrayed members of the dispossessed classes with sympathy, juxtaposed against their counterparts of the happier (read, wealthier) socioeconomic circles. Beginning, around the Reagan-Bush era, a new theme emerged: a hint that those "without" maybe really had more than the material-minded.

Introducing the theory of intracinematology as a means of examining filmic treatments, which will be explained in depth, this chapter analyzes seventy motion pictures dealing with the homeless and homelessness.

UNDERLYING THEORY: INTERCINEMATOLOGY

Going beyond traditional approaches to the analysis of motion pictures, "intracinematology" proposes both a theoretical perspective and a pragmatic means of analyzing the medium subcontextually. Although it has been applied to the five-volume series *Beyond the Stars: Studies in American Popular Film*, edited by Paul Loukides and Linda K. Fuller and published by Popular Press (1990–1996), this case study examining images of the homeless in motion pictures is the first time intracinematology is spelled out.

Coining a new word that goes beyond filmology (economic, political, social and technical causes and effects) or cinematology (the study of film itself), intracinematology penetrates into film to better understand both its manifest and latent content(s).[1] Introducing a new word and a new film theory into the dialogue, intracinematology is envisioned as penetrating into the deepest aspects of uncovering the many aspects and layers of film that can provide clues to our better understanding both its manifest and latent content. The idea is to explore film by means of conventionology.

Specifically, intracinematology can be applied to a number of different elements, including filmic characters (from stars to stock characters), filmic themes (conventions of plot), filmic "things" (the material world, such as cars, computers, and cigarettes), filmic places (locales ranging from kitchens to Cairo), filmic philosophies ("isms," doctrines, leitmotifs, and ways of thinking about the world), and or or filmic events (personal or world-shattering, time-bound or extending over a period of time). This subcontextual approach goes beyond aesthetics and personal response, asking the researcher to consider connections between social phenomena and social reality. Some examples follow:

Filmic Characters

Not necessarily stars and celebrities, but both leading and lesser personalities can inform the focus of this area of study. Those characters could be professors or prostitutes, babies or broadcasters, athletes or Army recruits, comedians or country folk, even doctors or dogs. Consider union members, for example, and how they have been treated from the days of *Norma Rae* (1979) to the more recent *Roger and Me* or even the award-winning documentary *American Dream*. Or take the stereotype of the heavy, face-flushed male Irish cop, now replaced oftentimes both in real life and in the movies such as *Back to the Future II* by the slender Hispanic woman.

While political correctness has encouraged deeper dissection of various typical filmic types, the exercise of exploring filmic characters by means of intracinematology has further value in helping to explain and explore various cultural milieu from which particular personalities emerge. Whether seen as an "extra," or in major or secondary roles, these figures enter our film-viewing consciousness; therefore, it behooves us to begin bringing awareness of these images into the open.

Filmic Themes

Conventions of plot, which in themselves key indices of cultural confirmations about our physical and social worlds, are further guideposts to revealing the symbiosis between film and the society it services. Whether the narrative attests to our fascination with the rise and fall of the sports hero, mistaken murder, the last-minute rescue, or the doomed love affair, the box office brings us parables to please.

We know, for example, that the cinematic serial killer, with the exception maybe of Jason of *Friday the 13th* fame, will always get caught—as, recently, in *The January Man, Criminal Law, A Shock to the System, Sea of Love, Stepfather II, Blue Steel,* and *Silence of the Lambs*—or that date rape will typically be depicted as occurring in lower working-class, rural, usually Southern settings, and that it will hardly come to terms with ugly hidden truths. Whether the victim is a complete innocent (the deaf-mute in 1947's *Johnny Belinda*), a tease (Sam Peckinpah's 1971 *Straw Dogs*, David Lynch's 1986 *Blue Velvet*), or someone who makes us uncomfortable at her self-examination (Jody Foster's awardwinning performance in *The Accused,* 1988), the plot device remains muddled in our minds because of Hollywood's twisted interpretations.

We have long liked age role-reversal films, and easily relate to fantasies such as Dudley Moore's *Like Father, Like Son,* Judge Reinhold's *Vice Versa,* George Burns' *Eighteen Again,* and most of all, Tom Hanks's *Big.* Again, as in real life, the Peter Pan syndrome persists. Intracinematology encourages subcontextual study beyond mere formulaic plot elements.

Filmic "Things"

The material world of motion pictures, its "stuff"—both used and abused—is probably the most obvious and at the same time the least analyzed. As much as we adore our automobiles in real life, in the movies we oftentimes drive them dangerously until we destroy them completely. Food, as another example, can connote sex, greed, lust, or living. Specific food can determine class—what one eats, how she or he eats it.[2] If a character orders a fancy French entrée but can't pronounce it correctly, it's a dead giveaway—often a comedic device. Pizza can signify fast food or ethnic preference (see *Mystic Pizza, White Palace*), and specific food is something else indeed from eating (see *Tom Jones, Eating Raoul,* even Henry Jaglom's recent documentary, *Eating*). Consider how images of cigarettes have evolved, from the macho mannerism of Humphrey Bogart to today's association with nervous, anxious losers. Clothing, computers, carpets, cocaine, chaise lounges, closets, and clarinets all provide invaluable time capsules to understanding society and its pursuit of material pleasures.

Another factor to be considered in the discussion of filmic "things" is the audience(s) for these images. As both cinema scholars and the corporate world begin to assess the impact of various products on the Big Screen, we are learning the value of both blatant and imbedded product messages. Examples of the notion of film as cultural artifact, a longtime but newly reconceptualized area of study (e.g., Sklar, 1922; Jacobs, 1968; Grogg and Nachbar, 1982; Jackson, 1986; Miller, 1990; Fuller, 1992) might range from inspecting interior decoration to monitoring modes of materialism.

Further, advertising is becoming evermore embedded in film scripts: see, for example, the ad nauseam mention of Dunkin' Donuts in Norman Jewison's *Other People's Money,* or the more subtle jabs at mall culture in *L.A. Story, Gremlins II,* or *This Is My Life,* or even instances where the movie itself is one big advertisement, such as *The Mighty Ducks* series to plug Disney's NHL franchise (Fuller, 1997). In this process, we need to realize that whether as background or actually plugged products, the world of "things" is omnipresent in American movies. As motion pictures enter their centennial decade, the innovation of the VCR affords us film documentarians a unique opportunity for visual recording and reflection on our world.

Filmic Places

Locales—whether London, laundromats, or literary hideaways, provide much more than setting in the telling of a story. Prisons, for example, have long been popular (e.g., *The Big House*, 1930; *I Am a Fugitive from a Chain Gang*, 1932; *20,000 Years in Sing Sing*, 1932; *We're No Angels*, 1954; *Birdman of Alcatraz*, 1961; *Cool Hand Luke*, 1967; *Papillon*, 1973; *The Longest Yard*, 1974; *Stir Crazy*, 1980; *The Thin Blue Line*, 1988). The South, Vietnam, the altar, and, recently, the Bronx are popular settings; *Pride of the Yankees* (1942) and Delbert Mann's *Marty* (1955) gave gritty portraits of its residents, *Fort Apache, The Bronx* of 1981 began a bleaker view of the borough, leading to films like *True Love*, *Five Corners*, and *Bonfire of the Vanities*.

Intracinematology encourages entering beaches and bedrooms, churches and cities, factories and fight arenas, borders and ballparks to see what has been and is now. Historically, economically, politically, and socioculturally, this approach allows us to look at the New South, or diners, or hospitals from a wide perspective.

Filmic Philosophies

Thematic or ideological conventions—the "isms," doctrines, leitmotifs, and ways of thinking about the world—provide yet another way the intracinematological approach encourages looking at subcontextual messages. Topics might deal with anti-establishment themes, hedonism and horror, pacifism, anti-Communism, biopics and American mythology, regeneration in sports films, homes and homelessness, consumerism, alienation, religion and secularism, ugly Americanism, racism, ageism, and so on.

Divorce, for example, has been a screen subject since the 1930s (*Dodsworth*, 1936; *The Awful Truth*, 1937), becoming more popular in the 1970s (*Scenes From a Marriage*, 1973; *An Unmarried Woman*, 1978; *Kramer vs. Kramer*, 1979), and really coming into its own in the 1980s (*Shoot the Moon*, 1982; *Twice in a Lifetime*, 1985; *Always*, 1985; *The Good Father*, 1987); and probably the most vicious of all, *The War of the Roses*, 1989. Class conflict has been around since the early days of Frank Capra's films, emerging also in films about the dispossessed like Fritz Lang's 1937's *You Only Live Once*, John Ford's *The Grapes of Wrath* (1940), Arthur Penn's *Bonnie and Clyde* (1967), or John Schlesinger's *Midnight Cowboy* (1969). The homeless, as an example of the dispossessed, make for a classic study. Examining cinematic history for its varied presentations of various ideologies presents an invaluable way of assessing fads and fashions, and enduring ideas.

Filmic Events

Specific or general, the "when" of an occurrence can be found to tell volumes about not only an event but about societal reaction to the event. That event might be instantaneous, such as the bombing of Pearl Harbor, or it might evolve slowly and insidiously, such as the advent of AIDS.

Conceived of as a means of dissecting events as they have been represented on celluloid, studies in this category might include fairs and festivals, the Oscars, losing one's virginity, bank robberies, spring break, the assassination of presidents, the Olympic Games, the crucifixion, and so on. The birthing event, for example, might be considered in terms of the act of giving birth, the birth process as a time of bringing couples together, the plot of switched babies in the nursery, and any other examples ranging from the comic to the sublime. The act of examining prayer as a cinematic event, according to Lindvall (1992), "takes us to diegetic movements in film where it functions as deal-making (in both *The End* and *Hannah and Her Sisters*, characters trying to bargain with God), as character signatures (from *Rage in Harlem*'s virginal hero to villainous hypocrites), as atmosphere (in *Tender Mercies* and *Trip to Bountiful*), and even as comic relief (*Witness*)." Ranging from the personal to the global, then, events can also provide yet one more means for intracinematic subcontextual film study.

As films from the United States flood the world in a kind of "cultural imperialism" neither predicted nor surpassed, and as images from our movies dominate both the domestic and international landscape, it is appropriate to examine them closely. The intracinematology approach adds a much-needed dimension to that investigation.

FILMOGRAPHY ON THE HOMELESS

Referring to the filmography in the Appendix, a number of general comments are made about filmic treatment of the homeless, and then specific detailing of various motion pictures are highlighted.

For starters, it is striking, as one reviews the more than seventy films identified here with images of the homeless, that practically every top director has tackled the theme, including the following: D.W. Griffith, Charles Chaplin, William Wellman, King Vidor, Jean Renoir, Lewis Milestone, John Ford, Preston Sturges, Luis Bunuel, John Schlesinger, Akira Kurosawa, Martin Scorsese, Martin Ritt, Hal Ashby, Hector Babenco, Melvin Van Peebles, Paul Mazursky, Mira Nair, Peter Yates, John Hughes, Mel Brooks, Lawrence Kasden, Martha Coolidge, Mike Leigh, and many others. Put another way, it is almost as if part of the auteur theory demands being able to deal with such a sticky subject.

The stories and screenplays presented here include works some of our greatest authors, counting among their number these famous names: Charles Dickens's *Oliver Twist* (1922), Elmer Rice's adaptation of his Pulitzer Prize-winning *Street Scene* (1931), Maxim Gorky's play *The Lower Depths* (1936), Mark Twain's *Prince And The Pauper* (1937), John Steinbeck's *Of Mice and Men*

(1939) and *Grapes of Wrath* (1940), Evan H. Rhodes's *The Prince of Central Park* (1977), Ernest J. Gaine's *The Sky Is Gray* (1980), Vincent Patrick's *The Pope of Greenwich Village* (1984), George Eliot's *Silas Marner* (1985), and William Kennedy's Pulitzer Prize-winner *Ironweed* (1987). Again, one is prompted to admire those willing to take on weighty topics.

The homeless themselves have been portrayed by such outstanding actors and actresses as the following: Charlie Chaplin (*The Tramp* (1915); *The Kid* (1921); *City Light* (1931)), Louise Brooks (*Beggars of Life* (1927)), Sylvia Sidney (*Street Scene* (1931)), Al Jolson (*Hallelujah I'm A Bum*, 1932), Jean Gabin (*The Lower Depths* (1936)), Errol Flynn (*Prince And The Pauper* (1937)), Burgess Meredith, Lon Chaney, Gary Sinese, and John Malkovich in various *Of Mice and Men* versions, Henry Fonda in *Grapes Of Wrath* (1940), Cary Grant in *None But The Lonely Heart* (1944), Mickey Rooney as ex-jockey in *National Velvet* (1944) and later as an elderly homeless man in *Home For Christmas* (1990), Dorothy McGuire in *Summer Magic* (1963), Dustin Hoffman and Jon Voight in *Midnight Cowboy* (1969), Barbara Hershey and David Carradine in *Boxcar Bertha* (1972)—Carradine also playing in *Bound For Glory* (1976), Cicely Tyson in *Sounder* (1972), Gene Hackman and Al Pacino as drifters in *Scarecrow* (1973), Tim Conway in *The Billion Dollar Hobo* (1977), Levar Burton in *Billy: Portrait Of A Street Kid* (1977), Anthony Quinn in *Children Of Sanchez* (1978), Jill Eikenberry in *Orphan Train* (1979), Dan Aykroyd and Eddie Murphy in *Trading Places* (1983), Eric Roberts and Mickey Rourke in *The Pope Of Greenwich Village* (1984), Ben Kingsley in *Silas Marner* (1985), Kris Kristofferson in *Trouble In Mind* (1985), Nick Nolte, Bette Midler, and Richard Dreyfuss in *Down And Out In Beverly Hills* (1986), Martin Sheen in *Samaritan: Mitch Snyder Story* (1986), Jack Nicholson and Meryl Streep in *Ironweed* (1987), Cher and Liam neeson in *Suspect* (1987), John Lithgow in *Distant Thunder* (1988), Mel Brooks in *Life Stinks* (1991), Jeff Bridges and Robin Williams in *The Fisher King* (1992), Jack Lemmon in *For Richer, For Poorer* (1992), Kevin Kline, Danny Glover, Steve Martin, Mary McDonnell, Mary-Louise Parker, and Alfre Woodard in *Grand Canyon* (1992), Kris Kristofferson and Martin Sheen in *Original Intent* (1992), Bill Paxton in *The Vagrant* (1992), Danny Glover and Matt Dillon in *The Saint Of Fort Washington* (1993), Burt Reynolds in *The Man From Left Field* (1993), Rae Dawn Chong in *Boca* (1994) and *Boulevard* (1994), Joe Pesci in *With Honors* (1994), and Patrick Swayze in *Three Wishes* (1995).

Documentaries, docu-dramas, and biographies are also well represented in the filmography. Lionel Rogosin's *On The Bowery* (1956) presents a disturbing view of depraved alcoholic nomads trying to manage day by day. Levar Burton plays *Billy: Portrait Of A Street Kid* (1977), while Anthony Quinn stars as a starving Mexican worker trying to keep his large family together in *Children Of Sanchez* (1978). Martin Bell's *Streetwise* (1985) documents young homeless pimps, prostitutes, and panhandlers. *Kanal* (1956), the second in Andrzej Wajda's World War 11 trilogy, tells of Polish resistance fighters, while *A Cry From The Streets* (1959) deals with the homeless children London social workers treat. *Streetwise* (1985) provides a grim documentary on Seattle's underbelly, while Lee Grant's *Down And Out In Beverly Hills* (1986) was an Oscar-winning expose on the "new poor." Mira Nair's *Salaam Bombay* (1988) follows in the steps of Hector Babenco's *Pixote* (1981) or Zalman King's *Boca* (1994), heartbreaking scenarios dealing with Brazilian streetchildren. *Monsieur Vincent* (1949) recounts the life of the 17th century social worker St. Vincent de Paul, patron saint of social workers. *Bound For Glory* (1976) recounts the work of singer or activist Woody Guthrie, as does *Samaritan: Mitch Snyder Story* (1986), a Vietnam veteran who launched a political crusade against homelessness. And *God Bless The Child*, a 1988 made-for-TV movie starring Mare Winningham as a young single mother forced to live on the streets with her seven-year-old daughter, is particularly poignant.

Another interesting part of the phenomenon of films about the homeless is the fact of its global nature. Reflecting so many different cultures and countries, this list includes films from the following places: Brazil (*Pixote*, 1981; *Boca*, 1994); Canada (*Boulevard*, 1994); France (*The Lower Depth*S, 1936; *Monsieur Vincent*, 1949; *Mon Homme*, 1996), Germany (*Orphan Boy of Vienna*, 1937), Great Britain (*Oliver Twist*, 1922; *A Cry From The Streets*, 1959; *Silas Marner*, 1985), India (*Salaam Bombay*, 1988), Italy (*Pardon My Trunk*, 1952; *Accatone!*, 1961); Japan (*Dodes Ka-Den*, 1970), Mexico (*Los Olvidados*, 1950; *Children Of Sanchez*, 1978), Poland (*Kanal*, 1956), and of course the United States.

Content-wise in the filmography, particular terms keep cropping up. Orphans, for example, abound: Jackie Coogan, the first child star, is adopted by Charlie Chaplin's Little Tramp in 1921's *The Kid*, then by Lon Chaney as Gagin, leader of a gang of pickpockets, in *Oliver Twist* (1922). We see the joy that an orphan girl brings to reclusive *Silas Marner* (Ben Kingsley) in the 1985 film version of George Eliot's novel, struggles others have adjusting to life in a German orphanage in *Orphan Boy of Vienna* (1937), orphaned Wisconsin siblings in *All Mine To Give* (1956), two orphans living in a tree in *The Prince Of Central Park* (1977) who are befriended by a lonely old woman, and New York City street kids taken out west to farm families in the mid-19th century in *Orphan Train* (1979).

Date- and context-wise, certain periods of time are quite evident in motion pictures depicting the homeless. While the Great Depression figures in *Hallelujah I'm A Bum* (1932), *Sullivan's Travels* (1941),1972 *Boxcar Bertha* (1972), *Bound For Glory* (1976), and *Ironweed* (1987), Vietnam appears to play a role in *Samaritan: Mitch Snyder Story* (1986) and *Distant Thunder* (1988). *Three Wishes* (1995), set in 1955, situates Patrick Swayze as a mysterious drifter appropriately entering the lives of widow Mary Elizabeth Mastrantonio and her two young sons just when they need a little magic.

Slums are the locale for *They Shall Have Music* (1939), *None But The Lonely Heart* (1944), *Los Olvidados* (1950), *Accatone!* (1961), *Dodes Ka-Den* (1970), and *Pixote* (1981). The streets, quite obviously, are where the action is—particularly those of New York City. As early as 1931, King Vidor's *Street Scene* introduced the world to images of immigrants struggling to move beyond the tenements. The next year found Al Jolson serving as the "mayor" of Central Park hobos in the musical comedy *Hallelujah I'm A Bum* (also known as I'm a Tramp)—until, that is, he is reformed by a beautiful woman (Madge Evans). *On The Bowery* (1956) takes place on the Lower East Side, *Midnight Cowboy*

(1969) and obviously *Times Square* (1980) in the 42nd Street area. Also from the Big Apple come *The Pope Of Greenwich Village* (1984), *Emanon* (1986), *The Fisher King* (1992), *The Saint Of Fort Washington* (1993), and *Sunday* (1997).

But this filmography in no way limits stories of the homeless to New York City. Also available are images from the Oklahoma Dust Bowl (*Grapes Of Wrath*, 1940), Wisconsin (*All Mine To Give*, 1956), Maine (*Summer Magic*, 1963), Arkansas (*Boxcar Bertha*, 1972), the 1930s South (*Sounder*, 1972), 1940s Louisiana (*The Sky Is Gray*, 1980), Philadelphia (*Trading Places*, 1983), Seattle (*Streetwise*, 1985), Albany (*Ironweed*, 1987), Washington, D.C. (*Suspect*, 1987), and noticeably in Los Angeles (*Down And Out In Beverly Hills*, 1986; *Up Your Alley*, 1989; *Life Stinks*, 1991; *Grand Canyon*, 1992; *Where The Day Takes You*, 1992; *Death Game*, 1996). Outside of the United States, we also learn of their plights in Bombay (*Salaam Bombay*, 1988), Italy (*Accatone*, 1961), London (*Oliver Twist*, 1922; *The Prince And The Pauper*, 1937; *None But The Lonely Heart*, 1944; *A Cry From The Streets*, 1959; *Silas Marner*, 1985; *Naked*, 1993), Mexico (*Los Olvidados*, 1950; *Children Of Sanchez*, 1978), Rio (*Pixote*, 1981) and *Boca* (1994), Tokyo slums (*Dodes Ka-Den*, 1970), Toronto (*Boulevard*, 1994), and Warsaw (*Kanal*, 1956).

While there is no particular genre associated with filmic depictions of the homeless, nevertheless certain themes and plot conventions predominate. Brigham (1996, p.173) claims that, while different characterizations prevail,

A discrete image does emerge: Contemporary American filmmakers routinely and most frequently portray the homeless as middle-aged or elderly, single (that is, not accompanied by significant others) white males, who are dirty and or or disheveled, who are—in most cases—suffering from alcoholism and or or mental illness—and only occasional physical health problems, and who are homeless either for unexplained or probably apocryphal. . .reasons—not due to the shortcomings of social institutions or the policies and power of the dominant social class. As will emerge from the following discussion, attitudes toward the homeless have made precipitous changes.

It is believed that the first motion pictures relative to this topic dealt with tramps, a character type that, Charles Musser (1990, p.40) reminds us, "was rooted in English and American popular culture." He elaborates.

During the late nineteenth and early twentieth centuries, the tramp was a stock character in the music hall and vaudeville (where W.C. Fields was a 'tramp juggler'), the comic strip (cartoon tramps included Happy Hooligan, Weary Willie, and Burglar Bill), pulp literature, and the newspaper. The motion picture debut of the comic tramp occurred in June 1897, when the American Mutoscope Company made *The Tramp and the Bathers*, a film in which the tramp steals the clothes of a man who is swimming in a small lake. Almost every production company had its tramp comedies at the turn of the century.

Of particular note is *The Twentieth Century Tramp* (1902), a 50-foot novelty film attributed to Edwin S. Porter; produced before movies were designed to tell a story, it features an airborne tramp figure holding onto a balloon and pedaling a bicycle, flying high above New York City. Nearly twice as long, the Edison short *A Romance Of The Rail* (1903) recounts a tale about a young couple aboard the Lackawana Railroad—a more likely place for where the homeless hung out (Anderson, 1923).[3] D.W. Griffith, considered by many film historians to be the most important auteur of the Silent Era, introduced his famous technique of parallel editing (or "switch-back") in the suspenseful story of *The Lonedale Operator* (1911).

Unquestionably, the person most associated with tramps is Charlie Chaplin. While prior to his presentations most movies depicted tramps as villains, Chaplin's efforts painted yet another portrait. For starters, there was his choice of clothing which, according to Jay Boyer (1990):

The costume itself seems to speak to the human condition. The little bristle of a moustache speaks to all our little vanities, the ill-fitting jacket and oversized pants to the difference between how we would have the world perceive us and how we actually look. And then too there's the bowler hat, dingy and worn, and the bamboo cane—not a gentleman's walking stick mind you, but just a poor bamboo cane. How better to remind us of our own sad attempts at finery? (p.79)

The Tramp (1915) courageously saves a young girl from crooks, then is cared for by her in return. A similar twist occurs in *The Kid* (1921), when the tramp adopts an abandoned baby boy whose mother, sometime later, comes to claim him. The silent masterpiece *City Lights* (1931) has the Little Tramp befriending a blind flower girl, prompting him to steal from a millionaire so that he can help her have an eye operation, culminating in a poignant fade-out. Contrast these plot devices with that of 1985's *Tramp At The Door*, where a transient poses as a distant relative of a family from whom he seeks food and shelter, wisely weaving fabricated stories that he thinks will win them over.

Charlie Chaplin's *The Idle Class* (1921) was probably the first film to introduce the notion of mixed identities; here, a tramp is mistaken for the husband of a lady. Mark Twain's *The Prince And The Pauper* (1937) mixes up a prince and a London lookalike street beggar. But in 1983, *Trading Places* brought the plot to a comic peak when two Philadelphia businessmen (Ralph Bellamy and Don Ameche) strike a bet that a Black street hustler (Eddie Murphy) can do better than their sniveling nephew investment broker (Dan Aykroyd)—and of course they're correct.

A twist on this twist is the notion of people pretending, in the movies, to be homeless. In 1941, Preston Sturges fakes a penniless hobo in the social comedy *Sullivan's Travels*—but finds out that homelessness is not quite so funny. Tim Conway has to live like a hobo in order to collect a multimillion-dollar inheritance in *The Billion Dollar Hobo* (1977). Then, in 1991, Mel Brooks brought us *Life Stinks*, which he co-wrote, directed, and starred in, about a feisty millionaire who bets he will relinquish all his earthly goods if he can life on the streets for a month. *For Richer, For Poorer* (1992) mimics the idea, with Jack Lemmon as a self-made millionaire who gives away all his money so he can remember what it's all about anyway.

A classic case for incorporating the homeless is film is found in the runaway character, usually from some authority figures such as Louise Brooks in *Beggars Of Life* (1927), hiding out from the cops even though she shot her adoptive father in self-defense. Otherwise, we mostly see the homeless wanting to run away from their situations, such as in *Street Scene* (1931) or *Times Square* (1980). Or, Hollywood shows us how you can't run away with evil intent; just look what happened to the *Midnight Cowboy* (1969) who wanted to hustle but got himself hustled instead. 1992's *Where The Day Takes You* deals with runaways in Los Angeles, banding together for support. Burt Reynolds plays a homeless coach, *The Man From Left Field* (1993), whose little leaguers help give his life new meaning. In *Boulevard* (1994), Rae Dawn Chong stars as a street-smart prostitute who befriends a young runaway, teaching her the tricks of survival. Then, *Home Of Angels* (1994) reverses the theme, when a young man helping his grandfather escape from a nursing home is aided by a homeless person when they are threatened by a street gang.

Can you imagine having a musical about the homeless? Premiering at the same time as *Little Orphan Annie* (1932), *Hallelujah I'm A Bum* (1932) greeted the Great Depression with Al Jolson performing for his fellow hobos. *They Shall Have Music* (1939) casts concert violinist Jascha Heifetz as a "pied piper" to help a music school in the slums. Hal Ashby's *Bound For Glory* (1976) chronicles Woody Guthrie's music along the railroads of Depression-era America.

Beginning around the 1980s, the homeless began to take on mythic proportions in the movies. Rather than being scared of them, or looking down on them, motion pictures encouraged us to learn from them. Although this thematic twist was introduced in Jean Renoir's *The Lower Depth* (1936, remade in 1957 by Akira Kurosawa), where an impoverished thief teaches a destitute aristocrat how to enjoy life without material things, or Clifford Odets' *None But The Lonely Heart* (1944), where a vagrant pulls himself out of the slums, we first see the poverty and pride combined in Stan Lathan's *The Sky Is Gray* (1980). In the case of Melvin Van Peebles' *Taking Care Of Terrific* (1985), the savvy one is a street musician. Kris Kristofferson plays an ex-cop who learns about life from a gang of homeless kids in *Trouble In Mind* (1985).

The 1986 comedy *Down And Out In Beverly Hills*, which derives from the 1925 French play demonstrating the triumph of bourgeois culture, *Boudu Saved from Drowning*, features Nick Nolte as a suicidal bum who chooses a swimming pool on the swanky property owned by Bette Midler and Richard Dreyfuss in which to drown his sorrows; predictably, we quickly learn who are the truly dysfunctional—even if we are left wondering who really are the truly rich. In *Emanon* (1986), the vagabond whose name in reverse belies itself is revealed to be none other than the Messiah. *El Derecho De Comer* (1987), which translates to "Right to Eat," features a good-natured vagrant who happens upon a purse filled with money and a love letter.

Liam Neeson plays a deaf or mute homeless veteran, the *Suspect* (1987) in a murder case, who enlightens the life of his public defender (Cher). John Lithgow also plays a veteran, in *Distant Thunder* (1988); a hermit traumatized by his Vietnam experience, his eventual return to society is meant to inspire. In *Up Your Alley* (1989), Linda Blair is a reporter assigned to a story on homelessness who ends up falling for a skidrow bum. Skid Row was the scene of the death of a military officer's brother, who recruits a platoon of homeless people to help find the killer, in *Bums* (1993). John Hughes' *Curly Sue* (1991) has the young ragtag con artist triumphing over her lawyer.

Of all the motion pictures dealing with the homeless, probably the one that best supports my notion of the trend toward having them painted as intellectually or spiritually superior can be seen in Terry Gilliam's *The Fisher King* (1992). The convoluted story has Jeff Bridges as a radio talkshow host whose comments have caused a tragedy, plunging him into despair and heading for the streets—where he meets up with Robin Williams and a search for the Holy Grail. More soul-searching is inspired by a homeless person in *Grand Canyon* (1992). In *Original Intent* (1992), we see a yuppie lawyer deciding, at great personal cost, to save a condemned shelter for the homeless from a greedy developer. That same year in *The Vagrant* we see a yuppie homeowner (Bill Paxton) being harassed by a homeless man who used to live there.

Mike Leigh's disturbing film *Naked* (1993) features a nihilistic drifter, alternately searching for sex and for shelter. About the only other recent negative view of the homeless comes in *Down, Out And Dangerous* (1995), when the befriended becomes a psycho killer. *The Saint Of Fort Washington* (1993) focuses on Danny Glover as a down-and-out and Matt Dillon as a would-be photographer schizophrenic making do with daily struggles in the city. The futuristic *Death Game* (1994) has street kids battling with cyborgs. Joe Pesci stars as a homeless person in Alek Keshishian's *With Honors* (1994); after finding Harvard student Brendan Fraser's honors thesis, which he holds in ransom, the two sides end up swapping a real education.

Mon Homme (1997) features a French hooker who picks up a homeless man whom she grooms to a new station in life by first building up his self-esteem. Gene Hackman is cast as an unscrupulous doctor in *Extreme Measures* (1997), trying to convince intern Hugh Grant that it's OK to perform research experiments on the homeless; "They're either lost of cold or stoned or worse. . .they have no families, nothing," he argues—until stopped by the authorities. And the most recent film dealing with the homeless is *Sunday* (1997), Grand Jury Prize winner of the Sundance Film Festival, which deals with another homeless man helped by a woman. Just as Peter H. Rossi (1990) has pointed out historical dichotomies between the old homeless and the new homelessness, so too has Tinseltown taken note.

CONCLUSION

In 1993, Catherine A. Lutz and Jane L. Collins scrutinized and deconstructed a venerable American institution in their *Reading National Geographic*, encouraging us to realize how editors attempt to guide us toward certain class considerations. A book reviewer made this observation:

National Geographic offered a kind of *Wunderkammer*, or cabinet of curiosities: A heterogeneous archive of natural specimens, both generic and peculiar, a collection summing up the Creation for the pleasure and instruction of its readers. But it also masked, under is high-minded pursuit of scientific knowledge, a thrilling prurience about other people's bodies, a fearful inquisitiveness about tribal rites and customs, a thirst for the primitive and the exotic. (Warner, 1993)

By the same token, movie producers and directors continually impose their ideological assumptions. Attitudes toward demographic variables like age, ethnicity, and socioeconomic status become subsumed by various biases. Consider: during the Silent Era the homeless were written off primarily as tramps, positioned as "other" by means of their villainous actions (Brownlow, 1990). In the same way that we as audience members are let off from caring about the homeless in this capacity, later representations of them as lowlife and or street-smart, worldly-wise mystics provide an equally easy allowance for keeping our distance from both the people and their problems.

In terms of the theory of intracinematology, one can see that a close reading of motion pictures dealing with the topic of the homeless reveals clear-cut demonstrations for dealing, or in this case not dealing with a difficult subject. In the early days of cinema it was easy to establish that person as villainous or comic tramp, whose life was so different as to make him "other"; later, that figure is again differentiated by being eccentric, albeit spiritually superior. As our society becomes evermore stratified in terms of both its economic and information gaps (Gallimore and Fuller, forthcoming), we unfortunately seem to be grasping at excuses for not dealing with the very people and problems that need our attention. It seems appropriate to conclude this discussion with a quotation from William Brigham's (1996, p.167) study of Hollywood's depictions of the dispossessed.

The myths of individualism and personal choice, institutional neutrality, absence of social conflict and class divisions, personal rather than institutional responsibility for social ills and immoral or unethical behavior all function to govern the production of popular culture products. The themes, characterizations, and plots of popular film adhere to these myths in the interest of ensuring continued obeisance to a social structure and process that benefits the elites.

APPENDIX

Filmography

1902 *The Twentieth Century Tramp.* Director: Edwin S. Porter
1903 *A Romance Of The Rail.* Director: Thomas Edison
1911 *The Lonedale Operator.* Director: D.W. Griffith
1915 *The Tramp.* Director: Charles Chaplin
1921 *The Kid.* Director: Charles Chaplin
1921 *The Idle Class.* Director: Charles Chaplin
1922 *Oliver Twist.* (British). Director: Frank Lloyd (Remakes: 1933, 1948, 1968, 1982, and 1985)
1927 *Beggars Of Life.* Director: William Wellman
1931 *City Lights.* Director: Charles Chaplin
1931 *Street Scene.* Director: King Vidor
1932 *Hallelujah I'm A Bum.* Director: Lewis Milestone
1936 *The Lower Depth.* (French). Director: Jean Renoir
1937 *Orphan Boy of Vienna.* (German). Director: Max Neufeld

1937   *Prince and the Pauper.* Director: William Keighley (Remakes: 1962, 1971, and 1978)
1939   *Of Mice and Men.* Director: Lewis Milestone
1939   *They Shall Have Music.* Director: Archie Mayo
1940   *Grapes Of Wrath.* Director: John Ford
1941   *Sullivan's Travels.* Director: Preston Sturges
1944   *National Velvet.* Director: Clarence Brown
1944   *None But The Lonely Heart.* Director: Clifford Odets
1949   *Monsieur Vincent.* (French). Director: Maurice Cloche
1950   *Los Olvidados.* (Mexican). Director: Luis Bunuel
1952   *Pardon My Trunk.* (Italian). Director: Gianni Franciolini
1956   *All Mine To Give.* Director: Allen Reisner
1956   *Kanal.* (Polish). Director: Andrzej Wajda
1956   *On The Bowery.* Director: Lionel Rogosin
1959   *A Cry From The Streets.* (British). Director: Lewis Gilbert
1961   *Accatone!* (Italian). Director: Pier Paolo Pasolini
1963   *Summer Magic.* Director: James Neilson
1969   *Midnight Cowboy.* Director: John Schlesinger
1970   *Dodes Ka-Den.* (Japanese). Director: Akira Kurosawa
1972   *Boxcar Bertha.* Director: Martin Scorsese
1972   *Sounder.* Director: Martin Ritt
1973   *Scarecrow.* Director: Jerry Schatzberg
1976   *Bound For Glory.* Director: Hal Ashby
1977   *The Billion Dollar Hobo.* Director: Stuart E. McGowan
1977   *Billy: Portrait Of A Street Kid.* Director: Steven Gethers
1977   *The Prince Of Central Park.* Director: Harvey Hart
1978   *Children Of Sanchez.* (Mexican-US). Director: Hall Bartlett
1980   *The Sky Is Gray.* Director: Stan Lathan
1980   *Times Square.* Director: Allan Moyle
1981   *Pixote.* (Brazilian). Director: Hector Babenco
1983   *Trading Places.* Director: John Landis
1984   *The Pope of Greenwich Village.* Director: Vincent Patrick
1985   *Silas Marner.* (British). Director: Giles Foster
1985   *Streetwise.* Director: Martin Bell
1985   *Taking Care Of Terrific,* Director: Melvin Van Peebles
1985   *Tramp At The Door.* Director: Allan Kroeker
1985   *Trouble In Mind.* Director: Alan Rudolph
1986   *Down And Out In Beverly Hills.* Director: Paul Mazursky
1986   *Emanon.* Director: Stuart Paul
1986   *Samaritan: Mitch Snyder Story.* Dir: Richard T. Heffron
1987   *El Derecho De Comer* (RIGHT TO EAT). Star: Arturo Correa
1987   *Ironweed.* Director: Hector Babenco
1987   *Suspect.* Director: Peter Yates
1988   *Distant Thunder.* Director: Rick Rosenthal
1988   *God Bless The Child.* Director: Larry Elikann
1988   *Salaam Bombay.* (Indian). Director: Mira Nair
1989   *Up Your Alley.* Director: Bob Logan
1990   *Home For Christmas.* Director: Peter McCubbin
1991   *Curly Sue.* Director: John Hughes
1991   *Life Stinks.* Director: Mel Brooks
1992   *The Fisher King.* Director: Terry Gilliam
1992   *For Richer, For Poorer.* Director: Jay Sandrich

1992 *Grand Canyon.* Director: Lawrence Kasden
1992 *Original Intent.* Director: Robert Marcarelli
1992 *The Vagrant.* Director: Chris Walas
1992 *Where The Day Takes You.* Director: Marc Rocco
1993 *Bums.* Director: Andy Galler
1993 *The Man From Left Field.* Director: Burt Reynolds
1993 *Naked.* Writer or Director: Mike Leigh
1993 *The Saint Of Fort Washington.* Director: Tim Hunter
1994 *Boca.* (Brazilian). Directors: Walter Avancini, Sandra Werneck
1994 *Boulevard.* (Canadian). Director: Penelope Buitenhuis
1994 *Home Of Angels.* Director: Nick Stagliano
1994 *With Honors.* Director: Alek Keshishian
1995 *Down, Out And Dangerous.* Director: Noel Nosseck
1995 *Three Wishes.* Director: Martha Coolidge
1996 *Death Game.* Star: Timothy Bottoms
1996 *Mon Homme* (French). Director: Bertrand Blier
1997 *Extreme Measures.* Director: Michael Apted
1997 *Sunday.* Director: Jonahan Nossiter

NOTES

1. "Cinematology," according to my sources at the G. and C. Merriam Company, producers of Webster's dictionaries, was a term first used in 1977 by James Monaco in his book "How to Read a Film" (Oxford University Press). The idea is that cinematology has to do with the study of film itself—as opposed to filmography, which deals with the economic, political, social, and technical causes and effects of motion pictures.

2. Carolyn Anderson (1996, p. 142) argues that, "Class markers are ubiquitous in all films, from set design to costume selection to ways of speaking."

3. Boyer (1990, p. 85) points out an interesting tie with commercialism in early film history: "Edison and Porter seem to have had a working relationship with the Lackawana Railroad, offering the company short, promotional films in return for services rendered. The film was probably intended to supllement a promotional campaign the railroad had underway. To counteract the image rail travel was acquiring as a hot, dirty, unpleasant form of transportation, the Lackawana Railroad employed a print campaign using photographer's model Marie Murray as Phoebe Snow, the Lackawana Girl. Phoebe was inevitably dressed in white, suggesting that a trip aboard the Lackawana would leave you white as snow."

REFERENCES

Anderson, Carolyn. 1996. "Diminishing Degrees of Separation: Class Mobility in Movies of the Reagan-Bush Era." In Paul Loukides and Linda K. Fuller (eds.) *Beyond the Stars V: Themes and Ideologies in American Popular Film.* (Bowling Green, OH: Popular Press): 141–163.

Anderson, Nells. 1923. *The Hobo: The Sociology of the Homeless Man.* Chicago, IL: University of Chicago Press.

Boyer, Jay. 1990. "Superfluous People: Tramps in Early Motion Pictures." In Paul Loukides and Linda K. Fuller (eds.) *Beyond the Stars V: Stock Characters in American Popular Film.* (Bowling Green, OH: Popular Press): 79–89.

Brigham, William. 1996. "Down and Out in Tinseltown: Hollywood Presents the Dispossessed." In Paul Loukides and Linda K. Fuller (eds.) *Beyond the Stars V: Themes and*

Ideologies in American Popular Film. (Bowling Green, OH: Popular Press): 163–186.

Brownlow, Kevin. 1990. *Behind the Mask of Innocence: Films of Social Conscience in the Silent Era*. London: Jonathan Cape.

Fuller, Linda K. 1992. "Seeing Cinema Cross-Culturally: *Gremlins* in Yugoslavia as a Case Study." Paper presented at the Northeast Popular Culture Association Meeting, Boston, MA.

Fuller, Linda K. 1997. "We Can't Duck the Issue: Imbedded Advertising in the Motion Pictures." In Katherine T. Frith (ed.) *Undressing the Ad: Reading Culture in Advertising* (New York: Peter Lang Publishing): 117–138.

Gallimore, Timothy A. and Linda K. Fuller. Forthcoming. *Telecommunications: Implications for Markets, Multiculturalism, and Media*. Quebec, Canada: World Heritage Press.

Grogg, Sam L., Jr. and John G. Nachbar. 1982. "Movies and Audiences: A Reasonable Approach for American Film Criticism." In Michael Marsden (ed.), *Movies as Artifacts: Cultural Criticism of Popular Film*. (Chicago: Nelson-Hall): 1–9.

Haining, Peter. 1982. *The Legend of Charlie Chaplin*. Secacus, NJ: Castle.

Jackson, Kathy Merlock. 1986. *Images of Children in American Film*. Metuchen, NJ: The Scarecrow Press, Inc.

Jacobs, Lewis. 1968. *The Rise of the American Film*. New York: Teachers College Press.

Lutz, Catherine A. and Jane L. Collins. 1993. *Reading National Geographic*. Chicago, IL: University of Chicago Press.

Miller, Mark Crispin. 1990. "Advertising: End of Story." In Mark Crispin Miller (ed.) *Seeing Through Movies*. New York: Pantheon Books.

Musser, Charles. 1990. "Work, Ideology, and Chaplin's Tramp." In Robert Sklar and Charles Musser (eds.) *Resisting Images: Essays on Cinema and History*. (Philadelphia, PA: Temple University Press): 36–67.

Rossi, Peter H. 1990. "The Old Homeless and the New Homelessness in Historical Perspective." *American Psychologist* (45): 954–59.

Sklar, Robert. 1922. *Our Movie-Made Children*. New York: Vintage Press.

Warner, Marina. 1993. "High-Minded Pursuit of the Exotic: How National Geographic Fashioned the World." *The New York Times Book Review* (September 19): 13.

Chapter 11

The Effect of Pictures on the Attribution of Homelessness

Andrew Mendelson

Photographs were used to bring the world to people soon after their invention. Stereographs and carte-de-visite of the second half of the nineteenth century and, more recently, magazines like *Life* and *National Geographic*, allowed people a glimpse of the world without ever having to leave home. Photojournalists realized that the camera could do more than just present travel pictures of the world. Pictures could be used to document social ills in order to bring about social change. For example, Jacob Riis (1971), in his book, *How the Other Half Lives*, and his public lectures, exposed the poor conditions that people lived under in the slums of New York City just before the turn of the century and helped bring about many health code changes (Goldberg 1991). Another photographer, Lewis Hine photographed child workers in southern textile mills for the National Child Labor Committee. Hine's pictures, combined with descriptive statistics and text, appeared in newspapers and magazines and helped to bring about national child labor laws (Goldberg 1991). Mary Ellen Mark's pictures of a homeless family brought in ten thousand dollars in donations (Goldberg 1991).

The purpose of such photography is to bring attention to these problems and hopefully bring about a change in these conditions on a societal level. As Hine said in reference to the power of a picture of a young girl laboring in a cotton mill, "With a picture thus sympathetically interpreted, what a lever we have for the social uplift" (1980, p. 111). One could say that the purpose of these stories is not to place blame on the individual, but on society for the situation and to stimulate social action. If readers place the blame on the individuals such documentary pictures and stories are nothing more than snapshots of a different world.

Due to the financial costs they impose and the lack of space available (the shrinking news hole), newspapers seldom run picture stories as large as the documentary projects mentioned above but newspapers still try to expose the poor conditions under which people live, usually by presenting a case study of an individual as representative of a particular problem in the form of a story with one or two pictures. The hope is, as with the larger format documentary projects, that the story will cause people to empathize with the individual and seek alleviation of the problem. These stories and pictures seem to say, "How can society allow this problem to exist?" or "Something must be done." This use of pictures seems to move the onus of responsibility for the problem from the individual to the greater society.

In looking at the documentary work of the 1930s, Stott (1986) echoed the view that such pictures were taken to bring about change in society. As he states in regard to the documentary works of the 1930s: "The point of all these books was the same: to make the reader feel he was firsthand witness to a social condition" (Stott, 1986, p. 214). It seems apparent that these works were not trying to show an isolated incident, but a widespread problem. Moreover, according to Stott, it was the pictures more than the text that was the real power of persuasion. "It was true that the photographs carried most emotional punch: while a text would often generalize, they the pictures were invariably particular" (1986, p. 215).

People do seem to be moved by what they see in the pictures in newspapers. If nothing else they seem to question the cause and possible treatments for the problem. At the very least, social documentary works show people that a problem exists. At the other extreme is social change. "Social documentary encourages social improvement," Stott said (1986, p. 21).

Current research on television suggests that such stories and pictures may cause people to attribute responsibility for both the cause and treatment of a social problem to the individual suffering from it, and not to societal factors like the economy. To draw on Hine's quotation, perhaps people do not or are not able to interpret pictures of social ills sympathetically when they portray those who represent the problem. This would seem to contradict many of the myths of the power of social documentary photography to influence people and bring about social change. Most of the research on attribution of responsibility derived from viewing television has been done by Iyengar (1991). He did not separate out the visual and verbal components. This study replicates Iyengar's overall results and examines how people differentially attribute responsibility for homelessness depending on which newspaper stories and pictures they view.

IYENGAR'S FRAMING RESEARCH

Iyengar concludes that the way television news frames a story can change the way we attribute responsibility for a social problem. The tendency to blame the individual, according to Iyengar, is as much based on the way television frames news stories about social problems as any other variables. "The ability of news frames to alter attributions indicates that attributions can be thought of as short-lived factors that co-exist in individuals' minds with a host of other important psychological cues, some of which have been internalized over the course of a lifetime" (Iyengar, 1991, p. 83).

Iyengar defined two types of news frames: episodic and thematic. An episodic news frame focuses on a specific event or particular cases of an issue such as a case study of an unemployed worker. A thematic news frame is one that places political issues and events in some general context (1991, p.2), such as a story that talks about the rise in unemployment nationally. It is from these two frames that people must be able to attribute responsibility for a social problem. As Iyengar stresses, no story is completely frame done way or the other, but in any story one usually dominates (1991, p. 14). As Iyengar's research used television, he did not distinguish between the visual and the audio parts of a story; they were viewed as one matched unit, that is, the picture and the story were either both thematic or both episodic. This is an important distinction.

Iyengar focuses on two kinds of responsibility for a social issue: causal and treatment. Causal responsibility focuses on who is responsible for the creation of the problem. Treatment responsibility looks at who is responsible for solving or alleviating the problem (1991, p. 3). Research on attribution theory has primarily focused on how people make causal judgments, whereas little research has focused on who is responsible for doing something for a problem. This is because most people assume that whoever is responsible for causing the problem is responsible for solving the problem. As we will see later this is not always the case when it comes to social problems.

Both causal and treatment responsibility can be attributed either to the individual or to the society or government. When people attribute responsibility to the individual, they focus on factors having to do with a person, like his or her education status, job skills, motivation or work ethic. When people focus on the society as the source of responsibility, they focus on factors like those stemming from the economy or the prevailing political climate, things outside an individual's control.

By changing a story frame from thematic to episodic, the viewer's attribution of responsibility changes. As Iyengar states: "The concept of framing refers to subtle alterations in the statement or presentation of judgment or choice problems, and the term 'framing effects' refers to changes in decision outcomes resulting from these alterations" (1991, p. 11). In his experiments, Iyengar manipulated the way the issue was framed; between thematic or episodic versions, taken from actual network newscasts. Subjects viewed these stories in the presence of many other "dummy" stories of different issues. The same dummy stories were seen by all subjects. After viewing this mock newscast, the participants were given an extensive posttest, which probed their attributions of causal and treatment responsibility (1991, Ch. 3).

In his attribution experiments, Iyengar claims to have found significant framing effects. When subjects watched an episodic news story, they were more likely to attribute responsibility to the individual. He was able to find some framing effects for many long term issues, including poverty, terrorism, racial inequality and, to some extent, crime. For terrorism, he showed subjects various stories (one episodic, two different thematic, and one control group) based on the TWA hijacking in Beirut. The results showed significant differences (p. 10) in societal attributions between one of the thematic conditions and the episodic condition, but not between the other thematic and the episodic.

In the particular case of poverty, he found that when the television newscasts used a thematic framed news story, explanations for poverty were mostly focused on the economy or governmental policies. When the media used episodic frames, explanations for poverty focused on the individual (1987, p. 822). It should be noted that the attributions also depended on the type of poverty depicted (1991, p. 67). Episodic portrayals of homelessness elicited the most individual causal and treatment attributions, whereas an episodic portrayal of an unemployed worker did not elicit a significant attribution in either direction (1991, p. 54–55). It is hard to tell if Iyengar was really comparing the same entities. Does a story just have to be in the "poverty" class or should he have compared an episodic homeless story with a thematic homeless story?

Iyengar's studies are part of a larger area of social psychology: attribution theory. To understand the processes at work when people make attributions of responsibility, we must briefly examine this area.

ATTRIBUTION THEORY

Attribution theory focuses on how people use incoming information to form judgments about the causes of events or situations. There are many important reasons for people to form attribution of causality. "Psychologists consider attributions to be important because they are the underpinnings of further judgments, emotional reactions, and behavior" (Fiske and Taylor, 1991, p. 54). If a person attributes the cause of homelessness to the laziness of an individual homeless person, this will affect how that person votes or reacts to a homeless person that is encountered. Different subsequent behaviors would result if the person attributes responsibility to the society for the homeless problem.

According to Kelley (1972), when people have little real world experience on which to form an attribution of causality, they rely on causal schemas to understand what they perceive. "A causal schema is a general conception the person has about how certain kinds of causes interact to produce a specific kind of effect" (Kelley as quoted in Fiske and Taylor, 1991, p. 39). This suggests that even for events that we have limited experience with, we are still able to form attributions. Most people have very little experience with the actual events they see on the news, yet this does not stop them from making judgments about the causes of these events.

As these schemas are representations of generalized cause and effect relationships, it seems reasonable that, given different information on which to base the attribution, a different schema might be called up, resulting in a different final attribution. This ties into the concept of framing; given a different context, the final attribution will be different.

Another area of research on attribution theory focused on the fundamental attribution error. Research in this area has shown that people tend "to attribute another person's behavior to his or her own dispositional qualities, rather than to situational factors" (Fiske and Taylor, 1991, p. 67). For many reasons, people tend to ignore context when attributing behavior and focus only on the individual. The fundamental attribution error would suggest that people would be more likely to blame a homeless individual for being homeless than the society they live in.

Tversky and Kahneman (1973) write that people use what is most available or accessible when making attribution assessments. If what is most available in memory is a reference to an individual, it is likely a person will attribute responsibility for a problem to individuals and not society (and vice-versa if what is most available is a societal cue).

In other research, Reyes et al. (1980) showed that "social judgments calculated from memory should be biased in the direction of relevant information that is highly available in memory" (1980, p. 3). He states that information that is easier to recall will then serve as a retrieval cue for associated information. Research has shown that pictures are easier to recall than words. It seems reasonable to conclude that pictures might serve as a retrieval cue for associated words.

More recent research in this area focuses on how people attribute responsibility for social problems and other events they see or read about in the news. Such attributions will have an effect on how a person votes in elections. If a person sees individuals as being responsible for their problems, that person will be more likely to vote against welfare programs. Thus, attribution theory gives us an explanation for why such framing effects occur. People seem to make attributions based on what they most readily recall. The next section argues that, based on past picture research, the frame of pictures should have a larger impact on the direction of attribution.

PICTURE EFFECTS

There has been much research to show that pictures in print facilitate understanding and are more easily recalled than text. In looking at still photographs, it has been shown that a content relevant (i.e., having to do with the text) picture can be used to facilitate the recall of information presented in text (Levie and Lentz, 1982). These results held for both children (Koenke and Otto, 1969; Levin and Berry, 1980; Levin and Lesgold, 1978; and Peeck, 1974) and adults (Alesandrini, 1984 and Anglin, 1986), and over time (Anglin, 1987).

Moreover, Holmes (1987) found that pictures were facilitative in inferential tasks, not just factual recall. With the aid of pictures, subjects could more easily fill in the blanks of inferential questions than without the pictures (p. 16). It was also found that pictures in a newspaper have an agenda-setting effect. Wanta (1988) concluded that a dominant photograph could lead to an increase in the importance readers assigned to that issue.

More recently, Wanta and Roark (1993) found that the type of photo can affect knowledge acquisition and predictions about future events. The more a photograph ties directly into the accompanying story, the more knowledge will be acquired. If the photos depict somewhat unrelated information, knowledge gain will be lessened (1993, p. 18).

Glenberg and Langston (1992) were able to show that pictures facilitate the comprehension and recall of text by aiding in the formation of mental models. Mental models are a representation of what the text is about, not the specific text used. A picture can assist in the construction of a mental model because the structure of the picture (the relations between the parts) are often identical to the required structure of the mental model (Glenberg and Langston, 1992). It should be noted that for his experiment they did not use traditional pictures, as in photographs. Their pictures were more like diagrams or outlines of the text. Pictures in newspapers might influence how the text is remembered and thus recalled for making attribution assignments. As this experiment was between a picture and no-picture group, Glenberg and Langston give no indication whether two different pictures with the same text will have differing effects on memory.

Pictures are also recalled more easily from memory than words. This implies that pictures are more heavily weighted than words when remembering information. Paivio and Csapo (1973) found that for free verbal recall, items presented as pictures are easier to recall from memory than items presented as words.

One last effect of photographs is the ability to serve as icons. Certain photographs take on greater significance. As Goldberg (1991) says, "But the images I think of as icons almost instantly acquired symbolic overtones and larger frames of reference that endowed them with national or even worldwide significance" (1991, p. 135). These photographs become symbolically tied to a larger issue. An example of such a picture was Dorthea Lange's "Migrant Mother." Though this picture was of a destitute mother with three of her children, it shortly came to represent the entire Depression. Another example cited by Goldberg is Joe Rosenthal's "Old Glory goes up on Mt. Suribachi." This picture of six soldiers raising the American flag immediately came to stand for victory and American patriotism (Goldberg 1991, p. 147). These two pictures serve as mental abbreviations for larger issues, such as the Depression, poverty, and the struggle for victory. These pictures helped people recall the larger events or issues for which they stood.

Thus, past research does point to significant picture effects. It is reasonable to conclude that pictures should play an important role in affecting a viewer's attributions. Pictures are not only remembered better, they have been shown to affect the memory of the text with which they are associated.

HYPOTHESES

Iyengar's research shows that exposure to a certain story frame determines to a significant extent how a person will attribute responsibility for poverty (as well as other issues) from watching a television news story. As Iyengar only had two conditions; a thematic story and an episodic story; his results could be shown in a model like this:

Figure 11.1
Additive Model: Television Viewing

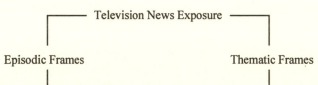

Iyengar does not differentiate between the verbal and pictorial elements in his study. These two elements are framed in the same way for any given story, either episodic or thematic.

Translating this to newspapers suggests an additive model where the effect of viewing elements framed in the same way add together to form an attribution effect, while elements framed in opposite way work to cancel each other out. In this model, the two episodic variables work together to produce the most individual responsibility attribution. This is most like the Iyengar episodic story on television, focusing totally on the individual. At the other extreme, are the two thematic components, working to produce the most societal/governmental attribution of responsibility. These two stories are the most focused on large, macro views of homelessness. The middle stories would seem to produce confusion in the viewer, because the frames are mixed, one being episodic and the other thematic: the two will negate each other. Such a model for newspapers would look like this:

Figure 11.2
Additive Model: Newspaper Viewing

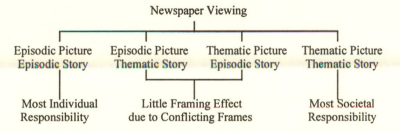

If the pictures and the words have truly independent effects with one dominating, two possible models would be the story-dominant and the picture-dominant. In these the attribution would go whichever way the dominant variable was framed that was viewed. For example, in a story-dominant mode, if a person read the episodic story, regardless of the picture seen, that person would attribute responsibility for homelessness to the individual. On the basis of the evidence from the Grimes (1990) study, these two possibilities seem unlikely. Grimes showed that the verbal and pictorial information interact in memory and are remembered more as one unit where either can change memory of the other element. For one element to have a dominating effect, that element would have to be remembered distinctly from the other.

Hypothesis One: The subjects' attributions to homelessness will follow the pattern proposed below in the interaction model.

Drawing on the research presented, I propose an interaction model. This model basically replicates the additive model (based on Iyengar), but it differs in how it deals with the mixed frame versions. I propose a model in which the picture is used to organize and cue recall of the text, thus affecting attribution. This model draws heavily on Glenberg and Langston's research and the largely qualitative research on social documentary.

As Figure 11.3 illustrates, the episodic picture/thematic story version is predicted to get the most societal attributions. Glenberg and Langston (1992) state that the picture helps organize a representation of what the story is about. Combining this research with the idea of an icon (a photo that symbolically is linked to a social issue) can explain why the episodic picture (a simple image of one person) with the thematic story (a social issue) would produce the most societal attribution. This individual homeless person would become the symbol or a "short-term icon" for the issue of homelessness. As pictures are more easily recalled than, this episodic picture, having been linked in memory to a social issue, would be recalled as a huge societal problem. I am not suggesting that this picture will take on the long-term significance of a picture like Lange's "Migrant Mother," but this picture should have this connection with the issue for the short term. This idea was also echoed by Stott (1986) above, that while the text would generalize (thematic), the pictures would be "particular" (episodic). The picture's strong emotional tone is directed by the context created by the text. According to Stott (1986): "If the pictures in a documentary book stimulated most emotion, though, the emotion was guided by the text" (p. 215).

Figure 11.3
Interaction Model

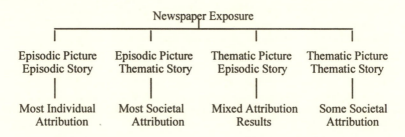

At the other extreme, that same episodic picture with the episodic story would be recalled rarely, perhaps attributable to something about that person. This picture would not be tied to a whole issue, but just one person. No short-term icon would be formed in memory. Since the picture and text both refer to one person, this will likely be a test of the Fundamental Attribution Error. Readers will be more likely to attribute that one homeless person's behavior (his being homeless) to dispositional qualities, rather than to situational factors.

The thematic picture with the thematic story would be like the television trend stories of the Iyengar studies. This would frame homelessness in terms of a societal issue, but without the symbolic neatness of the episodic photograph. Thus, there would be less societal attribution than the episodic picture with the thematic story.

Finally, the thematic picture with the episodic story could produce some societal attribution, if it is recalled as a political issue (the rally) with a human side, that is, homeless people are trying to be helped through societal change. But at the same time, it is likely that there could be some individual attribution, if people view this as a rally to help "one" person. That is, there are people working for change for something that is not widespread. This combination is not as likely to be seen in a real newspaper. But it will be close to the center in terms of attribution.

This hypothesis has two components: H1a: causal attribution, and H1b: treatment attribution. Both kinds of attribution were examined using the following controls: the subject's economic and social liberalness/conservativeness and religiousness. Also, the subject's attributions on the issue of racism were used as a control. This should represent a baseline measure of attribution as everyone was exposed to exactly the same version.

Hypothesis Two: Those subjects seeing the episodic picture will be more likely to state that they would send $5.00 to that homeless person.

While the above attributions address the idea of who or what should do something about homelessness and poverty in theory, it might be that there is a difference when a more specific treatment is offered. A specific case of the first hypothesis states that the version the subject sees will affect the extent to which the subject is willing to send money ($5.00) to the homeless person pictured or referred to in the story. It is more likely that the subjects who saw the episodic picture will be more likely to send the money than those who did not. They are able to attach a face with a problem. In some ways, regardless of who is responsible for the problem, people may feel it appropriate to send money. This will be controlled for by people's self-proclaimed views on charity and the average of their ideology toward economic and social issues (political ideology).

Hypothesis Three: Those subjects reading the thematic story will be more likely to say that homeless shelters are important.

There should be an effect on how the subjects rated the importance of homeless shelters depending on which experimental version the subject saw. This is another specific example of society being responsible for helping the homeless.

Hypothesis Four: Those subjects who read the newspaper more often will be less affected by frame differences than those who read less often.

One possibility that could affect results is how much the subject reads a newspaper. Those that read newspapers more often should be more likely to know the purpose of running any type of article on a social problem (i.e., to create awareness about a problem that needs correcting). They will be more used to version differences in the media. Someone not so used to these version differences will be more subject to their effects. This will be seen through an interaction between newspaper use and experimental group. Low users of newspapers will be more affected by the version they saw in the experiment, and high users will be less affected.

METHOD

The experiment took place during March and April 1993 at the University of Wisconsin, Madison. All of the subjects were undergraduate students enrolled in one of two journalism classes. In return for participation, the students were given extra credit points (as determined by the individual professor). Eleven subjects were drawn for the pilot test and seventy-nine were used for the actual experiment.

This experiment complied with all requirements of the University of Wisconsin Human Subjects Committee. As such, all participants were aware of what, in general, would be expected of them. Subjects were told that they would be participating in a newspaper learning study and that they would have to read a series of newspapers and fill out a questionnaire based on what they read.

For the pilot test, eleven subjects were run through the experiment over two sessions (seven and four per session) For the actual experiment, seventy-nine subjects were run over eight sessions (ranging from nine to thirteen per session). Each session lasted approximately one hour. There were four experimental groups (discussed in the following design section) and subjects were randomized between them.

MATERIALS

Stimulus Materials

The target issue that subjects were exposed to for attributions was homelessness. This is a topic that has been extensively covered in the past by documentary photographers and is still covered often by newspapers. This topic was also one that was examined in Iyengar's television research.

For this experiment, I manipulated both the stories and the pictures in terms of their frames (whether episodic or thematic). Drawing on Iyengar, the episodic story was a profile of a homeless person living on the streets of Madison. The thematic story focused on the difficulties in dealing with homelessness on a governmental level in Madison. Both stories were written by a University of Wisconsin journalism graduate student, who teaches undergraduate reporting classes and has worked as a newspaper reporter. Both stories were approximately the same length. The episodic story had 579 words and the thematic story had 460 words.

The pictures used were selected from the picture library of the *Wisconsin State Journal* and *Madison Capital Times*. The episodically framed picture was of an individual homeless person sitting outside warming himself over a small garbage can fire. The thematic picture was of a rally against homelessness. The picture was of a number of people holding signs. My reason for using the rally photograph as thematic was that it, more than any other picture, seems to set the issue of homelessness in a societal/governmental context. It shows that other people feel that the government must do something about homelessness. All pictures used were black and white images, mainly to save printing costs.

Figure 11.4
Four Conditions of Attribution Measurements

Episodic Picture Episodic Story	Thematic Picture Episodic Story
Epsodic Picture Thematic Story	Thematic Picture Thematic Story

The stories and pictures were combined to form the four different conditions in this experiment. To make each picture/story combination fit together, the headlines and captions were altered. As seen in Figure 11.4, the headlines and captions added no new information, but either generalized what was in the story or restated what was in the story or picture.

To fill out the rest of the newspaper pages that the subjects viewed, distracter stories were selected, some just to fill space and others to serve as alternative attribution measures. None of these distracter stories (or pictures) addressed in any way the issue of homelessness or poverty. All these stories were pulled directly from past issues of the *Wisconsin State Journal* and *Madison Capital Times*. The pictures that originally went along with these stories were used also.

To examine people's attributions of responsibility to other social issues, a thematic story and picture about racism was used and an episodic story and picture about crime was used (though the final questionnaire did not examine attributions for crime). They were used as they originally ran in the *Wisconsin State Journal*.

Each subject saw three newspaper pages. The first and third were distracter pages that were exactly the same for all subjects (page 1—racism; page 3—crime). The second page was held constant except for the type of homeless picture and story.

The finished pages (mock-ups of the *Wisconsin State Journal* front pages) were laser printed on 11″ x 17″ paper. Cost prohibited printing the pages on full newspaper-sized broadsheet paper. The quality of the printing was good enough so that all the detail in the pictures was recognizable. The final product simply looked like a reduced photocopy of the *Wisconsin State Journal*.

EXPERIMENTAL PROCEDURES

The same procedures were used for the pilot test and the actual experiment (with minor changes). When subjects came in, they signed two volunteer consent forms, one of which they kept and the other I kept. They were given the three newspaper front pages (face down), and they were given twenty-five minutes to "go" through them. The pilot test was originally twenty minutes. The word "go" was used so as not to stress reading over looking at pictures.

Though many finished all three pages in that amount of time, some did not. All subjects were reading at least somewhere on the third page when time was called. They were also told not to talk to anyone else or read anything else during the experiment. No picture or story from the third page was probed in the questionnaire.

After twenty-five minutes, the pages were collected and the subjects filled out the questionnaire. Subjects were given as much time as necessary to complete the questionnaires. When everyone was done with these, the group was debriefed as to what this study was designed to find out. The entire experiment lasted approximately one hour per group.

CODING

Regardless of the version of the newspaper seen, every subject filled out the same questionnaire. The first set of questions probed the subject's beliefs on homelessness and poverty. These questions formed the basis for the dependent measure of responsibility attribution. These questions could be broken down into two sets, those that probed causal responsibility and those that probed treatment responsibility (four questions each).

In coding these open-ended questions, each distinct idea given was coded in one of four categories: those responses that blamed the individual, those that blamed the society, those that put responsibility for the problem to fate, and those that fell into none of these categories. Individual responses for the causal responsibility questions focused on characteristics of the homeless person (e.g., lack of motivation or lack of education). Societal responses for the causal responsibility questions focused on shortcomings of institutions in our society such as government or the economy. For treatment responsibility, the same categories were used. These categories were based on those used by Iyengar.

For each of these questions there was a code for the number of each type of response. These codes were added together to get a total number of attributions. To get the dependent measure for causal responsibility, all the individual attributions for questions two through five were added together and divided by the total number of responses for these four questions. This is the same type of measure Iyengar used, the percentage of responses that attributed causal responsibility to the individual. For the treatment responsibility, the dependent measure derived in the same way from the societal responses to questions six through nine. The four questions for each section were combined as one to give a stronger, more reliable measure of attribution. There was no reason to think that poverty was thought of differently than was homelessness based on the responses given.

The next series of questions examines people's views on homeless shelters. This is one of the main treatments that society has used for homelessness, so it gives another way to examine attribution of responsibility for this problem.

The racism questions were included to serve as a baseline measure of the subject's attribution of responsibility. As everyone saw the same story and picture, this can serve as covariate for preexisting beliefs about the responsibility for social issues. These two questions were coded in the same way as the homelessness questions, giving a percentage of responses that were either individualistic or societal.

Next, a series of temperature scales of favorability was used, examining a variety of groups of people. Another question examined whether people felt that they would donate $5.00 to a homeless person they read about or saw in the paper. It may be that people's feelings of charity are independent of the feelings of responsibility of homelessness.

The end of the questionnaire examined media usage and a variety of other demographic variables, such as political ideology, religion, income, age, and gender.

RESULTS

Power Analysis

Prior to the experiment, a power analysis was conducted using Iyengar's results to determine the proper sample size. As Iyengar only published sample means and the level of significance, power was determined using the t-value for which Iyengar's level (.01) and sample size (n = 86) met. These numbers were based on the t-test in Iyengar's Poverty Experiment 1 conducted between the homeless episodic condition (mean = .65; amount of individual causal attribution for poverty) and the national poverty thematic condition (mean = .18). These two categories were the closest to the categories I am using in my experiment (1991, p. 55).

Using the above t-value, I was able to generate a formula: $r^2 = (t^2/(n-2))/(1 + (t^2/n-2))$. This resulted in $r^2 = .0766$ (and thus $r = .2767$). To ensure the detection of an r of this size at = .05 and power = .80, we would need approximately n = 84. This translates to about twenty-one subjects per cell. This is only an estimate based on a similar study, and was only used as a guide as to how many subjects to run through the experiment. In the end, seventy-nine people participated (20, 20, 20, 19) in this experiment. With slightly less than the eighty-four subjects from the power analysis, this experiment may be under-powered and potential significant differences may not be detected because of this (type II error).

Descriptive Statistics

This section looks at the descriptive statistics for the variables. Across the four questions (added together) that probed the attribution of causal responsibility, the number of individual attributions ranged from 0 to 18 (mean = 5.06; sd = 3.32). For the social attributions for these questions, the number of responses ranged from 0 to 11 (mean = 3.82; sd = 2.35). The total number of attributions to these questions (the sum of the individual, social, fatalistic and other responses) ranged from 4 to 28 (mean = 9.99; sd = 4.06). Lastly, the percentage of individual attributions for these questions out of the total number of responses ranged form .0 to .93 (mean = .49; sd = .24). The percentage that attributed to society ranged from 0.00 to 1.00 (mean = .40; sd = .24).

Looking at the questions that probed the attributions of treatment responsibility, the number of individual responses ranged from 0 to 7 (mean = .81; sd = 1.38). The social responses ranged from 1 to 12 (mean = 6.33; sd = 2.09). The total number of responses ranged from 4 to 12 (mean 7.21; sd = 1.94). The percentage of the total responses that attributed responsibility for homelessness to society ranged from .125 to 1.00 (mean = .886; sd = .18). The percentage of the total that attributed homelessness to individuals ranged from 0 to .875 (mean = .105; sd = .17).

Reliability

Reliability measures were determined for the open-ended questions. High reliability is important because it shows consistency in how responses to the questions are being interpreted.

A coding guide was created prior to coding to cover both the open-and close-ended questions. The coding of the responses to the questionnaires was conducted by two people. A sample of eight questionnaires (two from each exposure condition, determined randomly) of the seventy-nine total sample was used to establish intercoder reliability measures for the open-ended responses. These eight were coded independently by both coders.

On the first coding attempt, the intercoder reliability was unacceptable. For the second attempt, a new second coder was trained. A new set of eight questionnaires was selected for reliability and coded independently by this second pair of coders.

The intercoder reliability was determined using Cronbach's Alpha. After the initial reliability analysis of the second coding set, 41 of the 48 open-ended variables were above the .70 level of reliability (mean reliability for these 41 variables = .919). If the other seven variables with lower reliabilities are included, the mean reliability for all 48 variables drops to .827.

For the final analysis of data the results of each individual question were added with its counterparts so as to increase reliability. Thus the reliability of these low variables was examined when they were added to a related variable. This analysis resulted in acceptable levels of reliability.

Multiple Regression Results

To investigate the above hypotheses, multiple regression techniques were employed. The results of the regressions were analyzed using a type II error, which holds the error term constant for all steps of the regressions.

For Hypothesis 1, a number of data analyses were conducted so that both causal and treatment responsibility could be examined. In addition, a number of third variables were also examined to identify possible individual differences due to exposure. The initial run simply looked for differences on level of attribution depending on which newspaper version was seen, without any controls.

The first dependent measure of attribution was the ratio of the total number of responses that attributed the cause of homelessness to the individual to the total of responses given. This was analyzed without the addition of any controlling variables. Looking at the regression, the overall F test of the R^2 = .0512 is not significant (F = 1.31; F = 2.74; = .05; df = 3.73). This means that neither of the main effects nor the interaction can be examined for significance (See Table. 11.1 for the cell means).

Even when controlling for other factors, specifically political ideology, the subject's religiousness, and the subject's views on the cause of racism, no significant effects were found. (political ideology, F = 1.23; F* = 2.74, = .05, df = 3,72) (religiousness, F = 1.31; F = 2.74, = .05, df = 3,72) (subject's views of racism, F = .81, F = 2.74, = .05, df = 3.70).

In looking at the results from the analyses for the effect of the different versions on the causal attributions, we see very little in terms of effects. When run without controls, none of the effects reached significance. Only the story's main effect was even close. Perhaps with a larger sample size (i.e. increased power), this effect would have been significant. This half of H1 is not supported. There was no significant difference between attributions of causal responsibility based on which newspaper version was seen. More specifically to this study and the effects of pictures, the two different pictures did not elicit different responses nor did they have more of an effect in directing attributions than the stories (as predicted above). Furthermore, the effects of individual differences in political ideology, religiousness, and views on racism had no significant effect in bringing out response differences.

One final note, the fundamental attribution error suggests that people are more likely to make causal attributions to dispositional factors rather than situational factors. This idea is not supported by this research. Looking at the mean for the causal attributions, ignoring the paper version seen, we get a value of .4878, which suggests that about 50 percent of the respondents blamed the individual for homelessness and 50 percent blamed society for homelessness.

Moving on to the attributions of responsibility for the treatment of homelessness, the ratio of total number of societal responses to the total number of responses was used as the dependent variable. The overall F-test for the $R^2 = .0457$ shows that it is not significant (F = 1.16; F = 2.74; = .05; df = 3,73). Again, since the overall F test is not significant, we cannot look at the various mean comparisons (for means see Table 11.1).

As above, the controls had no effect on the attributions. (for political ideology, F = 1.21; F* = 2.74, = .05, df = 3,72) (for religiousness, F = 1.26; F* = 1.996; = .05; df = 3,72) (for racism attributions, F = 2.67; F = 2.74, = .05, df = 3.70).

Table 11.1
Cell Means for Each Analysis

Dependent Variable	Control Variable	EP* and ES* N = 20	EP and TS* N = 20	TP* and ES N = 20	TP and TS N = 19
Treatment Attribution Ratio	None	.9034	.896	.822	.923
Casual Attribution Ratio	None	.566	.447	.513	.427
Send Money Rating	Charity Rating	4.64	5.86	4.03	6.26
Send Money Rating	Political Ideology	5.09	6.33	4.57	6.81
Send Money Rating	None	4.56	5.90	4.05	6.34
Homeless Shelter Support Rating	None	8.21	9.00	8.31	9.11
Causal Attribution Ratio	LNP* Use	.511	.489	.472	.476
	HNP* Use	.697	.192	.605	.274
Treatment Attribution Ratio	LNP Use	.855	.898	.800	.905
	HNP Use	.986	.878	.840	.972

*EP = Episodic Picture; ES = Episodic Story; TS = Thematic Story; TP = Thematic Picture; LNP = Low Newspaper Use; HNP = High Newspaper Use

The treatment responsibility, like the causal responsibility analysis, shows no significant effect of newspaper version on responses. This also holds true when the third variables are controlled. The frame of the pictures did not produce a main effect for attribution.

For this analysis, the means do not follow Iyengar's pattern. From most social attribution to least, we see: the thematic story/picture, episodic story/picture, thematic story/episodic picture, and episodic story/thematic picture. This pattern does not follow any of the hypothesized patterns.

These results do not support H1. The causal attribution results might replicate Iyengar's results, given a larger sample size. Also given a larger sample size, the fundamental attribution error might be supported. Just looking at where the dependent variable scores fell for the two analyses, ignoring the groupings, the subjects were more likely to attribute responsibility for the cause of homelessness to the individual and responsibility for the treatment of homelessness to the society.

One last item to examine is the correlation between the subjects' causal and treatment attribution scores. These two variables have $r = -.035$, which is not significantly different from 0 ($t = .306$, $t = 1.994$; $df = 73$; $= .05$). Thus, whom a person blames for the cause of homelessness does not necessarily predict who the subject believes is responsible for doing something about homelessness.

Hypothesis 2 examines whether there is a difference in responses to a specific case of treatment—namely, whether the subject would send \$5 to the homeless person mention in the article and/or shown in the picture, depending which version was examined.

The overall F-test of this regression was significant ($R^2 = .1478$; $F = 4.10$; $F = 3.13$; $= .05$; $df = 2,72$). Due to this significance, we may look further at the main effects and any interaction effect. The main effect of the story had a $t = 3.24$, which was significant at the $= .05$ level (thematic story mean $= 6.12$, episodic story mean $= 4.30$; $t = 1.994$; $df = 71$), but neither the main effect of the pictures ($t = .62$) nor the interaction between the pictures and the stories ($t = 1.34$) were significant. (See Table. 11.1 for means and see Figure. 11.5 for a graph of the means.) This effect was not altered when controlling for the subjects' beliefs in charity or political ideology.

These results suggest that the type of story, more than the type of picture, can affect people's willingness to give money to homeless people. Unlike what was hypothesized, it was not the personal profile that caused more willingness to give, but the story on the growth in the number of homeless. Having a face to attach to a problem made no difference. This seems to go against many of the ideas of social documentary and muckraking—that, personal accounts of social ills will move people to help.

It should be pointed out that there is the appearance of interaction in the means. With the thematic story, the addition of the thematic picture increases the subject's willingness to give \$5.00 when compared to the same story with the episodic picture. The opposite is true for the episodic story. With this story, the thematic picture lowers the subject's willingness to give. Perhaps with more subjects, this interaction would be significant. This might be because the thematic picture ties in better to the thematic story than to the episodic story.

Comparing these results to the ones above for treatment responsibility, we see that there is more of an impact of the frame when the treatment is a specific action by the subject (giving money), rather than when it is only theoretical (who should do something). Further, the r for the treatment responsibility dependent variable and the willingness to give \$5.00 dependent variable is .130. This value is not significantly different from 0 ($t = 1.15$; $t = 1.994$; $df = 73$; $= .05$). This suggests that there is no correlation between what a person believes should be done about about homelessness and his/her personal act of charity.

Looking at the r between willingness to send money and the causal score, we again see that the correlation is not significantly different from 0 (r = .035; t = .304; t = 1.992; df = 77; = .05). Thus, there is no correlation between who a person blames for homelessness and his/her willingness to lend support.

Figure 11.5
The Effect of the Newspaper Frames on Subjects' Willingness to Send $5.00

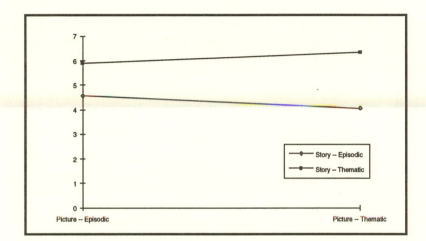

In Hypothesis 3, another example of a specific treatment for homelessness is examined, namely, the importance the subjects placed on homeless shelters. The independent measures of interest were again the contrast codes relating to newspaper version. These results were also controlled for subjects' views on welfare and, as above, political ideology.

The overall F-test (R^2 = .0778) in this regression was not significant (F = 3.04; F = 3.13; = .05; df = 2,72), based on a regression with only the codes for the two main effects entered (See Table 11.1 for the means). Again the model was not affected by the presence of controls (in this case, welfare beliefs and political ideology).

According to these results, seeing the different pictures or reading the different stories did not affect whether a person supported homeless shelters or not. Part of this may be because most people said they supported homeless shelters (mean = 8.62, on a 0–10 scale). This could be evidence of a ceiling effect. All the opinions are so close to the top of the scale that there is not much room for variance.

Homeless shelters are a specific societal treatment for homelessness. Looking at the correlation between the shelter score and the treatment score, we see an r = .218, which is not significant (t = 1.907; t* = 1.994; df = 73; = .05). It does seem that the more likely people are to call on society to do something about homelessness, the more likely they are to be in favor of homeless shelters. This correlation might have been significant with a few more subjects.

Hypothesis 4 refers to the effect of newspaper use on the attributions the subjects gave to the causes and treatments of homelessness. The expectation is that there should be an interaction between newspaper use and the attributions. Through regression analysis we can interpret this as an ANOVA design between the number of minutes per week spent reading newspapers and the newspaper form that the subject viewed in the experiment. Low users will be more affected by the version they saw, because they are less used to the format of the medium. High use of newspapers should negate any version effect.

Looking at the regression analysis for causal responsibility, the main effect of newspaper reading is not significant (F = .245; F* = 3.99; = .05; df = 1,66). This was interpreted using a model II error term. The overall test of the group codes was also not significant (F = 1.07; F = 2.75; = .05; df = 3.66), nor was the interaction between the group codes and newspaper usage is not significant (F = .89; F = 2.75; = .05; df = 3.66).

Figure 11.6
The Effect of Newspaper Use and Newspaper Frame on Causal Attribution of Homelessness

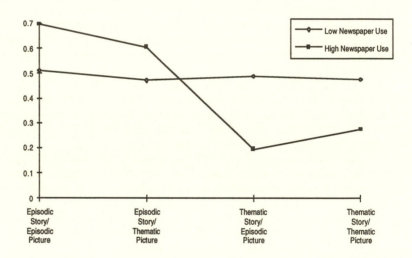

Moving on to the analysis of treatment responsibility, the main effect of newspaper usage is not significant (F = .04; F = 3.99; = .05; df = 1.66). The group differences are also not significant (F = 1.29; F = 2.75; = .05; df = 3.66). Finally, there is no significant interaction effect (F = .08; F* = 2.75; = .05; df = 3,66). (See Table11.1 for means of both analyses).

The above analyses show that there is neither a significant effect of newspaper use nor any interaction, however, a closer look at the means in both analyses is worthwhile. For the causal analysis, there is no significant difference between the means for low users of newspapers. This was determined through a Newman-Keuls analysis (q = .70, between Form 1 and Form 3; q = 3.74 for 4 steps; df = 66; = .05). On the other hand, there is a significant difference between the means scores for high users of newspapers based on which story they saw. This suggests a story-dominant model. Four out of the six comparisons were significant. The ones that were not significantly different were the ones with the same story version.

As seen in Figure 11.6, this finding is exactly opposite of the hypothesized one—it appears that high users of newspapers are much more sensitive to the frames of the stories found in newspapers, while those who are not as familiar with newspapers are not so susceptible. Those seeing the thematic story were significantly less individual (thus, more societal) in their blame for the cause of homelessness, than those subjects seeing the episodic story. Again, the pictures had little effect on the attributions of people who read the newspaper more or less frequently. These results, as they are based on a non-significant regression analysis, should be further examined with a larger sample, to see if the overall Fs might become significant with more power.

CONCLUSION

The results of all the above analyses fail to support the idea of the interaction model, nor do they support the idea of pictures having a greater effect on a subject's attributions, at least for the issue of homelessness. While there was a suggestion of support (given more power) for the additive model in a number of places, it is hard to say whether this lends support to what Iyengar found. As previously mentioned, it is unclear whether his results were based on real framing effects of comparable subject matter or if they were based on differences due the content of his segments.

Looking at the these results, there was no overall effect of either the stories or pictures for the causal attributions, nor did controlling for the subjects political ideology, religiousness, or views on racism affect these results significantly. The means did appear to fall in the direction predicted by the additive model, but none were significantly different from each other.

This causal attribution analysis was predicted to show support for the fundamental attribution error, where people are more likely to blame dispositional factors rather than societal ones as causes of behavior. This was not supported by the data. Half of the responses to the causal questions were societal in nature. For the treatment attribution, there again was no significant effect of stories or pictures. Further, the means did not fall into any predicted pattern (nor was there any significant difference between any of the means).

The results of Hypothesis 2 suggest that people might be willing to do something personally about homelessness, without wanting society to get involved. There was a significant effect of the newspaper version looked at and the level of willingness to send $5.00 to a homeless person. The likelihood was greater when the subject looked at the thematic story, rather than the personal profile. This effect was not found when controlling for the subject's ideology or beliefs in charity.

The correlation between this dependent score and the treatment attribution score show that they are independent variables. This suggests that persons who feel that society should not do anything about homelessness might still be willing to help out a homeless person themselves. This correlation result also suggests the need for a more discriminating way to score treatment attribution. The measure used only compared societal attributions to individual attributions. Perhaps societal responsibility should be split between government and private (non-homeless) citizens acting on their own. This would allow someone to support private action to treat homelessness, without government action, or the homeless just trying to help themselves.

Hypothesis 3 examines the effect of the newspaper version on a specific societal treatment. When looking at support for homeless shelters, there was not a significant effect of the stories or the pictures, though the means did follow the pattern predicted by the additive score (but they were not significantly different from each other). The correlation between shelter support and societal treatment attribution was not significant. This suggests, though, that people may theoretically support government assistance in the fight against homelessness, but not support specific government programs.

Finally, when looking at how newspaper usage affected attributions, we see interesting results. While there was no significant effect of either usage on the attributions or the interaction with the version on attributions, the causal attribution analysis does suggest a puzzling interaction. The high users of newspapers seem to be more affected by the frames than the low users. Perhaps the low users are not familiar enough with the style of the newspapers to realize the difference in the frames; treatment attribution means showed no such interaction.

PICTURES REVISITED

Overall the interaction model received no support. One thing is clear—pictures were shown to have little effect on the direction of subjects' attributions. There was no short-term icon seen, which goes against much historical data from the work of Hine and Riis to the present.

There are a number of reasons why a stronger picture effect was not seen. First, the subjects were not specifically told to "read" through the newspaper versions, therefore they might have focused more on the text to the exclusion of looking at the pictures. The subjects, knowing a questionnaire was to follow, might have decided that the questions would focus only on the text.

Second, one picture alone probably is not powerful enough to create a framing effect and move a subject to action. The single photograph may not have been telling enough to create a framing effect. However, multiple pictures of the same frame might create a significant framing effect. As Goldberg (1991) states: "Photographs most often achieve their force by addition or multiplication. A single photograph may be powerful but it seldom does the job alone" (1991, 175). Future research must look at how either a multiple picture story or a number of pictures spread out over time would affect attributions. Perhaps it is possible that people are able to combine cognitively a number of different episodic scenes into a thematic social problem. At what point do people say that a number of case studies equals a widespread problem? Neither this research nor Iyengar's investigated this possibility.

Perhaps still pictures do not have the power they once had. In this age of television and movies, perhaps people have become so reliant on moving images they are no longer "literate" to the meanings in still pictures. This would have to be investigated in a larger study designed with both television and newspaper groups.

Anecdotally, television magazine shows, especially "60 Minutes," are often cited for their impact on people and their ability to motivate people to do something. Less seems to be said about this kind of impact from shorter, television news pieces. The effects of these magazine stories could be due to their length or their medium. Future research needs to focus on comparing across media. The same "story" should be presented in both print and television.

Finally, perhaps subjects need to put themselves in the actor's (the homeless person's) place when they read an article and look at a picture about a social problem. Fiske and Taylor (1991) state: "Observers induced to empathize with actors become more situational in their explanations. Personal involvement in an actor's plight yields similar effects" (1991, 74). Perhaps this is where the power of case studies lies. For an episodic story to move people to demand social change, perhaps the story/picture must be such that they invite the reader to become involved with the actors.

The results suggest that a single photograph may not be worth a thousand words. Its power to move people to do something about a social problem may be more limited than anecdotal evidence suggest. It is true that today's photojournalists are still using episodically framed pictures to tell the stories of social problems in this country. This is evident from looking at the winning pictures in the National Press Photographers Association "Pictures of the Year" competition (1993). Almost all of the winning pictures reveal social problems through case examples of those problems. It is hard to imagine, though, that all these photographers are shooting this way in vain.

REFERENCES

Alesandrini, K. L. (1984). Pictures and Adult Learning. *Instructional Science* 13, 63–77.
Anglin, G. J. (1987). Effect of Pictures on Recall of Written Prose: How Durable Are Picture Effects? *ECTJ* 35, 25–30.
Anglin, G. J. (1986). Prose-Relevant Pictures and Older Learners' Recall of Written Prose. *ECTJ* 34, 131–136.
Bennett, W. L. (1992). White Noise: The Perils of Mass Mediated Democracy. *Communication Monograph,* 59, 401–406.
Fiske, S. T. and Taylor, S. E. (1991). *Social Cognition.* New York: McGraw-Hill, Inc.
Garcia, M. R. and Stark P. (1991) *Eyes on the News.* St. Petersburg, FL: The Poynter Institute for Media Studies.
Glenberg, A.M. and Langston, W. E. (1992). Comprehension of Illustrated Text: Pictures Help to Build Mental Models. *Journal of Memory and Language* 31, 129–151.
Goldberg, Vicki. (1991). *The Power of Photography: How Photographs Changed Our Lives.* New York: Abbeville Press.
Graber, D. A. (1990). Seeing is Remembering: How Visuals Contribute to Learning from Television News. *Journal of Communication* 40, 134–155.
Grimes, T. (1990). Encoding TV News Messages into Memory. *Journalism Quarterly* 67, 757–766.
Hine, L.W. (1980). Social Photography. In *Classic Essays on Photography*, edited by A. Trachtenberg. New Haven, Connecticut: Leete's Island Books, 109–113.
Holmes, B. C. (1987). Children's Inferences with Print and Pictures. *Journal of Educational Psychology* 79, 14–18.
Iyengar, S. (1987). Television News and Citizens' Explanations of National Affairs. *American Political Science Review* 81, 815–831.
Iyengar, S. (1991). *Is Anyone Responsible? How Television Frames Political Issues.* Chicago: University of Chicago Press.
Kelley, H.H. (1972). *Causal Schemata and the Attribution Process.* New York: General Learning Press.

Koenke, K., Otto, W. (1969). Contribution of Pictures to Children's Comprehension of the Main Idea in Reading. *Psychology in the Schools* 6, 298–302.

Levie, W.H., Lentz, R. (1982). Effects of Text Illustrations: A Review of Research. *ECTJ* 30, 195–232.

Levin, J. R., Berry, J. K. (1980). Children's Learning of All the News that's Fit to Picture. *ECTJ* 28, 177–185.

Levin, J. R., Lesgold, A. M. (1978). On Pictures in Prose. *ECTJ* 26, 233–243.

National Press Photographers Association. (1993). *The Best of Photojournalism: #18 The Year in Pictures.* Durham, NC: National Press Photographers Association.

Paivio, A., Csapo, K. (1973). Picture Superiority in Free Recall: Imagery or Dual Coding. *Cognitive Psychology* 5, 176–206.

Peeck, J. (1974). Retention of Pictorial and Verbal Content of a Text with Illustrations. *Journal of Educational Psychology* 66, 880–888.

Postman, Neil. (1985). *Amusing Ourselves to Death: Public Discourse in the Age of Show Business.* New York: Penguin Books.

Reeves, B., Chaffee, E., Tims, A. (1982). Social Cognition and Mass Communication Research. In *Social Cognition and Communication*, edited by M. Roloff and C. Berger. Newbury Park, CA: Sage.

Reyes, R.M., Thompson, W. C., Bower, G. H. (1980). Judgemental Biases Resulting from Differing Availabilities of Arguments. *Journal of Personality and Social Psychology* 39, 2–12.

Riis, J. A. (1971). *How the Other Half Lives: Studies Among the Tenements of New York.* New York: Dover Publications, Inc.

Stott, W. (1986). *Documentary Expression and Thirties America.* Chicago: University of Chicago Press.

Tversky, A., Kahneman, D. (1973). Availability: A Heuristic for Judging Frequency and Probability. *Cognitive Psychology* 5, 207–232.

Wanta, W. (1988). The Effects of Dominant Photographs: An Agenda-Setting Experiment. *Journalism Quarterly* 65, 107–111.

Wanta, W., Roark, V. (August 1993). *Cognitive and Affective Responses to Newspaper Photographs.* Paper presented at the Association for Education in Journalism and Mass Communication annual conference, Kansas City, MO.

Chapter 12

Japanese *Furoosha* (Bums) and *Hoomuresu* (Homeless): Living in the Shadow of Wealth

Richiko Ikeda and Eric Mark Kramer

In the early morning of January 24, 1996, employees and policemen of the Tokyo Municipal Government cleaned up the homeless from the street in the basement of the east side of the Shinjuku Station. The government had decided to build a moving walkway on that street. Although the homeless and their supporters resisted the power of the authorities, they were expelled. The Tokyo Municipal Government offered a shelter for the homeless. However, they could stay in the shelter only until the end of March. Of the more than 200 people removed, only 43 expressed any interest in moving into the shelter (Shinjuku no, 1996, p. 11). On the next day, the government announced that they would place steel bars between pillars along the walkway so that the homeless could not come back to their previous home even after the construction was finished.

Japan has suffered from an economic recession since 1991. This recession, the worst in the post World War II era, is called the *Heisei* recession. Increased rates of corporate bankruptcy and unemployment have threatened ordinary people with the specter that they might become homeless. In the modern corporate society, having a place of employment and a domicile are very closely related. This specter of having a tenuous grasp on employment and home was exacerbated by the mass media's reporting of the Shinjuku clean up (Morikawa, 1994). Although the distinction between wealth (having a home) and poverty (being homeless) is clear, the perception that the possibility of losing one's home has increased during the *Heisei* recession has also increased. The actual likelihood that a typical worker could end up homeless has never been calculated and it is probably quite remote. Nevertheless, the high visibility of homeless people, combined with the real anxiety caused by the recession has compounded to make the existence of the homeless almost unbearable. The row of homeless people on the street in the west side of the Shinjuku station both signifies and symbolizes the perceived threat (likely or not) of severe economic deprivation. As thousands of smartly dressed salary-men and women pass by every day, the contrast between those who have a job and home and those who do not is profound. Since the recession, the presence of the homeless makes the recession even more disturbing to the armies of workers passing by. The homeless are a constant reminder of what could, no matter how remotely, happen to those who loose their place in the system.

Since the *Heisei* recession, the threshold between the homed and homeless has fallen. The economic and psychological distance between the two populations, like the physical distance between the people living on the street and those salary employees marching by, has become too close for comfort. Japan's economic miracle, like most miracles, has been exposed as a myth by the presence of the homeless. Their simple existence shakes the psycho-economic confidence of those who see them both personally and on television. Certain prosperity has died during the *Heisei* recession. The result is anxiety for a whole generation of workers who have come of age without knowing anything other than constant growth.

The mass media sensationally suggests to their viewers that they too could experience a homeless life in the near future, the media also describes incidents where the homeless have been treated as garbage. The incident described at the beginning of this paper is one such warning. The Tokyo Municipal Government threw the homeless away just as one would dispose of bulky garbage. The phrase bulky garbage (*sodaigomi*), which is commonly used in Japan, refers to the difficulty one has in disposing of unproductive and unwanted people such as the homeless and the aged. Such unwanted people present a moral dilemma which makes dealing with them difficult in a way similar to removing large unwanted objects like broken refrigerators and old automobiles. The shop owners in the Shinjuku Station area and most of the commuters using the prommenade welcomed the clean-up. The incident of the Shinjuku homeless made the front pages of several major newspapers such as the *Asahi Shimbun*.

The term homeless (*hoomuresu* in Japanese) is borrowed from English. It only recently gained currency in the Japanese lexicon since the late 1980's and early 1990's. During the 1980s and before, the term bums (*furoosha* in Japanese) was commonly used to signify people without permanent employment and domicile. Both bum and homeless designate the Others. But there is a significant difference in connotation. Bums were more tolerable than homeless.

The existence of Others may seem an unfortunate contingency. However, these categories, which collectively signify Others among us, actually serve a purpose for group cohesion and identity. According to the binary logic of identity and difference, the Other, which is a fashionable way to say the outsider, is necessary for the insider to exist. The outsider is essential to the consolidated identity and presumed harmony among the insiders. Insiders feel safe and secure in their identity as so defined. They recognize their wealth when they see the impoverished Others.

However, the homeless, signifies more than simple otherness. As is implied in the incident described above, it also signifies a threat to the Japanese people. The homeless are a threat to *Wa* (harmony) on many levels including the desire for a coherent reality, the desire for group cohesion, and the desire for a psycho-economic sense of equilibrium, stability, and identity. Moreover, the linguistic shift from bums to homeless reflects a change in popular attitude among most people that may be related to the uncertainty of the *Heisei* recession.

This chapter examines this linguistic shift and explains what it signifies. It is suggested that the actions of the authorities and the shift in linguistic valence indicates a fundamental relationship between modern identity and economic status. This analysis will reveal the changing attitude of the Japanese people through the semiotic analysis of bums and homeless, not merely as words, but as those people who are living in the shadows cast by the oft cited Japanese miracle.

BUMS AS OTHERS/OUTSIDERS

Outsiders are created by and for insiders so that insiders can survive and maintain their identity. Since this dialectical structure is necessary for the existence of such identities (they are co-constituting), those who benefit by the sacrifice of the Others, that is the insiders, will work in their own interest to maintain that structure (Kramer, 1993). The poor state of the outsider can be quite valuable to the system as a warning to all who might entertain any ideas of deviance. But if the gap between the inside and the outside becomes too small for comfort, then the use-value of the outsiders is outweighed by feelings of dissonance. Consequently, the outsiders have outlived their use as scapegoats and should be removed. Insiders typically feel superior and perhaps even secure in their identity when they see the inferior situation of the Other. However, this sense of security is maintain only in so far as the outsiders are a clearly distinguished group of Others. So long as the difference between being an insider and an outsider is obvious, then the existence of such a clearly defined outside serves the interests of the inside. But what if the difference begins to fade? What if the boundary appears to be permeable so that the diametrical positions of insider and outsider begin to mix? The result is that the two identities begin to disappear because they are not so apparently different. When this occurs, then the existence of the outsider no longer serves the purpose of defining and discriminating the identity of the insider. Instead, the insider might begin to identify with the so-called outsider, and in this case, the result is very disturbing for the insider. The insider is loosing her identity as such. (S)he can begin to see herself in the face of the outsider (Levinas, 1994). As is almost always the case with outsiders (by definition), to see oneself becoming one of them or like them is repugnant.

Furthermore, if the insider believes that his or her identity, as such, is contingent on forces beyond their control, then the presence of the outsider may actually be threatening and disturbing. The predictable consonance or harmony the insiders presume may be confronted by potential disharmony and consequent dissonance. From a comfortable distance, insiders may feel sorry for the Others' miserable situation at least so long as it seems unlikely that they themselves (the insiders) could become an outsider. However, insiders are moved to take action when they feel threatened and wish to consolidate or expand their power. When a crisis of identity occurs, appeals to harmony, order, and reason, in a word *Wa*, are made. Demonizing the Other, helps to consolidate the sense of in-group identity and cohesion (*Wa*). The once relatively harmless and even pitiful Others are transformed into a dialectical opponent expressed as It's us or them. The *or* is the key, or operant term. Or implies mutual exclusion, not mutual co-existence. To be homeless is a frightening and unacceptable alternative. If becoming one of them appears to be emerging as a possibility, then it must be excluded from the universe of options.

The shift from being relatively harmless and even worthy of pity to being an object of scorn, disgust, and evil (disharmony) is profound. The shift manifests a psychological and semantic distancing. One must keep in mind that since the time of Isocrates, and including Sapir and Whorf, and Merleau-Ponty (and many others) the distinction between some invisible psyche and expression has been questioned. The expression and the expressed are identical so that a linguistic shift manifests a shift in attitude and/or way of thinking. The separation, or distancing between the homeless and the homed, which leads to a ·sense that one type of person is somehow more human than the other, begins when one looses the fundamental sense of identity that constitutes a unified community (Gebser, 1949/1985). While there is no distance between one and the other in the magic, unidimensional world of extended family, the beginning of one's separation from the other is found in the mythic ambivalent world of the emergent mass or city-dwelling individual (Gebser, 1949/1985). For a magic person, there is no sense of isolation or identifiable self as different from other people or nature or supernature. Magical expression is identifiable in that the signifier and the signified are identical. In the magic world or mode of communication, there is no semantic distance. For example, magic artifacts do not refer to or symbolize some force that exists elsewhere. Sacred artifacts manifest magic. They *are* magic so that if the artifact is lost, so too is the magic. Likewise, the one who possesses (and is possessed by) magical power is identical with it. Such a person is said to be literally (not figurally or symbolically) holy or magical. Because such a person is holy, bits of them, or even the entire body is preserved and religiously worshiped. Examples include the mummification of famous Buddhist monks, bits of the bodies of saints faithfully preserved in churches and cathedrals, the display of pseudo-religious leaders like Lenin and Stalin, and the hypervaluated preservation of pieces of paraphernalia that belonged to rock and movie stars. The cult of personality is essentially a magic mode of expression and is quite alive in the twentieth century. In the case of magic power, the holy or magical person *is* authority. An example of the identification of the person with their magical artifacts is the *kuruta*, or the sacred gown, which Shoko Asahara, a leader of the Aum religious cult, wore. For the true believers, it does not have a symbolic distance from him. There is no separation between him and his sacred gown. When his *kuruta* is taken from him, he gets upset because it is not simply an arbitrary piece of clothing or even a more emotionally charged symbol, but it is a talisman (a sacred and powerful object). There is a unity or, to put it in another way, there is no sense of Otherness in the magic world. One cannot loose one's magical identity. It is primordial.

Ethnic and or clan identity is one of the oldest types. It is essentially a magical phenomenon so that one is identical with the extended family. The same blood flows through all the veins of the clan. For instance, I may move away from Japan, speak a different language, and hold a different citizenship, and yet, on the magical level, I am and always will be Japanese by inherent nature, by blood and clan identity. Such a self exists prior to nationality or other legalistic (perspectival) designations. Practically all people harbor a dimension of magical identity as an integral part of their self concept. Whether it be Japanese or Italian or Mayan or Muslim or Black (or whatever ethnic group), ethnicity is a complex magical phenomenon people use to trace their sense of inherent identity to a common origin. Magic rituals to make individuals brothers, which means to have very intense emotional commitment, very often have blood and the mixing of blood in the process. An example would be when the leader cuts him or herself and cuts the initiate and they compress the two wounds together so that their blood mixes or when the initiate must drink the blood of the founder. The magical belief is that with the consumption of the flesh and blood of the Other they become one, the qualities are inherently transferred as when a magic person eats a certain kind of animal or part of an animal in order to become that animal.

Magic identity is a sense of being part of one single and unifying bloodline. People who appeal to a need to assure and defend the purity of the race or the religious or ideological dogma are manifesting magical consciousness structure. It is evinced in their actions and other forms of expression (rituals, ceremonies, war, arts, laws, and so forth). Patriotism and religionism are common expressions of magical consciousness in the modern world. Magic is highly affective and is the root of most attempts to justify actions typically believed to be immoral such as mass murder and the disposal of Others. Genocide has been justified because the existence of the Other threatens the aggressors pure identity. An example is the many prohibitions against interracial marriage around the globe and the prohibition against blood transfusion between races, a practice followed in the United States which had segregated white from colored hospitals until the mid-1960's. Even the sharing of food or drink (drinking fountains) was believed to lead to contamination. These are just a few examples of magical consciousness and its intensely emotional expression in the modern world. Magic identity is intensely emotional because the very sense of self is at stake.

On the other hand, the mythic world introduces a nascent separation of pseudo-individual ego identities. They are not yet expressed as dualistically discrete, as in the perspectival modern world, but in the mythic world nascent independence appears as a polar structure. The polar structure is characterized by mutual implication of one for the other. Hence the existence of sides (a spatial metaphor) begins to emerge. The inside implies the existence of an outside. The Other is somehow different from not one's own kind, which is magical, but different from one's self. The nascent realization of self-identity makes it possible to recognize the Other as well as his or her group identity. Mythical people realize that they belong to a group, *sui generus*. Identity, which is utterly presumed and invisible for magic people, becomes evident *sui generus* in the mythic world, although it is not yet a crisis as it is in the case of the perspectival world where suicide becomes common despite relatively heightened material comfort. Mythic people see themselves as no longer brothers with other animals, nor as possessed of and by spirit beings. Rather, the spirits have left the world to take up a distant residence on a mountain top or some astral realm. While the magic world is thoroughly animate such that everything has a spiritual dimension and the universe is full and finished (i.e., rivers have spirits, the sky or wind has a spirit, the trees have spirits, in short everything is the same—spiritual), the mythic world is characterized by the onset of a process of dissociation, which has extended in the Western European Renaissance style of perspectival dualism (articulated first by Aristotle and again by individuals like Francis Bacon and Rene Descartes).

In the mythic world, great schisms and clashes emerge with the articulation of master discourses, mythological systems (including the great religions) which are ultimately (logically) mutually exclusionary. The signifier and the signified begin to separate. The primordial problem of interpretation emerges. Meaning and communication as such comes to be seen as complex and problematic. The simple magical identity gives way to debate about the meaning of signs. This realization was the impetus for the invention of academic critical thinking about the meaning of texts and communication as such, in the form of ancient hermeneutics (derived from Hermes the winged messenger god who not only translated but *interpreted* divine messages), and endless commentaries on the sacred texts such as Talmudic exegesis. Thus institutional religion emerges as magical identity breaks down allowing for conflicts of interpretations and the felt need to defend a dogma (a position).

In the magical sense, one does not belong to the Christian church for instance, but *is* a Christian. The possibility of choice, which presupposes the emergence of a critical distance, emerges as mythological ambivalence. For instance, rituals such as communion and baptism are magical forms of idolic communication as well as a mythical forms of symbolic communication. Thus, one can recognize a sedimenting of forms of consciousness which co-exist. This kind of sedimentary complexity also exists in the meaning of bums and homeless.

Via mythical implication, when one tries to maintain the solidarity and clear (pure) identity of the inside, such communal solidarity works to exclude or distance outsiders. The insiders (*uchi*) work together in order to maintain their harmony or *Wa* and, at the same time, to protect their communal bonds, by excluding outsiders (*soto*). While insiders offer extensive service and emotional support to their own group members, they are very cold and indifferent to outsiders. Insiders will even sacrifice themselves for the benefit of the group. Sacrificing themselves is, however, not an accurate expression. Since individual ego or awareness of individual self is irrelevant to the members of the mythic *uchi* community, they do not think that they are sacrificing themselves. Rather than being unsung heroes, they are seen as rewarded martyrs to be envied. This is why the magic and mythic logic of cult suicides, like the Heavens Gate mass suicide in San Diego, California, in the Spring of 1997, often completely escapes the understanding of perspectival analysts. From the point-of-view of the perspectival consciousness structure, such intense dedication to (or more accurately identification with) a cause, seems wholly irrational and impossible to understand. In a different, but to some extent no less suicidal way (if one tries to understand the suicidal efforts of soldiers during the Second World War), members of *Ie*, or the mythic all encompassing family of Japanese, for example, do not think that politically arranged marriages are a sacrifice, but rather a necessity (Ikeda, 1992). Mythic people simply accept such marriages as natural. From the perspectival point-of-view this is fatalism. To those involved, the purpose of marriage is to preserve the system of *Ie*, not to express or achieve their individual desires or to assert their independence. In the magic and mythic world, nothing could be worse that to be independent or outside of the group. To be independent is to have no magic or mythic identity. Independence, which is freedom, is arbitrary and therefore extremely uncertain, which is very disturbing to magically and mythically minded people.

Bums, like other minority groups everywhere (not just Japan, for being marginal is what minority means), are treated as outsiders. A necessary condition for their existence is the continual maintenance and belief in sides. On the side of good are the normal, Japanese people who maintain their harmonious identity, or *Wa*, against the threat of discordentant elements both inside and outside the country. Japanese identity as *Wa* is dependent upon the creation and maintenance of the outsider (Kramer and Ikeda, 1997). The character *Wa* signifies harmony as well as Japan itself. The concept *Wa* has been a guiding principle for Japanese people at least since it was institutionalized by Prince Shotoku in his *Seventeen Article Constitution*,[1] which was compiled around 600 A.D. It says: *Wa o motte tattoshi to shi, sakaraukoto naki to seyo* (Harmony is to be valued, and avoidance of wanton opposition is to be honored) (translated by William Aston, 1956, in *Nihongi*). Although Prince Shotoku imported the idea of Buddhist compassion and expressed it in the concept *Wa*, Buddhist compassion came to be expressed, practiced, and identified with the order of the imperial system. It did not, and does not extend beyond the edges of the system (see Kramer and Ikeda, 1997). Compassion stops at the edge of the system. If one acts *out*, or is a foreigner, then compassion and identification is limited.

The *Wa*, or harmony, that Prince Shotoku had in mind, was more specifically the state of order under the emperor. The edicts required that the people pay respect to the emperor so that order, or the hierarchy of the system, namely *Wa*, should and would be maintained. This gave a moral dimension to identity. But moral behavior, or morality in general, tended to not be extended to those outside the group. The alternative to the good, which was hierarchical, rational order, was evil, meaning chaos or irrational anarchy. The emperor was considered the (common) source of all Japanese identity. This system then created and controlled Others in order to sustain the system. Such Others include the *buraku* people, the *Ainu*, Koreans in Japan, the handicapped, and so forth.

Since then, Others have been purposefully created by the authority in the modern or perspectival structure. In the modern perspectival world, difference is recognized as arbitrary. But for rhetorical purposes, authority appeals to magic and mythic identities that are supposedly inherent. Thus, authority cannot be blamed for the subservient status of the Others because the authorities did not make it happen. Thus the rhetoric of naturalism is used to inoculate the authorities from being responsible for arbitrary decisions they have instituted. One is not arbitrarily inferior, which would suggest that one could change one's status (the idea of the mutability of the individual), but rather on is naturally and inherently inferior. Given such conditions, the law of society is thus seen as merely harmonizing with the law of nature which after all is the moral and rational thing to do. Resisting nature is foolish. The good state is the one that most accommodates the tendencies of human nature. It is no one's fault, and certainly not the fault of the authorities who are innocently interested only in law, order, and justice, that one group of people is inferior to another. And how could it be just, that inherently unequal people have equal power? This would be nothing short of unnatural, a sin against nature itself. To resist nature is totally irrational. To presume that everyone is equal is utterly irrational, nothing short of ridiculous. Thus, the authority (defines) recognizes the inherent and immutable otherness of Others, as such, in a presumably reasonable, objective, and detached (innocent) way (see Kramer and Ikeda, 1997).

As a consequence of this rational organization, in the early 1600s, the To-kugawa government, established a strict caste system and ranked the *buraku* people at the bottom of the system by merely recognizing their natural place relative to other subgroups, and this order was acceptable by all involved (at least until the perspectival ideas of individual rights and merit came from the West) including the *buraku* themselves. In this way, the feudal administrators could not only avoid responsibility for the inequalities of the social structure, but even claim to have honorably fulfilled their duty by properly and respectfully recognizing the order of nature. Once one was identified with a caste, not as an arbitrary member but as the personification of the caste, such a status was passed down from generation to generation. That which was arbitrary, became ines-capably inherent. This is the magical dimension of rationalization exploited by the perspectival form of power through dissociation and ordination. The political and religious authorities legitimized the lowly status of the *buraku* people by announcing that they were identified with death, and as such were naturally (ob-viously and unquestionably) polluted and impure. This status was presumed to be inherent in their very nature and so it was hereditary, it was an ascribed not achieved status.

In mythical thinking causation can go in both directions so that it was un-clear, and in a way irrelevant, whether being an animal butcher and hide tanner was the cause or the effect of being *buraku*. In any case, the status designation was not seen as an arbitrary decision, but determined and in accordance with the Buddhist understanding of natural order.[2]

As a result of mythic legitimization, people come to accept the reasons for the identification of themselves and Others in certain ways and to discriminate accordingly. They do not doubt the order of things, or their own identity, nor do they hesitate about or question whether such discrimination may be wrong. This explains the process of normalizing *Sabetsu*, which is justified discrimination against others, and *Ijime* or justified bullying of others.

Bums came to be defined as Others in the second half of the 1960s (Akasaka, 1991, pp. 76–77). By then, the Japanese economy had recovered and had even begun to enjoy pronounced success. Defining bums as the Others coincided with Japan's economic success. Until then, the distinction between the insider of the community, and the outsider, such as bums, had been ambiguous. Like the me-dieval village idiot or drunk, a person might not be a paragon of virtue by the communities' standards but he or she was still, and unquestionably, a member of the community. Ambiguity is characteristic of a mythic relationship.

Although the distinction between one and the other (the signifier and the sig-nified) begins in the mythic awareness, a residual yet ambiguous identity is found in the mythic sense of appropriateness. While the symbol stands in for the thing symbolized, thus indicating an ontological distinction, it is still meaningful to discuss the appropriateness of a symbol such as a metaphor. For instance, a metaphor must reveal some sense of the truth of a phenomenon while it differs from it, or it is said to be inappropriate. In other words, there is still a sense of unity and identity in the mythic symbolic relationship even though the relation-ship is ambiguous and am-bivalent. A mythic person still cares very much about the symbol. For example, if one's national flag is destroyed, one may realize that it is merely a symbol of national identity and yet it is not arbitrary. For the mythic person there is yet emotional attachment with the symbol. While there is no distance between a magic person and their world, for the mythic person there exists a nascent sense of distance or differentiation between his or herself and the world. The unambiguous distinction between self and Other, subject and object presumes perspectival arbitrariness and emotional dissociation (dualistic abstraction). For instance, a perspectival modern does not care much (identify with) the binary computer code of 0,1. The code is purely arbitrary.

By contrast, mythic ambiguity is well expressed in the Chinese symbol, *Tai-chi*. The circular *Tai-chi* symbol consists of a dark hemisphere, called *Yin*, and a light part called *Yang*, each of which includes a small spot of the other part. This symbol captures the mythic quality which is not oppositionally dualistic but mutually implicate. The relationship between *Yin* and *Yang* is thus ambiguous.

Just as the *buraku* people were not strictly, inescapably defined as outsiders, but marginals, *before the Tokugawa era*,[3] bums were never completely seen as outsiders or Others in a strict sense. Due to the ambiguity and am-bivalence of mythic consciousness, some social mobility in and out of the *buraku* community (identity) was possible. The status (identity) of the *buraku* was not fixated in the form of bureaucratic written record keeping, which traced and maintained their status at the bottom of the social structure from one generation to the next, until the advent of the Tokugawa administration. As Harold Innis (1986) has argued, writing, which is a necessary condition for bureaucratization, is externalized memory. Record keeping is the origin of empire. Writing enables institutionalization, institutional memory, and official identification. It is linear, categorical; in a word perspectival.

Under the tyranny of well organized bureaucracy, one finds it more and more difficult to escape from one's official identity. In the mythic world, the *buraku* people were not permanent outsiders or Others. But with the advent of bureaucratic reason and order and its calculating use of natural rationalizations, the *buraku* became trapped. Escape became possible only when the idea of individual merit and individual civil liberties entered the Japanese consciousness. With the notion of arbitrary rather than inherent value comes the idea that individuals can change their social station through free will and achievement. Thus, postmodernity has enabled the permeability of categorical boundaries that demarcate identities. Hyper-valuing the individual as someone more than a group member has enabled various kinds of mobility which means that identity is no longer fixed by collectivistic, mythic and early modern thinking.

In a similar way, in the feudal mythic world bums were not strictly identified as outsiders. Although they did not have the same status and privileges as fullfledged insiders, bums were allowed to be in the community. There were places (physical, social, economic, spiritual, and semantic) for bums in the mythic community. Indeed, they sometimes where seen to have endearing qualities. At the time of village festivals, bums appeared in the confines of shrines and begged for food and money. They were thus integrated into village life (Akasaka, 1991, pp. 77–78). People gave the bums food and allowed them to live in temples and shrines and even under the eaves of their houses. Even though people occasionally beat them, the mainstream people did not try to expel the bums from the community. Bums accepted such treatment *as a rule* in order to receive shelter and food. The relationship between mainstream people and peripheral bums in the community seems to be cruel from the modern or perspectival sense of propriety; however, the relationship cannot be judged as right or wrong. The two loosely identified groups (for some bums were vagabond samuri, maverick monks, poets, and others of high esteem) co-existed, just like people and nature do. In the feudal world, identity was not reduced to economic status as much as it is in the current corporate world. One could be poor but yet respectable. In such a way, *Wa* or harmony was maintained within the community.

Mythic harmony was broken when the modern or perspectival idea of self-dependent individualism and competitiveness, especially economic competitiveness, became the dominant criteria for identity. Modernity is obsessed with competitiveness and efficiency (both economic concepts). In the modern or perspectival world, being productive and efficient is considered good, while being slow or inefficient is bad. The more one can produce per unit time, the more he or she is rewarded. Even time, which is essentially energy (Gebser, 1949/1985), is spatialized or measured and expressed as a quantity. In modernity, qualitative differences are reduced to quantitative ones. Thus, those who are not productive or efficient in material terms, including children, women, the elderly, the handicapped, and so forth, are considered useless, worthless, and inefficient. Such persons are not worthy of respect. Bums are also considered to be peripheral to value as it is expressed by quantitative productivity. In the modern perspectival world, Bums came to be regarded as useless appendages of the society. They came to be valuated as non-productive, thus they are identified as nothing more than an (economic) burden on society—essentially parasitic. What may have once been acceptable as a wondering poet or minstrel, free laborer, or sword for hire, is now unacceptable. One must have a permanent place within the system or be perceived as problematic. Thus, life time employment is an expression of having a permanent place within a stable system. Even the mobility of free labor, so common in previous times, is considered suspect or of dubious value. In the modern Japanese economy, much of the floating labor is made up of foreign workers who are not regarded as integral to the in-group. Such workers are not Japanese. They are contingent and, as such, expendable. In times of economic downturn, foreign labor was the first to go.

However, when the specter of lay-off began to touch in-group members, a crisis of membership and group identity emerged. The presence of homeless *Japanese* came to be a very disturbing symbol of economic weakness and instability. And since Japan has staked its pride almost exclusively on its economic prowess to the exclusion of other ways of displaying dominance such as military might, population size, or land size (common criteria used by many other countries such as the United States, China, India, Brazil, Russia, and so forth), when its economic engine began to stall the consequences went to the very heart of what it means to be Japanese. Made in Japan had become a label of pride world wide. Japan remains the only G7 nation in Asia. But such bragging rights are being eroded. When the sense of self-esteem is threatened, especially by economic problems, scapegoating is commonly observed all over the world, and Japan is no different.

In the modern Japanese milieu, with its emphasis on material production and economic power, people came to the idea that any burden, meaning any net expenditure to society, should be terminated. Belt tightening and cost-cutting take the form of getting serious, and getting tough. In such a singularly motivated society, reorganization reaches all aspects of the social world. Getting strong and staying strong is the name of the game. As eugenics prospers in the modern or perspectival world, people try to eliminate those who are inferior. Under the Eugenic Protection Act established in Japan in 1948, people have expressed a felt need to terminate inferior genes. Under the principle of eugenics, people have come to the conclusion that bums are inferior, and as such should be eliminated. In modern society where waste is valuated as bad, people began to attack bums. People started to see bums as discrete Others, not as mythic, ambiguous Others.

ATTACKING OTHERS

In 1983, the media sensationalized a report about a group of junior high school students who attacked and killed bums in Yokohama. The media described the attacks as being a game, or for fun. One of the students commented: Bums were irresistible and they just ran away when we attacked, which gave us a thrill. We enjoyed ourselves by throwing stones at them and hitting the bums (translated by the author) (*Furoosha Shugeki wa*, 1983, p. 11). Another boy said: If we played in a game arcade it cost money, but we didn't need any money in the game of attacking bums and it was fun (translated by the author) (*Joshi Chugakusei mo*, 1983, p. 23). These comments remind one of the kind of senseless killings commonly reported in Western countries, such as wilding, drive by shootings, and the like (Kramer and Ikeda, 1997). In cases of wilding, juvenile males in search of momentary gratification, make a woman, any woman, the target of impulsive attack. After the attack she is discarded because she is dead (or unconscious) and gives no more gratification to the player(s) or attacker(s). Drive-by shootings are also impulsive and violent attempts at self-gratification at the expense of others. The targets are often anonymous and objectified, which means that they hold no inherent value worthy of respect for their attackers. This is late-modern or even post-modern crime in that anonymity is a come quality of the targets, there is no premeditation, no planning, and there appears to be no rhyme nor reason for the selection of targets with the possible exception that such brutal youth avoid people that might appear to be able to fight back. Other than this criterion of selection, according to police interviews, targets are utterly random—arbitrary. In the post-modern world, where everything, including meaning, is arbitrary, and quality is considered a medieval chimera, the Other has become a devalued and disqualified object (Buber, 1970). Senseless killing is a manifestation of post-modernity, and killing bums is one expression of this attitude (Kramer and Ikeda, 1997).

In the mythic world, which thrives on spectacle, pageantry, ceremony, and patriotic emotion, killing can have great semantic import. It can make one a hero or butcher. Most histories are the narratives of power-politics and war. War has been deemed worthy of great sacrifice, many memorials, and countless volumes of books and movies. Post-modern murder, on the other hand, appears to be an utterly senseless, rather than sense-making behavior. It manifests a level of dissociation and alienation that defies rational explanation. Even the best efforts at explanation fail because post-modern murder seems utterly meaningless. It is a form of killing that lacks motive or intent. The target is not a worthy opponent or a hated enemy, but anyone who happens by.

Modernity or the perspectival world is expressed as a separation between self and the Other (estrangement). In the post-modern world, arbitrariness is, quite contradictorily, taken to absolution. In the modern world one comes to be aware of himself or herself as an individual being. But the logical relationship between freedom and responsibility yet holds. The ambiguous distinction between self and the Other in the mythic world becomes more distinct in the modern perspectival world (Gebser, 1949/1985). In other words, the ambiguous relationship of the mythic symbol becomes the arbitrary sign. The relationship between the signifier and the signified is accidental at best—unmotivated. The sign, has no emotional identity. What is polarity in the symbol becomes stark and discrete duality in the sign. There is no ambiguity in the dualistic world. Everything is white or black, yes or no, either or, 0,1. Code switching is not problematic because one does not care when the world is totally arbitrary. The sign has no inherent internal cohesion, meaning, or value.

Arbitrariness leads to quantitative unitization. In the arbitrary world, units are interchangeable. Even people are reduced to functional equivalencies. Meaning exists only as operation. Identity is reduced to operation within a structure. I am a computer programmer, I am a lawyer, I am a marketing agent... When one's position within the structure is lost, so too is one's sense of self. Hence, lay-off are devastating for the modern individual.

In the post-modern world, everything is equal; qualitative differences are irrelevant (Kramer, 1997). Thus, the unitized object, such as a woman in wilding, a target in drive-by shootings, a bum, a general issue soldier (not mythic warrior), etc. can be carelessly replaced (Kramer and Ikeda, 1997). Only the number of conquests matters. How many soldiers does it take to win a battle is computed in cost or benefit analyses. Style is replaced by brutal efficiency such as the biggest bang for the buck. While feudal warriors expressed a unique identity in their coats-of-arms, their colors, and the style of their armor and fighting, modern soldiers are regimented and anonymous. Human beings have become resource base. Humans can become obsolete. They must retool. Increasingly, machine language is applied to human interaction. Communication is replaced by informatics and cybernetics, whereby feedback is used to maintain order (equilibrium). Discordant and deranged individuals must be corrected and arranged.

Perhaps the most disturbing aspect of the juvenile attacks was that the media reported that the students who killed the bums showed no emotion or sympathy for those they tormented and murdered. Some suggested that they did not, or perhaps could not, understand that they had killed human beings (Aoki, 1985). When one of the boys was asked why he killed bums, he answered with a grimace that bums were dirty and smelled bad (Aoki, 1985). Another said that he used bums as objects for practicing his fighting skills (*Kenka no*, 1983, p. 23). Many readers and viewers were irritated by the juveniles' unreasonable reasons. None of the boys, however, were held legally responsible, even though five of them were 16 years old, which is old enough to be charged as an adult according to Japanese criminal law. The police declared that the boys did not have any intention of killing the bums. As startling as it may seem, the police may be right. In the post-modern world motive, intent, and meaning are not real. The police accepted the unreasonable reasons for justifying the killings.

In the case of the bum killings in 1983, despite the attitude taken by the police, a majority of Japanese people did not accept the boys' reasons for killing, and they expressed their frustration in the media. An outpouring of humanistic reaction against the killers was expressed. Humanistic ideas are modern Enlightenment ideas. In the modern world, humanity has been conceptualized *sui generus* and emancipated, which means that humanism emerged as a discrete ideology which, in turn, gave birth to the social sciences, modern jurisprudence, and democratic modes of discourse like blind and refereed science. According to the French philosophies and Enlightenment thought, humans must be released from myths, superstition, blood-based power legitimization, and other so-called irrational phenomena. Minorities, such as women, non-Caucasians, the handicapped, and others, have demanded equality and individual rights. This is only possible when one is aware of his or her individual self. This, reawakening or rebirth (which is the meaning of the word Renaissance) of self-awareness was manifested in the American and French Revolutions, and various civil rights and post-colonial movements, globally. The idea of equality leads to humanistic ideologies. If someone is not given an equal opportunity by the power structure, humanists feel empathy and sympathy for that person and may try to help him or her. In the modern or perspectival world, a rather contradictory tendency exists such that individualism promotes civil liberties as the basis of a just community, and at the same time it tends toward post-modern isolation.

Although such a humanistic tendency was expressed by many in their public reactions to the case of killing bums in 1983, the reaction was rather hypocritical. People felt sorry only after the media revealed the killing case. In everyday life, they avoided the bums in their own communities. They were indifferent to the plight of the homeless. Furthermore, bums were generally considered to be dirty, useless, waste, et cetera. In short, the popular attitude toward bums was basically the attitude expressed by the killers. The Juvenile's may have seen their actions to be justified by the common sense regarding bums.

As is typical, it didn't take long for the media to forget about the 1983 incident. After the incident, only occasional and short articles about bums appeared in newspapers. Nevertheless, the 1983 incident was a catalyst for an emotional outpouring from the general population. Feelings of shock, guilt, and remorse where common themes in the media. This reaction is quite in contrast to the case of killing homeless (persons) in 1996.

The Linguistic Shift from Bums to Homeless: From Modernity to Post-Modernity

At the end of 1995, the mass media reported two cases in which youngsters killed homeless (persons). In the first case, two males (24 and 25 years of age) threw a 63-year-old homeless man off of a bridge and into a river. The homeless man drowned. In the second case, three teenagers attacked a 69-year-old homeless man and killed him. These cases were, however, treated as trivial in the media. Major networks reported them briefly in news programs; major newspapers spared only little space for reporting these incidents in the social sections of their pages. Around the same time the media was enthusiastically focused on the details of a series of trials of Aum religious group members. The two cases of killing the homeless were not, by media measurement, regarded as important news. What and how the media reports an issue creates the perception of its import. According to the theories of agenda setting and status conferral, if the media treats a case as trivial, it becomes a trivial case. As in the case of all sensationally based forms of knowledge (as opposed to purely logical forms of knowledge), if an incident is not perceived it simply does not exist. The media and their consumers suffer from the tree falling in the woods syndrome.

While the media coverage of the 1983 case of killing bums generated a great deal of public reflection and outrage, the lack of media attention to the 1995 cases muted reaction. The result of an apparent lack of status conferral by the media concerning the 1995 cases correlates to an apparent indifference on the part of the public. Between 1983 and 1995, have people become more disinterested and or more desensitized to such crimes? Is this an indicator of increased alienation and carelessness so commonly attributed to modern urban living? It has been suggested by many scholars and media pundits that overdevelopment and overurbanization has created a condition where people increasingly care more about things and manipulate people than care about people and manipulate things. A rather uniform set of editorial criteria and decisions across the commercial media in Japan was evident in the content and coverage of the 1995 cases. Apparently, it was concluded by editors and producers that coverage of the killings of homeless people would not be of much interest to the general consuming public and would therefore not sell. The relative indifference toward the 1995 cases may be a manifestation of extreme me-ism and of an increasing inability to have a qualitative relationship with Others. I am the center of the universe and do not care about others. While the Aum Shenrikio attacks could directly effect the consuming public, news consumers were more interested in coverage of the cult trials than the murders of homeless, and essentially harmless, street people. Several Japanese scholars and writers (Miyadai, 1994; Kramer and Shimomisse, 1991; Sakurai, 1986) have suggested that the vitality of the modern or perspectival world where an individual self not only enjoys rights and privileges but also recognizes responsibilities to the larger collective may be waning. Caring about, and the willingness to sacrifice personal desires for, the collective good seems to be decreasing.

The deficiency (fragmentation) of the modern or perspectival world is indicated by the shift of terminology from bums (*furoosha*) to homeless (*hoomuresu*). While the term bum was used in the 1983 cases, the term homeless is found in the reportage of the 1995 cases. According to a search of two major Japanese newspapers (the *Asahi Shimbun* and the *Yomiuri Shimbun*), the linguistic shift from bums to homeless can be located in the mid-1990's. This linguistic shift occurred in the middle of the *Heisei* recession.

The rapid recovery of the Japanese economy after World War II enabled Japanese people to improve their lives. Since the 1960s, survey after survey has indicated that about 90 percent of Japanese believe that they belong to the middle class. They have also believed that each new generation will have a better economic situation than the last. The Japanese economy even overcame the recession which immediately followed the Oil Crisis of the 1970s. Japanese people believed that the Japanese economy would never fail. The *Heisei* recession, however, hit Japan after the prosperity of the bubble economy and destroyed the myth of endless prosperity. Perhaps the most important bubble that was deflated, was the psycho-economic faith people had had in the economy. The Japanese system of life-long employment, seniority, and large annual bonuses could no longer be taken for granted. The restructuring of the economy, the financial system, the political system, companies, and perhaps most importantly, the restructuring of the expectations of the Japanese people, began in earnest during the 1990s. The unemployment rate has steadily risen since 1991. It was 2.1 percent in 1990 and 1991, 2.2 percent in 1992, 2.5 percent in 1993, 2.9 percent in 1994, and 3.2 percent in 1995 (Shitsugyoritsu, 1996, p. 2). The rate in May 1996 was 3.5 percent (Rising Unemployment, 1996, p. 15). This is a very sobering reversal of fortunes for the Japanese people. For the first time since the Second World War, the Japanese people feel threatened. It became conceivable to the average laborer or student that even they could become homeless in the future.

During the recession, the media has reported an increasing number of homeless in major cities. In the Airin district in Osaka, for example, the number of homeless in 1991 was 253; it increased to 485 in 1992, and to 692 in 1993 (Hoomuresu Kyuzo Osaka Airin-Chiku, 1993, p. 15). In Nagoya, the number of homeless on May 7, 1993 was 403, while the average number of homeless in April and May of 1992 was 250 (Hoomuresu Kyuzo 400nin o Toppa, 1993, p. 23). Between January and October of 1993, in Shinjuku, Tokyo, more than 1,850 visited the welfare office of the Shinjuku Ward seeking food and medication. This number was twice what it was in 1990 (93nen Ato 10ka, 1993, p. 19). Beginning in October 1994, the Salvation Army started to serve food in Shinjuku every Thursday. In the beginning, 250 meals a day were enough for the homeless there; toward the end of 1994, even 350 meals were not enough (Shiwasu Fukikomu, 1994, p. 11). According to a survey conducted by the Tokyo Municipal Government in February 1995, there were 3,300 people living on the streets in Tokyo (Aoshima-san Motto, 1996, p. 5). A support group for the homeless estimated that in May 1995, about 850 people a day slept on the streets of Shinjuku (Hoomuresu 3000nin Toppa, 1995, p. 30). Although the total number of homeless is hard to estimate, newspaper articles in the *Asahi* and *Yomiuri Shimbun* indicate a clear trend of increasing numbers of homeless in Japan.

At the same time (during the 1990s), articles reporting the situation of the homeless in the United States, were also increasing. To name but a few, an article on January 11, 1992, described the increasing number of homeless and their problems (Seijuku Shakai *no*, 1992, p. 7); and an article dated October 7, 1992, reported on poverty and the homeless in relation to the Presidential election (Daitoshi no Hinkon, 1992, p. 6). Feature stories about the United States included the term or phenomenon, homeless. A series called A Portrait of America explained the situation of Mr. Roberts who entered a homeless shelter after coming back from the Gulf War (Kikyo Ernest Roberts-san, 1993, p. 10). An opinion piece from a reader described some of the well-facilitated shelters for the homeless in the United States, as compared to the ones in Japan (Hoomuresu ni Yasashii, 1993, p. 5). Poverty and homelessness constituted a significant aspect of the image of the United States in the Japanese media.

Accordingly, the term homeless, has become associated with the image of a declining United States. Japanese people know through the media that the United States suffers from a high rate of unemployment and a large number of homeless. They are afraid that Japan will follow the pattern of the United States. The borrowing of the word, *hoomuresu* (homeless), expresses this fear that the Japanese people have. Or it may be that their heightened anxiety about the *Heisei* recession (which appears to have no end in sight) compelled editors to choose the term homeless, instead of bums. The Japanese have begun to identify their predicament with a perceived predicament in the United States. Not only have Japanese editors followed the linguistic lead of the United States, but that has suggested that the term homeless is also applicable to the Japanese situation. It is feared that Japan is following the U.S. which is a regular source of news about massive lay-off and down-sizing.

The term homeless signifies that anyone, irregardless of their own personal effort, can become homeless. While the status of being a bum tended to be considered the fault of the individual as lazy or stupid, being homeless connotes a consequence of a systemic force beyond one's control. Economic disjunction is not well understood and is poorly explained in the press. Economic forces have a tendency to be mystified and mystifying. The economy is practically a magical phenomenon. We are all parts of it. The fear that comes from lack of understanding and real or perceived consequences is felt as personal vulnerability and anxiety. The term homeless may reflect such uncertainty in Japanese society. Being uncertain results in fear or anxiety (Berger and Calabrese, 1975).

Such fear is manifested in the reaction to the clean-up of the homeless in Shinjuku by the Tokyo Municipal government described at the beginning of this paper. Those who work in Shinjuku support what the government did, partly because the existence of the homeless reminds them of their own vulnerabilities in the face of anonymous, often mysterious and massive economic forces. They recognize that they too could become homeless, and therefore they do not like to look into the face of a potential self (Levinas, 1994). Thus, they abhor the homeless as dirty, useless, lazy, as essentially disturbing of their personal mental harmony. They want to expel the homeless from their awareness. Personal affective equilibrium should be in consonance with the larger world stability. The magical identification with such a disturbing life situation motivates the authorities to remove the symbol and sign of decline and threat. The homed pedestrians do not care what happens to the homeless after being expelled from the street. They try not to be too be empathetic for that leads to the pain dissonance. A selfish person—one with a hypertrophic ego in Gebser's (1949/1985) terms—only cares about him or herself, and seeks to maximize his or her own emotional equilibrium. Just like a vanishing point in the perspective of post-Renaissance painting, one can see only a point, and this small slice of reality is inflated to mean the whole of life. Out of sight, out of mind. So long as Others are not within one's perspective they cannot disturb one's peace-of-mind. The humanistic ideology of appreciating the equal rights of Others—a positive element of modernity or perspectivity—is sacrificed for the sake of self-comfort. The late-modern world of selfishness and alienation has become dominant, and it is manifested in the shift of terminology from bums to homeless.

CONCLUSION

Through the semiotic analysis of the words *furoosha* and *hoomuresu*, and the linguistic shift from the former to the latter, Japanese society is expressing a post-modern attitude.[4] Extreme selfishness and alienation have become dominant in Japanese urban life. People have become dissociated from each other effecting the quality of community and interpersonal relationships. It seems to have become acceptable, even desirable to deny the existence of Others as meaningless objects.

If Japanese people expel the homeless or the Others from their community, can they enjoy themselves? Can they enjoy their prosperity and wealth? They should know that extinguishing Others means to extinguish themselves. The existence of the Other is a necessary condition for the existence of the self. They are co-constituting, and as such, meaningful identities. Urban life flourishes only when the city allows diversity. Difference enriches everyone.

Furthermore, even if the government can drive the homeless away from certain areas or from the urban centers, they cannot make the homeless the home owner. Those who were expelled must settle down somewhere else, and they will still be homeless. Cleaning-up the homeless, which really is nothing more than relocation, cannot solve the fundamental problem. It is only a temporary and localized treatment of the symptom of anxiety which the presence of the homeless cause in the minds of the homed and employed. What the government, the people should do is generate jobs for the homeless and to offer shelter for those who are unable to work. The perception that the Japanese economy is bursting or collapsing is based more on journalistic sensationalism than economic fact. But the problem is less one of money than one of attitude.

Perhaps a new point-of-view should be taken. One might make the argument that the success of an economy is measured by the number of homeless that exist. However, people will probably always make new Others. The problem of intense dissociation in late modernity and post-modernity would probably continue even if the homeless problem were solved. Dissociation is the basic problem while alienation and homelessness are the symptoms. A mutation in attitude, a new awareness of relationships will be necessary for things to change fundamentally (Gebser, 1949/1985).

What we need to do in order to solve the problem fundamentally is to constitute qualitative relationships or systatic relationships (Gebser, 1949/1985). In order to survive, one must constitute a systatic relationship between One and the Other. Different modes of relationships constitute systatic relationships. To be a bum used to have a complex and ambiguous meaning(s). Jesus Christ could be seen as a bum or homeless. In India, the homeless are considered sacred beings. There are different modes of relationships in being bums and the homeless. One must unfold different meanings in them. Then, one can appreciate the differences that Others present, which gives us an enriched existence. This is what we choose to call the aperspectival integral world (Gebser, 1949/1985; Kramer, 1992; 1997). The aperspectival is a mutational shift from the modern mentality. The so-called post-modern, so popular in current academic fashion, is actually a linear, logical extension of modern individuation to disintegration (which amounts to the absurd idea of absolute perspectivism). Post-modernism is more accurately labled late-modernism (Kramer, 1997). The integral is a completely different mutational shift from the logical consequences of hypertrophic modernism (post-modernism).

NOTES

1. Some scholars argue that Prince Shotoku's Seventeen Article is a moral book, a constitution in the modern sense of the term, because it does not include any penal code

(Sidney Brown, Personal Communication on December 28, 1995; Umehara, 1981).

2. The buraku people were forced to live in isolated areas. They consist of two groups: *eta* and *hinin*. The former usually dealt with animal skins and dead people, thus they were considered to be polluted. The latter were criminals who were driven to isolated areas after serving prison terms.

3. More precisely, Toyotomi Hideyoshi's land survey fixed the predecessor of the buraku people in such a status. Hideyoshi began to form a centralized nation after ending civil wars, which lasted about 100 years. As one of his policies, a nation-wide land survey was conducted between 1585 and 1598, which resulted in binding people to the land and their status.

4. Another possible explanation for such linguistic choice is that in general Japanese people prefer borrowed words pronouncing them according to the Japanese phonetic system and expressing the borrowed terms in katakana, one of the three writing systems in Japan.

REFERENCES

Akasaka, N. (1991). *Haijo no genshogaku* (Phenomenology of exclusivity). Tokyo: Chikuma Shobo.

Aoki, E. (1985). *Yatto mietekita kodomotachi* (Children who can be finally understood). Tokyo: Asunaro Shobo.

Aoshima-san motto atatakami o (Mr. Aoshima, more compassion). (1996, January 25). *The Asahi Shimbun*, 5.

Aston, W. G. (1956). (trans). *Nihongi, chronicles of Japan from the earliest times to A. D. 697*. London: George Allen and Uniwin.

Berger, C., and Calabrese, R. (1975). Some explorations in initial interaction and beyond. *Human Communication Research*, 1, p 99–112.

Buber, M. (1970). *I and thou*. New York: Charles Scribner's Sons. Daitoshi no hinkon (Poverty in metropolitan). (1992, October 7). *The Asahi Shimbun*, 6.

Furoosha shugeki wa chugakusei shudan (A group of junior high school students attacked bums). (1983, February 12). *The Yomiuri Shimbun*, 11.

Gebser, J. (1985). *The ever-present origin* (N. Barstad, and A. Mickunas, Trans.). Athens, OH: Ohio University Press. (Original work published 1949)

Hoomuresu kyuzo Osaka Airin-chiku shuhen de 700nin (Rapid increase of the homeless in the Airin district in Osaka). (1993, December 6). *The Asahi Shimbun*, 15.

Hoomuresu kyuzo 400nin o toppa Nagoya (Rapid increase of the homeless, more than 400, Nagoya). (1993, May 22). *The Asahi Shimbun*, 23.

Hoomuresu ni yasashii beishisetsu (Shelters in the U. S. kind to the homeless). (1993, October 20). *The Asahi Shimbun*, 5.

Hoomuresu sanzanna natsu (Miserable summer for the homeless). (1994, July 15). *The Yomiuri Shimbun*, 35.

Hoomuresu 3000nin toppa (More than 3000 homeless). (1995, Jun 20). *The Yomiuri Shimbun*, 30.

Ikeda, R. (1992). *Ie to kazoku: A shift in the communication pattern of the Japanese family*. Master's thesis, University of Oklahoma.

Innis, H. (1986). *Empire and Communication*. Toronto: Press Porcepic.

Joshi chugakusei mo ita (Female students also involved). (1983, February 14). *The Yomiuri Shimbun*, 23.

Kenka no renshudai (Practicing a fight). (1983, February 15). *The Yomiuri Shimbun*, 23.

Kikyo Ernest Roberts-san (Ernest Roberts came home). (1993, January 9). *The Asahi Shimbun*, 10.

Kramer, E. M. (1993). Understanding co-constitutional genesis. *Integrative Explorations: Journal of Culture and Consciousness*. Vol. 1, No. 1, p 41–47.

Kramer, E. M. (1997). *Modern/Postmodern: Off the beaten path of antimodernism.* Westport, CT.: Greenwood.

Kramer, E. M., and Ikeda, R. (1996). Fatal mistakes in crosscultural communication: The case of Yoshihiro Hattori. *Proceedings II of the 5th Japanese/American Phenomenology Conference*, p 73–87.

Kramer, E. M., and Ikeda, R. (1997). What's a Japanese?: Diversity, culture, and social harmony. In E. M. Kramer (ed.), *Race relations in a postmodern world*, Westport, CT: Praeger, p 79–102.

Kramer, E. M., and Shimomisse, E. (1991). Crisis in Japanese domestic relations: temporal stress and the disruption of domestic communication patterns. Unpublished manuscript delivered at the conference Communication in Japan and the United States, March 14, California State University, Fullerton.

Levinas, E. (1994). *Outside the subject* (M. Smith, Trans.). Stanford, CA.: Stanford University Press.

93nen at 10ka (10 days left in 1993). (1993, December 22). *The Yomiuri Shimbun*, 19.

Miyadai, S. (1994) *Seifuku shojotachi no setaku* (The choice of the high school girl). Tokyo: Kodansha.

Morikawa, N. (1994). *Anata ga hoomuresu ni naru hi* (The day when you become homeless). Tokyo: Sandoke Shuppankyoku.

Rising unemployment rate cause for serious concern. (1996, July 3). *Asahi News* (Internet), p 15–17.

Sakurai, T. (1986). *Kazoku no mitoroji* (The mythology of the family). Tokyo: Shinyosha.

Seijuku shakai no byori (Pathology of mature society). (1992, January 11). *The Asahi Shimbun*, 7.

Shinjuku no wagaya kieta (Home in Shinjuku disappeared). (1996, January 24). The Asahi *The Asahi Shimbun*, 11.

Shitsugyoritsu nao saiaku 3.4 percent (The unemployment rate is still the worst, 3.4 percent). (1996, January 30). *The Asahi Shimbun*, 2.

Shiwasu fukikomu "kamino ie" (The end of year blows through "cardboard houses" (1994, December 17). *The Yomiuri Shimbun*, 11.

Umehara, T. (1981). *Shotoku Taishi II, Kenpo 17jo* (Prince Shotoku, the Constitution of 17 articles). Tokyo: Shogakukan.

Index

Contributors

RICHARD CAMPBELL is director of the School of Journalism at Middle Tennessee State University. His research focuses on textual analysis of television, audience analysis, and cultural studies.

JAMES A. DANOWSKI is an associate professor at the University of Illinois at Chicago. His research focuses on statistical analysis of large textual and speech corpora, textual effects on audience cognitive/emotional responses, user information retrieval behavior, and network analysis.

JOHN FISKE is a professor of communication at University of Wisconsin-Madison. His research focuses on cultural studies, reception theory, and textual analysis.

LINDA K. FULLER is an associate professor in the Communications Department of Worcester State College. Her research focuses on media representations of minorities and underpriviledged groups. She is also interested in cross-cultural communication.

RICHIKO IKEDA is an assistant professor at International Christian University in Japan. Her research focuses on intercultural communication and gender studies.

ERIC MARK KRAMER is an associate professor of communication at University of Oklahoma. His research focuses on phenomenology of communication. He has taught in Japan, Singapore, and Bulgaria.

SOOBUM LEE is a senior researcher at Korean Broadcasting Research Institute in Korea. His research focuses on critical studies and intercultural communication.